The Shattered Silents

THE SHATTERED SILENTS

How the talkies came to stay   *Alexander Walker*

'The trouble with the
whole industry is that
it talked before
it thought.'

JOSEPH M. SCHENCK

WILLIAM MORROW AND COMPANY, INC.
NEW YORK   1979

Library of Congress Catalog Card Number 79-88931

ISBN 0-688-03544-2

Printed in the United States of America.

First U.S. Edition

1   2   3   4   5   6   7   8   9   10

For Margaret Gardner and Charles Champlin

Contents

Preface

Almost every history of Hollywood's movies contains an embarrassing gap in the record. It is of a few years only, from mid-1926 till round about the end of 1929. But it is as if the film historian's needle has jumped violently several grooves in response to a severe jolt that the system has suddenly suffered. There are a few stuttering references of an obligatory nature – Vitaphone . . . Al Jolson . . . *The Jazz Singer* . . . *The Lights of New York* . . . *Broadway Melody* . . . John Gilbert . . . King Vidor . . . *Hallelujah* – and then, with audible relief, one is back on the track with the guide lines of the new era again observable (and probably, for most readers, all too familiar). The missing years I am referring to are the ones when the silents were shattered.

They are the short but amazingly eventful months that saw Hollywood changing from an industry that turned out silent films to one that produced talkies. There has been no revolution like it. It passed with such breakneck speed, at such inflationary cost, with such ruthless self-interest, that a whole art form was sundered and consigned to history almost before anyone could count the cost in economic terms or guess the consequences in human ones – and certainly before anyone could keep an adequate record of it. There has never been such a lightning re-tooling of an entire industry – even wartime emergencies were slower – nor such a wholesale transformation in the shape and acceptance of new forms of mass entertainment – even television's later, total conquest of hearts and (sometimes) minds, was achieved at a virtual snail's pace by comparison. The shape and especially the sound of cinema movies today was decided during those few years. Not in any cool-headed, rational fashion: but amidst unbelievable confusion, stupidity, accident, ambition and greed. Somewhere at the bottom of the Pandora's Box of talking pictures there was, fortunately, a resilient particle of artistic endeavour; and seeing it survive, though not necessarily triumph, gives the revolution its redeeming feature. On almost all other grounds, the story of the shattered silents is one to confirm the cynic and delight the sceptic. The human panic was on the same scale as the financial earthquake that hit Hollywood as sound undermined the old ways of working and living. The imperative of speech was thrust on those whose fame and fortune – and in the heady era of the 1920s both were at a height seldom achieved or at any rate sustained with such arrogance in later years – had been created in conditions of silence. They knew not what dire or disastrous fates threatened the pampered security of their lives now that they had to do what the common folk did naturally (and for no pay) every day of their lives – namely, *talk*.

These years are interpretable in many ways. In human, artistic, economic and even moral terms. As success story or tragedy. Yet the fact is they seldom have been interpreted at all. They are more often than not 'given a miss' in the history books that otherwise deal so thoroughly and illuminatingly with the silent or the talkie eras. This was a puzzle to me when I conceived the idea of this book. The puzzle was very quickly solved when I began writing it. It took precisely twice as long to write as I had first judged necessary: and I could still be researching it, but for the contractual deadlines every author must meet. It is not just that guide lines are few: though they are. The one scholar who is a notable forerunner, and to whom I pay envious tribute, is Harry M. Geduld, Professor of Comparative Literature [*sic*] at Indiana University, whose scrupulously researched book *The Birth of the Talkies* is the model work on the period. Well, on *part* of the period. Even Professor Geduld's book, subtitled 'From Edison to Jolson', unfortunately chooses to 'cut out' just as the major Hollywood studios have got the 'okay for sound' and are rushing to beat each other to the box-office jackpot, with all their glorious errors, vanities (and successes) still ahead of them. Frederick Thrasher's large picturebook actually entitled *Okay for Sound*, first published in 1946, is revealing, but necessarily condensed. And of course Lewis Jacobs, doyen of cinema historians, puts one in his debt (not for the first time, either) with his masterly précis of the changes sound brought with it in his 1939 classic *The Rise of the American Film*. For a period so rich in consequence, these are few enough source books.

The trouble and challenge (as well as a good deal of the excitement) begins when one seeks out the primary sources. A lot of movie history must be written with one's eyes on the films themselves. That is difficult enough, to begin with. General readers, as well as movie buffs, know how shamefully incomplete the world's film archives are – how even the studios that made the movies have often neglected to keep copies, or, even worse, deliberately destroyed old prints to make way for new. The problem is multiplied when it's not just a question of seeing old films – but of *hearing* them, too. To research this transition period is to know all the frustrations of trying to catch lost sounds. The wax discs or optical tracks that gave the early talkies their voice have not survived well – if at all. I sometimes thought I had located a movie that was an important and popular early talkie, only to find that it was the *silent* version that had survived in the archives. I can only honestly report that I saw as many of the films of this period as I needed – but not as many as I desired. There is a powerful consolation, however. For writing about a period that may not be so long ago in time, yet seems centuries away in experience, requires an imaginative empathy that can only come from the whole variety of sources that a film historian uses. The sound track is only one of these. Nor is it necessarily the one to be most trusted. Nothing can bring back the *actual* sounds that audiences in the last year of the 1920s heard issuing from the lips of stars – because nothing can now reproduce the acoustics in a cinema of that time, or the fidelity of a Vitaphone amplifier, or even an audience's shock, delight or embarrassment at hearing, actually *hearing* those Hollywood divinities uttering mortal words. We can easily guess how the later talkies were received, the ones from 1930 onwards, because a greater proportion of those films is extant, here to be seen and heard, and because the audiences that originally saw and heard them were not very different from ourselves.

I suspect that proportionally more silent films have survived in good or reparable condition than early talkies. After all, who knew that silents might not come back? For a short but significant time, Hollywood itself believed the talkies were a fad. Silent pictures were not junked quite as quickly as those first stuttering, hissing attempts at talking features whose rapidity of improvement, getting better by the month, was actually a kind of in-built death warrant.

To recreate these hectic years when all was novelty we have to evaluate whatever source reports are available. That is where the hardship starts. There is as yet simply no index to these transition years, apart from the few books I've mentioned. It is as if a fragmentation grenade has gone off: bits of it are embedded everywhere in a mass of unannotated material, on film and in print. One great asset I enjoyed was to begin this book just when microfilming was making many old and relatively inaccessible sources at last available again. Chief of these, as the reader will soon discover, is the American showbusiness weekly *Variety*, now microfilmed by arrangement with my own old University of Michigan, at Ann Arbor. For this (or any other) period, it is an essential research tool. I have pointed out in the text – but it bears repeating – that *Variety*'s reporters were writing for those in the film industry and were therefore more forthcoming with just those facts, figures and opinions which the historian values than were the professional film critics writing in other journals simply to inform or amuse their lay readership. I am most grateful to *Variety*'s present Executive Editor, Syd Silverman, for letting me quote liberally from earlier issues of his journal.

I think I have included more contemporary material in this book than in any of the earlier studies I have made of the Anglo-American film scene. History is partly a matter of sifting evidence and making judgments: that is the most important part. But the historian also has a duty to let the period in question speak for itself, so that the colour and texture of the times can emerge in the narrative. I hope the reader will find the greater part of the material I have quoted fresh and revealing: it certainly was so to me when I researched it. I have treated the period chronologically. Grouping events thematically is attractive: but it would impose its own falseness on them if applied in this case. So much happened so quickly, sometimes almost simultaneously, that a sense of sequence is vital if cause and effect – or, more likely in the movie industry, success and imitation – are to be perceived. For the same reason, I have been generous with dates. To my mind, nothing is more irritating that finding amidst a text such phrases as 'a few months later' or 'that same November' – one cries out to know 'later than *when*' or 'November *which* year?' The first mention of most of the major movies is followed by a date, generally that of their New York opening. It may not be their actual première date: such things at that period were by no means as precisely arranged as they are now when promotion and advertising have to be synchronised months or even a year ahead of the event. Some of the early talkies were given public previews – at which the critics also caught them – to test the acoustics of the cinemas where they were to open: they might then be withdrawn for 'adjustments'. But the dates given are handy reference points amidst the turbulence of the talkies. Since converting dollars into sterling would make for an unattractive text, I have left all sums of money in their original denomination (generally American). British readers may care to know that between 1925 and 1930 the official dollar-sterling exchange rate was 4·87 dollars. The equivalent sterling purchasing power of 100 dollars was 65 pounds in 1925 and 72 pounds in 1930.

A full list of professional and personal acknowledgements will be found elsewhere. But it would be an act of discourtesy, as well as omission, to fail to acknowledge here and now the encouragement of my editor Colin Webb who pushed me into expanding a short chapter from my earlier book *Stardom* into this full-scale account; Richard Schickel who supplied me with a title and much relevant material; and Kevin Brownlow who has shown in his own book on silent Hollywood how one can bring a lost era to life again – in this case, I hope, to audible life.

ALEXANDER WALKER
Davos, 1976–
London, 1978

Acknowledgements

Grateful acknowledgement is made of quotations from articles in the following newspapers and periodicals:

Cinema, Film Spectator, Film Weekly, Fortune, Harper's, Motion Picture, Moving Picture Classic, Moving Picture World, The New York Times, New York World, Photoplay, Sight and Sound, The Silent Drama, Theatre Magazine, Variety.

Many of the illustrations come from stills issued to publicise films made by or distributed by the following companies: Columbia, Metro-Goldwyn-Mayer, Paramount, RKO-Pathé, Twentieth Century-Fox, United Artists, Universal, Walt Disney, Warner Communications. The author expresses his gratitude. With films made so long ago, copyright is sometimes obscure and although every effort has been made to trace the present holders, the author apologises in advance for any unintentional omission or neglect and will be pleased to insert the appropriate acknowledgement to companies or individuals in any subsequent edition of this book.

In addition to those named in the Preface, the author wishes to express his warm thanks to the following people and institutions for the personal assistance they rendered him in researching and writing this book:

Miss Brenda Davies and Staff, Reference Library, British Film Institute; Miss Michelle Snapes and Mr Markku Salmi, Stills Section, National Film Archive; Mr Jeremy Boulton, Viewing Service, National Film Archive; Chief Librarian and Staff, British Museum Newspaper and Periodical Library; Mr John Kobal; and Mrs Leatrice Gilbert Fountain (John Gilbert's daughter).

The Shattered Silents

'Who the hell wants to hear actors talk?'

To any New Yorker opening his *Times* on 29 March 1928, the newspaper's sedate selection of the day's radio programmes gave little hint of the extraordinary event that was to take place that evening on the other coast of America. As the season was Lent, the air waves offered a noonday service, the Rev. H. Emerson Fosdick officiating. Then came sermons of a more worldly temper, though still related to human frailty and redemption: a broadcast from the Federal Grand Jury Association's luncheon. As dusk fell, the U.S. Marine Corps band took over. . . . Then at precisely 9.00 p.m., from his Illinois home, one Edgar G. Wilmer, President of Dodge Motors of Detroit, prepared to introduce the brand-new Standard Six model to the American public on his company's sponsored radio show, which was to be broadcast on over 55 stations in or linked to the NBC network.

Unfortunately, a plan to have the Edison Co. record the broadcast on disc fell through; so there is no certainty of knowing if Mr Wilmer suffered from the new-ish ailment of the radio age, 'mike fright'. Probably not – for he talked for half-an-hour. And he expressed his total conviction, backed by guarantee, in his six-cylinder automobile's ability to perform as advertised. In this respect at least he had more self-confidence than the amazing line-up of guests who followed him on the *Dodge Brothers Hour*. They included the most famous, the highest paid names in American motion pictures, some of them already part and parcel of the history of the movies – but all of them now more concerned about the future than the past. From mid-afternoon, since Pacific time was three hours behind New York, they had been gathering in a mood of fretful nervousness behind the locked doors of Mary Pickford's bungalow on the United Artists' studio lot in Hollywood. Besides Miss Pickford and her husband Douglas Fairbanks Sr, there were Charlie

Chaplin, the director D. W. Griffith, John Barrymore, Dolores Del Rio, Norma Talmadge and Gloria Swanson. For taking part in the broadcast, they were collectively being paid a mere 50,000 dollars – divided equally. The amount of the fee hardly interested them – an unusual situation where their services were concerned – since some of them spent that kind of money at their dressmakers in a week. The value of the occasion, which was costing 250,000 dollars to stage, was infinitely greater than the cash: so were the risks. For the Big Broadcast of 1928 was designed to demonstrate to millions of Americans, listening in at home or across the nation in cinemas which had been specially wired to receive it, that these Hollywood stars, these public idols whose unique qualities sustained an industry then conservatively valued at sixty-five million dollars, possessed one thing which had never been regarded as remotely necessary to that industry's prosperity or their own celebrity, namely *a voice*. They were there, in short, to prove they had what it took to meet the challenge of *talking* pictures.

As they listened to Mr Wilmer boasting how Dodge factories were turning out 1,000 vehicles a day, most of them may have wished their own voices were as dependable as those vaunted six cylinders. When their sponsor's spiel had at last stopped and Paul Whiteman's orchestra in New York had played a reprise of 'Together', Douglas Fairbanks took over as host. The published programme suggests that the fellow stars he introduced all did things highly characteristic of their famous selves. Doug, for instance, the apostle of physical prowess and optimistic pep, addressed 'the youth of America', and declared, 'It's not hardening of the arteries that makes us grow old, but hardening of the ideas.' D. W. Griffith, like the Great Victorian he still was, discussed 'love in all its phases, eschewing the sex angle completely'. Mary Pickford seems to have just talked 'intimately' to women: they asked no more of America's Sweetheart. Somewhat more specific, John Barrymore recited a *Hamlet* soliloquy: it is unidentified, but one suspects it was indeed *that* one. Chaplin told 'humorous anecdotes in dialect' – i.e. Jewish and Cockney. Gloria Swanson advised girls against trying to gatecrash Hollywood, something she herself had done with great success. Norma Talmadge discussed 'fashion and the films'. And Dolores Del Rio, who had a new film in release called *Ramona*, opted to sing and chose a ballad called – 'Ramona'. It all apparently passed off without a hitch or any of the 'awkwardness' which had been caused in an earlier *Dodge Brothers Hour* when Al Jolson had cracked an off-colour joke about Clara Bow sleeping cross-ways in bed. These stars were less used to live audiences than the irrepressible Al. When it was over everyone in 'the broadcasting chamber' collapsed in various states of nervous exhaustion or euphoric relief. Chaplin declared he had 'nearly died of mike fright'. Barrymore, on the other hand, courted the suspicion that he had fortified himself in advance with the then prohibited liquor by announcing that he was totally indifferent to the effect he had made and didn't really take 'this radio thing' seriously.

Outside reaction to the broadcast was, well, tetchier. The Press were particuarly huffy. This may have been due to the newspapermen's resentment at being locked out of the 'studio' – not even United Artists' executives were allowed in to the broadcast – and being forced to listen in to the stars' voices over amplifiers amidst the vaulting horses and punch-balls in the United Artists' gymnasium where Doug Fairbanks kept himself in shape. Reports were soon rife of substitute voice 'doublers' being used, particularly for the female stars. It was suspected that a professional singer had sung the lyric for Dolores Del Rio, and that someone else had given Norma Talmadge's fashion chat for her. The first rumour was soon proved untrue; the second remained widely accepted, since Miss Talmadge was notoriously speechless at public functions. Joseph Schenck, President of United Artists, and the man who had helped arrange the broadcast, can hardly have been pleased by the belated revelation that the opportunity to appear on the show had previously been offered to stars of Paramount, Metro-Goldwyn-Mayer and First National whose executives had all turned it down after conferring with their publicity chiefs. As things proved, their caution was amply justified. Simply no one had foreseen the calamitous conjunction on the night of the broadcast of the year's worst electrical storms and the equally turbulent response to hearing their favourite stars which came from the public assembled in those cinemas which had halted their advertised programmes to pick up the broadcast. *Variety*, the leading show-business weekly, later published a full-page round-up of nation-wide reactions: it must have made film industry chiefs tremble as they read how intemperately patrons had responded to the grand strategy of proving that the well-loved but silent stars were equal to the task of talking.

In some small theatres, demonstrations had occurred amongst resentful audiences bored out of their minds by the flood of stilted loquaciousness: occasionally the loud-speakers had to be turned off and admission money hastily refunded. 'After ten minutes of the Coast colony stuff,' reported the manager of the State Theater, Boston, 'the entire audience started to razz and the theater had to switch back to its regular performance.'[1] Static was so heavy over Buffalo that most of the show was (fortunately) inaudible. In Rochester, Mr Wilmer's paean of praise for his new car was greeted with 'moans and boos'. The programme was 'yanked' even before Fairbanks's closing remarks. In Memphis, the only star they stood for was Barrymore: the manager reported that 'they don't want radio advertising stunts mixed with their entertainment in this burg'. In Detroit, where static caused sniggers, Norma Talmadge was openly cat-called. 'They paid some heed to Fairbanks with his chatter about optimism', but refunds were demanded when the hapless Mr Wilmer spoke again. Baltimore was more polite,

[1] *Variety*, 4 April 1928.

3

but it was agreed that it had been a mistake to take the public behind the Hollywood scenes and 'let them listen to entertainers whose talents are essentially visual'. All in all, it was a bad omen for the talkies. *Variety*, though, offered this consolation: only in the smaller towns did the broadcast being carried by the new enemy, radio, adversely affect box-office business at the cinemas. Small comfort, perhaps: but absolutely radiant news compared with the message which Edgar G. Wilmer had to relay to shareholders a few months later. The sales of Dodge cars had dropped thirty million dollars below the 1926 figures! Whatever else it had done, the broadcast certainly hadn't proved that stars sell cars. But of much more immediate anguish to the stars who had taken part in it, and indeed to all of Hollywood in those early months of 1928, was the colossal conundrum of whether an industry that had been mute all its life could now sell voices from the screen to a public that had never in its life had to listen to them. What lay ahead was 'the talkie revolution', which *Fortune* magazine, after the earthquake was over and everyone who had survived it was drawing breath again, was to characterise without exaggeration as 'beyond comparison the fastest and most amazing in the whole history of industrial revolutions'.[2] One need only add, '. . . and the most panic-stricken as well'. A few months after the broadcast, one of Hollywood's most perceptive residents would survey the panic then being precipitated by the talkie revolution in full spate and later on comment in his memoirs on the state of mind of just such superstars as those who had 'tried their voices' at the mike. 'Through no fault of their own, they were finished, washed up, out. The gaiety and glitter of Hollywood was theirs no longer. The adoring crowds would soon forget they had ever lived, the gorgeous homes with swimming pools and tennis courts would pass into the hands of others who had the right voices. It was tough.'[3] It was also not quite the whole truth. But who was to know that in 1928?

What is often overlooked in writing about the history of this perplexed period is that the talkie revolution in the cinema was preceded, and indeed prepared for, by the talkie revolution in the home. Behind both events was – radio.

Americans in the early years of the 1920s were for the first time hearing voices and music that didn't emanate from vaudeville or the stage of the live theatre, but entered their eardrums through the headphones of the early crystal sets and then, before long, as vacuum tubes arrived, expanded from inside the individual's head to fill the living-room, drug store, business office or barber's shop. A nation which had hitherto read its news now more and more *listened* to it; people who had socialised conversationally now kept their own mouths shut while disembodied voices talked to them; the broadcaster's voice

[2] *Fortune*, Vol. 2, October 1930.
[3] *Hollywood Saga*, by William C. de Mille (E. P. Dutton & Co., New York, 1939), p. 287.

was so swiftly accepted as part of a change in public awareness that inside a few short years it was hard to recall a time when silence had been the golden rule except when the telephone shrilled or the phonograph uttered its scratchy melodies – and both of these were essentially personal devices for communication, unlike public radio. By 1923, according to the historian Llewellyn White, 'no fewer than 556 broadcasting stations (in America) were making the ether crackle with strange sounds'.[4] By 1924, the manufacture of receiving sets had become a fifty million dollar industry; its gross value three years later was put at four hundred and twenty-five million dollars. The expansion of broadcasting was phenomenally swift. It was something else, too: it was phenomenally easy. Setting up a radio station in the early 1920s, if one knew how to go about it, took little time and not much more money.

Four men who were obliged to acquire such cost-conscious knowledge quickly by 1925 were Sam, Harry, Albert and Jack Warner. Two years earlier they had set up Warner Brothers Pictures Inc., and had parlayed their assets of one canine star (Rin-Tin-Tin) and one Shakespearean actor (John Barrymore) into healthy box-office grosses. They had expanded into more studio space and wider distribution by erecting a Broadway picture palace and buying the old and ailing Vitagraph Co. production lot. This created a need for stepped-up publicity. What was the latest, the most exciting medium for this? Why, radio! With the economical sense of cost-cutting that was to give their films, at best, their down-to-earth efficiency, and keep a couple of generations of stars complaining of the Brothers' cheese-paring attitudes, they hired a sound engineer at the cheapest possible price. Major Benjamin Levinson, formerly of the Signals Corps was then Pacific Coast director for Western Electric, the manufacturing subsidiary of the American Telephone and Telegraph Co. His brief: to build a studio and radio transmitter on Warners' Sunset Boulevard lot using second-hand equipment from a recently bankrupt station – Warners were taking no chances.

Station KFWB, Los Angeles's third, started broadcasting on 3 March 1925, introduced by a male singer who was none other than Jack L. Warner himself, an estwhile boy soprano. Love of music ran almost as deep as love of profit in the souls of the Warner quartet: and it is this conjunction that explains the next move – and its revolutionary consequences. Major Levinson brought back news of experiments going on at A.T. & T.'s research branch, the Bell Laboratories, New York. The telephone company had been refining its lines so as to carry the human voice more clearly across the continent; the labs had also been encouraged to seek more outlets for the new and clearer sound system which had been snapped up by the major phonograph companies – and they had turned to the one medium that seemed to them to need sound, the movies. This shows an almost transcendental innocence as regards

[4] *The American Radio*, by Llewellyn White (University of Chicago Press, 1947), p. 13.

the big-business motives of Hollywood, where sound films would have immediately written down the value of the motion picture industry's twenty-five year investment in silence. But that, amazingly, did not sink into the heads of those pure researchers at Bell Labs till later, and meanwhile Major Levinson was enthusing to Sam Warner about a short test film he had seen in which one could hear, actually *hear*, a piano being played while watching the pianist – even the audible snap of his glove buttons as he removed them came forth from the screen with breathtaking authenticity. It was all due to two synchronised motors, one moving the film through the projector, the other turning a wax phonograph disc.

Sam Warner, the 'technical' brother, hurried to New York to see – no, to hear – for himself. 'I had heard and seen so much about talking pictures that I would not have walked across the street to look at one,' he later recalled. 'But when I heard a twelve-piece orchestra on the screen at the Bell Telephone Laboratories I could not believe my own ears. I walked in back of the screen to see if they did not have an orchestra there synchronising with the picture. They all laughed at me.'[5]

Harry Warner, who ran the 'business' end of things, got interested immediately his brother reported that here was a way of opening up the cinemas that at present wouldn't play Warner products by generously saving them the cost of the house orchestras which accompanied the silent film shows with suitable mood music: Warner films would henceforth come with their own synchronised recorded accompaniment. No need for live musicians. Why, they could even offer a 'canned' concert or vaudeville show to towns without a 'legitimate' theatre. The show would be on the screen! Jack L. Warner, the 'producer' brother, has recorded the ensuing conversational exchange. It must take the all-time prize for non-prescience. '"But don't forget you can have actors talk, too," Sam broke in. "Who the hell wants to hear actors talk?" Harry asked testily.'[6]

Agreement for further research into sound pictures was signed between Warners and Western Electric in June, 1925: at which point Warners discovered that an entrepreneur called J. Walter Rich had already signed a prior agreement to do exactly what they hoped to do. But Rich agreed to go along with them 'on a share and share alike' basis for a fee of 72,000 dollars, just twice the sum he had spent unsuccessfully trying to interest other movie companies in sound. He was thus the first to be enriched by the device that was named the Vitaphone; and as things turned out for Warners, it looked within a year that they might be the first to be bankrupted.

Movies accompanied by sound were by no means an untried novelty

[5] Sam Warner, quoted by Stanley McConnell, Bulletin of the National Film Music Council.

[6] *My First Hundred Years in Hollywood*, by Jack L. Warner and Dean Jennings (Random House, New York, 1964), p. 168.

in 1925. Due to his own increasing deafness, Thomas Edison had been more concerned with developing a hearing machine called the phonograph than a seeing machine which was to be named the Kinetoscope; but it took only a commercial entrepreneur not disadvantaged by such sad personal afflictions to mix sound and vision and the Kinetophone became the talking-picture show of 1894. Its novelty value was short and unprofitable. In the new century several synchronised devices were available for sale or hire: two records, each for a dollar, went with Sigmund Lubin's production of *The Bold Bank Robbery* in 1904: a phonograph to play them on was thrown in free. But amplification remained more of a problem than synchronisation. It wasn't satisfactorily solved till Lee De Forest invented the audion amplifier in 1907 which allowed sound to be increased to auditorium volume. As Harry M. Geduld makes so abundantly clear in his meticulously researched history of the early sound film, *The Birth of the Talkies*,[7] Lee De Forest was a genius who still hasn't won the recognition he deserves since his commercial sense was blunter than his inventive acumen. He developed the forerunner of the modern sound track by photographing sound waves in black and half-tones directly on to the margin of the film strip, then converting them back into audible sound by the photoelectric cell as the film ran through the projector. He made his first talking picture (of himself) in 1921. By 1923 he was exhibiting the Phonofilm, as he called his invention, not only in New York but in several dozen East Coast towns, using songs and comic sketches by artists like Eddie Cantor and W. C. Fields as material. He even put a synchronised music track on to James Cruze's silent Western epic *The Covered Wagon* in 1924. By 1927 he had 'produced' more than 1,000 shorts. But he failed utterly to create a commercial basis for sound movies simply because the more tenacious and conservative entrepreneurs who ran the industry saw them more as a threat than a promise. A whole industry, a huge audience, had been geared to accept the silent mime in which players projected the emotions, sub-titles supplied the dialogue, spectators imagined the voices, and musicians, who might range from a single pianist to a complete orchestra depending on the capacity of the house and the pretensions of the drama, supplemented the psychological mood or matched their instruments to the physical action. It was this combination, at best a beautiful unison of art, industry and imagination, that sound was about to shatter.

The Warner brothers next move in 1925 anticipated – though no one then was aware of it – one of the most devasting consequences of the early talkies. Namely, the overweening power of New York or, rather, Broadway. Jack L. Warner stayed out in Hollywood producing the romantic drama *Don Juan*. It had been begun as a silent film: when it was decided to add a Vitaphone music score to its swashbuckling ardours, its budget was increased from 500,000 to 700,000 dollars, making it

[7] *The Birth of the Talkies*, by Harry M. Geduld (Indiana University Press, 1975).

Warners' most expensive film to date. But the really pioneering work in sound was done in New York, where Sam Warner set about filming and simultaneously recording a series of high-class concert items, eight 'acts' in all, to be presented in the same bill as *Don Juan* as evidence of Vitaphone's power to hold audiences in thrall, as well as sell itself to other producers and exhibitors. Art, dignity and the hard buck were inseparable parts of the package.

New York was then – and still largely is – the business end of the movies, where the cinema chains reported, the book-keeping was done, the accountants ruled, and there was a deeply entrenched antipathy towards those prodigals out on the West Coast who didn't know the value of money outside their own inflationary contracts. Actually, there was much truth in this view. A U.S. Government statistical review of the mid-1920s estimated that the return on a two and a half billion dollars investment in producing, distributing and exhibiting movies was a puny 1·9 per cent, well below the average profitability of other major industries. Production and studio overheads were identified as the holes through which the profits leaked. Sam Warner's decision to put the Vitaphone half of the bill together in New York, not Hollywood, under the eye of the East Coast money-men, was like adding another set of muscles to that end of the tug-o'-war. In plain truth, though, he had no choice. Instrumental and singing talent from concert hall and opera house was to be found in the East, not the West. To bring such artists to Hollywood still involved a three-and-a-half day train journey: to keep them there would add thousands of dollars on to the million or so it was to cost Warners to hire them for the film, in some cases buying them out of exclusive contracts. Besides, all the recording know-how was still in the East: it would be a relief to have Bell Labs on the doorstep if Sam got into difficulties. As he very soon did. . . .

Trains rumbling by on the subway forced him to move from the thin-walled Vitagraph Studios in Brooklyn to the Manhattan Opera House where the Vitaphone recording apparatus was squeezed into a reputedly sound-proof cubicle usually used by the tenor John McCormack for 'warming up' before he went on stage. Then blasting began at a nearby construction site, causing the stylus to jump out of the groove it was tracing. Jack Warner claims in his memoirs that it was he who suggested the cure for this – 'Record at night'. And why not? After all, back in Hollywood, where actors weren't under Equity's or any other union's protection, the studios worked artists round the clock, day and night, in conditions that for all but the few pampered stars resembled sweated labour. Less easily 'cured' were a host of unexpected 'noises-off'. To everyone's surprise, the Vitaphone apparatus kept picking up strange snatches of radio programmes that were drifting inaudibly around in the Brooklyn ether. These intrusive waves were only repulsed when the recording machines were sheathed in metal. Then the arc lights 'sizzled' and an incandescent type of illumination had to be devised – all this in

Above, Filming of a Vitaphone musical short at the Manhattan Opera House, turned into an improvised sound studio, probably in early 1927. Flats and drapes muffle the echoes; three microphones are suspended from the flies; the camera box, without its side wall, is mounted on castors to permit some mobility. *Below*, Jolson in 'white face' for a change, playing the part like one who already knows he is the star of the show. In no sense did *The Jazz Singer* make him a star, but it amply confirmed his stage celebrity in another medium and started the rush into pictures with dialogue.

double quick time. The wax records themselves developed a surface 'hiss'. But worst of all was the whirring mechanism of the motor-driven cameras. These had replaced the old hand-cranked machines which wouldn't have preserved the regularity of speed essential if sound and image were to be perfectly synchronised. The sòlution was drastic. The camera along with its operator was exiled from free-ranging contact with the action and incarcerated in a sound-proof shed of cramped dimensions, limited mobility and suffocating interior temperature. In the front of it was a square porthole; and the captive lens now shot the picture through sheets of optical glass specially imported from Germany. Instead of transmitting emotion, the first edict of the new order was to smother noise. For those who stopped to think, it was a bad omen.

Lee De Forest had stopped to think, way back in 1923, when he was asked what sound would mean to feature film production. 'They'll have to direct films by sign language,' he replied. 'What will happen is that they will have to use real artists – actors who have a voice as well as a camera face. I think it will add brains to the movies.'[8] A shrewd prophecy: but still a long way from fulfilment. If asked what sound was adding to *their* movies in the spring and summer of 1926, Warner Brothers might have answered, 'Not brains, headaches.'

Don Juan's score, a remarkably sophisticated one, full of instrumental colour and variety of mood, had been composed the previous winter: it was recorded in the Opera House by the New York Philharmonic Orchestra. Henry Hadley led the 107 members through it as the movie was projected on the screen behind them: eyewitness reports make it sound a strangely modern scene. The Vitaphone concert bill had had less time devoted to it, just three months – probably due to all the technical snags – and it was finished a mere few days before the scheduled première date, 6 August 1926; at which time Warner Brothers had run themselves heavily into debt. To produce their new wonder, they had spent a massive three million dollars; and at that date they had only one cinema in the world equipped to show it. Fifty selected seats at the thirteen-hundred-seat Warner Theater had been equipped with earphones for the hard-of-hearing; again no chances were being taken.

Paradoxically, the one thing scarcely mentioned at that hugely successful première was the single quality that was soon giving its name to the revolution Warners started. Practically no report of it refers to *talking* pictures in the offing – at least they don't seem to have been uppermost in the audience's mind on that opening night. What emerges with startling clarity amidst the diverse reactions is that Vitaphone's novelty lay not in its power to 'talk', but to purvey music – and self-consciously *quality* music at that. *The New York Times*'s critic, Mordaunt Hall, deemed it 'a marvellous device' and reported that 'it stirred a

[8] *A Conqueror of Space*, by Georgette Carneal (Liveright, New York, 1930), p. 283.

distinguished audience . . . to unusual enthusiasm'; but he didn't give the slightest indication that 'talkies' were now a practical possibility. His account continued: 'The natural reproduction of voices, the tonal quality of musical instruments and the timing of the sound to the lips of singers and actions of musicians was almost uncanny. . . . The future of the new contrivance is boundless. . . .' But the future for what? For dialogue pictures? No: '. . . for inhabitants of small and remote places which will have the opportunity of listening to and seeing grand opera as it is given in New York'[9] It is quite true that as the lights dimmed at the première, the first thing heard from the screen was speech. Or, rather, a throat being cleared in preparation for speech. Standing to attention between a decorative chair and a table laden with (decorative?) books, Will H. Hays, the former Postmaster-General in President Harding's Cabinet who had become a president himself, heading the Motion Picture Producers Association, began to speak. 'No story written for the screen is as dramatic as the story of the screen itself.' It sounds in retrospect uncomfortably like one of those over-rehearsed 'giant step for mankind' utterances. But his words, congratulating all and sundry, were perfectly synchronised, his authentic tones won acclaim. 'There was no muffled utterance or lisping,' said the *Times*. 'It was the voice of Hays, and had any of his friends closed their eyes they would have immediately recognised his voice.' At the end of his speech, Hays stood in silence. The audience applauded spontaneously. Whereupon, the figure on the screen actually bowed! Witnessing this marvel of realism, one spectator later observed, 'No closer approach to resurrection has ever been made by science.'

Perhaps: but it was still a long way from suggesting to anyone present the inherent possibilities of talkie *dialogue*. What reaped bushels of praise was the musical fare. It was itemised by the *Times* with awe. The Philharmonic Orchestra had 'thrilling volume . . . the screen scenes swayed (*sic*: 'cut' was not yet commonplace in reviewers' vocabulary and 'pan' would have been incomprehensible to readers who were cued to view the Vitaphone as a proscenium event) from those of the whole body of musicians to small groups as each instrumental choir took up its work.' Mischa Elman, violinist, played Dvořák's *Humoresque*, 'every note synchronised with the gliding bow'; Marion Talley sang an aria from *Rigoletto* and 'as she retreated from the front of the stage, her voice became modulated'; Roy Smeck on banjo, ukulele, harmonica and Hawaiian guitar provided a light interlude in which 'every note appeared to come straight from the instrument'; Giovanni Martinelli sang an aria from *I Pagliacci*, 'nothing like it had ever been heard in a motion picture theatre . . . the invited gathering burst into applause . . . the singer's tones appeared to echo in the body of the theater as they rose from a shadow on the screen'.

What is of special interest here is the comment on Marion Talley's

[9] *The New York Times*, 7 August 1926.

voice becoming 'modulated' as she moved away from the camera and microphone: what would have been deemed faulty in a phonograph recording turned (for some at least) into stunning realism when a singer could at last be heard as well as seen moving away into long shot. On the other hand, this section was the most criticised part of the film. *Photoplay*'s reviewer was downright disrespectful. 'The one frost of the evening was Marion Talley, the "Kansas City canary". Miss Talley sang the "Caro Nome" from *Rigoletto* and her voice was far from attractive. As for her face, the producers made the mistake of allowing the camera to come too close to (her). Long shots – and good, long ones – were just invented for that girl.'[10] *Variety*'s reporter didn't lose his head, either. He noted that the hapless Miss Talley 'looked to be grimacing her way through', dismissed the divertissement of Russian songs and dances entitled *An Evening on the Don* as a failed effort, and chided the Philharmonic for weak brass. He also wrote that Harold Bauer (piano) and Efrem Zimbalist (violin) in variations on Beethoven's *Kreutzer Sonata* 'did not register well', although the *Times* man found 'every note audible'. This discrepancy is in all likelihood due to a simple matter of where the respective critics were sitting: poor acoustics were to haunt the talkies right into the 1930s: it's hardly to be wondered at if all wasn't right on the opening night. What everyone agreed on was the success of the finale in which Anna Case sang 'La Fiesta' accompanied by the Cansino dancers, the Metropolitan Opera Chorus and the one hundred and seven-piece Philharmonic – though Harry Warner's later admission that an eighty-piece orchestra produced a better recording tone than a one hundred and seven-piece one, leads one to doubt if quite *everyone* was present and correct. Not that the audience felt undersold. *Variety*'s headline 'Vitaphone Bow Is Hailed As Marvel'[11] confirmed the success of the evening.

Extra assurance came to the Warner brothers swiftly. After a public opening at ten dollars a seat, the box-office generated a record 13,787 dollars for only five performances. The top evening prices were 3·50 dollars, which was 1·50 dollars more than the top price for a silent movie 'special' at other cinemas: ticket scalpers were selling them at 5·00 dollars and more to huge crowds. The show was to run nearly eight months, be seen by over half-a-million and gross almost 800,000 dollars.

Don Juan, the accompanying feature film directed by Alan Crosland, was overshadowed by the Vitaphone concert attractions even though, at ninety minutes, it ran half-an-hour longer and had a genuine star of the cinema, not simply the stage, in the title role. It also drew mixed notices. Barrymore's distinguished reputation in classical roles in the theatre frequently made critics a little contemptuous of his crowd-pleasing screen parts. What Stark Young had said of him in *The New Republic* was typical of the reviews he was accustomed to getting from some lofty

[10] *Photoplay*, October 1926.   [11] *Variety*, 11 August 1926.

quarters: 'Artistically, the only thing we could say about Mr Barrymore's performances is that he brings to them tricks and mannerisms that stiffen them slightly and perhaps convey a sense of acting to a public that has seen but little of it.'[12] His energetic Don didn't allay the feeling that he was squandering his talents and even aping a little too slavishly Douglas Fairbanks Sr in the swordfights and his athletic leaps down staircases and over balconies. 'Hey, Mr Fairbanks, come home quick,' *Photoplay* advised, 'John Barrymore is stealing your stuff.'[13] He was reputed to have bestowed 127 kisses on the various ladies in the film during production, a figure brushed disdainfully aside by defenders of Rudolph Valentino. Barrymore, incidentally, played not only the Don, but the Don's father, whose bad experience with women during the prologue was designed to whet the audience's appetite for the son's overt misogyny following the intermission. Valentino in *The Son of the Sheik*, whose production overlapped with *Don Juan*, had also played both 'son' and 'sheik' and suspicion that their idol was being plagiarised as well as burlesqued irritated Valentino fans – his death in New York just seventeen days after the première of *Don Juan* probably didn't help them warm to Barrymore, either.

Owing fewer sentimental debts to the deceased holders of the 'Great Lover' patent, we can be more relaxed about Barrymore's lively and amorous interpretation, while agreeing with Edmund Wilson's cool sarcasm that 'as for the Hollywood version of *Don Juan*, it differs strikingly from those of Byron, Mozart and Molière'.[14] That degree of difference was emphasised by the refurbished Warner Theater whose foyer was dominated by a 'gigantic apotheosis' of Barrymore kissing a girl amidst the clouds, while on the street front blue and red lights flashed on and off, artfully illuminating blow-ups in which naked females who were invisible in the red glow sprang into lubricious prominence in the blue. In such a gaudy context, it is perhaps understandable if few of the reviews dilated on *Don Juan*'s specially composed score. After all, Barrymore could only make love – the Vitaphone stars could make music and song.

Significantly, the concert part of the programme was determinedly 'up market'. Possibly the only concession to popular taste was the novelty guitarist Roy Smeck: yet the audience was so enthusiastic over his act that it was to have great influence on the contents of the next Vitaphone programme. But the vulgarity of vaudeville was not (yet) allowed to sully the 'quality' entertainment. There was not even a song in English – which must have been of help to the lip synchronisation. There is one other aspect – and it is a cruelly paradoxical one – to an evening that Warners could justifiably boast of as 'The Greatest

[12] Stark Young, quoted in *The Barrymores*, by Hollis Alpert (W. H. Allen, London, 1965), p. 263.

[13] *Photoplay*, October 1926.

[14] *The American Earthquake*, by Edmund Wilson (W. H. Allen, London, 1958), p. 84.

Sensation in the History of Motion Pictures!' adding in the advertisements 'PUBLIC THRILLED – CRITICS AMAZED'. Far from immediately sensing that Vitaphone was a clear and present threat to their livelihood, musicians and singers alike, in the immediate aftermath of it, shared the initial euphoria and actually welcomed the invention that was so soon to put thousands of them out of work. What they chose to see on that heady evening was a God-given device for disseminating their talents and reputation across the nation and even overseas. One or two Vitaphone 'short subjects' a year, and they could sit back and draw royalties as the recording stars already did without the grinding need to tour 'in person'. The performing image would stand in for them. Reality soon dashed that dream: but such was the talk on the night, and even on the morning after. As with so much else that had to do with the coming talkies, everyone sensed, to quote *Variety* again, that 'they were present at what might be the première of a new era in the amusement business'. But equally truly, nobody really understood into what immense changes the new era was about to plunge them.

2

'The music – that's the big plus about this.'

'There is so much to the Vitaphone as it may affect the show business that most of it will come in little driblets of comment,' said *Variety* cautiously, fully two weeks after the première. Then, even more hesitantly, the paper alluded to what might, just *might* be an outcome.

> One novel angle thought of by a *Variety* reviewer (Schader) is that, since Will Hays' speaking voice on the Vitaphone is a faithful reproduction, the best 'talking picture' ever heard as to talk only, the Vitaphone might be adapted to picture players, permitted them to talk 'titles', thus doing away with the written titles. Just how far that might start a panic among picture players who can't talk and have no dramatic experience or knowledge of elocution or diction is problematical. Its effect might reach far and also open up a more ready picture field for dramatic actors.[1]

For anyone believing that the talkies were absent one day and then there the next, invented overnight, such passages are useful correctives. The possibilities of talking pictures were barely glimpsed by the industry they were to turn upside down. What overshadowed most speculation about the future of Vitaphone were the enormous profits it was making in the here and now. 'Why change a good thing?' might well have been the reaction to *Variety*'s tentative forecast. In the second week of the Warners' double-bill, an amazing gross of 29,000 dollars was produced: the highest single week's business ever done by a Broadway cinema. Just as dramatic was the impact on Warner Brothers' stock, which had been as low as 14 before the première, but moved up to 32 within three days of it, then soared to 54 by the end of the month. After a 'four-wall deal' had been done for the Vitaphone programme with a Chicago theatre –

[1] *Variety*, 25 August 1926.

Warners had few outlets of their own and had to 'buy the house', so to speak, at a special price to get other cinemas to show their films – the stock raced up to 69¼, six times its price just two months earlier. Other companies' film stock was behaving excitably, too, suggesting that banking interests were buying into a business that Wall Street had hitherto treated with often well-founded reserve. Something big was definitely stirring. No one knew quite what, but the financial feelers were being put out. But by the end of September, the stock slumped to 45: amongst those burned were numerous Warners' executives, film directors and actors who had bought it at 60. Those deeper in the know said that the price would not rise again until the next Vitaphone programme, due for its première on 5 October 1926, at Warners' newly equipped Colony Theater, Broadway. In some ways, this show was an even greater successs than the first: it had far more relevance to the future of sound films. For one thing, the second bill of fare was much broader in appeal. 'Better Than Vaudeville', said *Variety*'s front-page.

The Philharmonic Orchestra opened the hour-long show; but now the music wasn't *Tannhäuser*, but 'The Spirit of 1918'. This overture was followed by a concert baritone, Reinald Werrenrath, but instead of a foreign opera aria he sang such homestead favourites as 'The Long, Long Trail' and 'The Heart of a Rose'. Also on the bill were The Four Aristocrats with 'jazzy songs and melodies'; Elsie Janis perched on an army truck with a chorus from the 107th Infantry as support forces; Eugene and Willie Howard in a comic sketch; and George Jessel doing a monologue and singing an Irving Berlin song. But the hit of the show was undoubtedly the blackface singer Al Jolson.

During the intermission, and before the synchronised feature film, *The Better 'Ole*, which was part of the accompanying programme, the Colony lobby buzzed with excited talk about how much it would cost a vaudeville house to present such artists in person. 'There were mighty few theatres in the land that could stand a tab as enormous as that (would mean),' *Variety* declared. The estimates then quoted are revealing; they showed the impressive salaries already reached by artists in the older branch of entertainment which the talkies were shortly to eliminate. The Philharmonic Orchestra alone would cost 6,000 dollars a week. For Werrenrath to stoop to vaudeville entertainment would mean a sweetener of 2,500 dollars. Jessel, Janis and the Howards were reckoned to pull in 3,000 apiece for their acts. As for Jolson, he would be drawing 5,000 dollars. The weekly bill for the cluster of talents would total 23,000 dollars; and if the theatre where they appeared also wanted to show *The Better 'Ole*, a broad bit of silent slapstick starring Syd Chaplin as Bruce Bairnsfather's First World War Tommy, 'Old Bill', scripted by Charles F. Reisner and Darryl F. Zanuck, and provided with a 'patriotic' music score and sound effects, then the theatre would have to add another 8,000 to 15,000 dollars to its salary sheet. *Variety*'s report made the ominous comment, 'How much business the average vaudeville show that plays a town like Schenectady, New York, Dakron, Ohio, Richmond, Virginia, or Providence, Rhode Island, would do if stacked up against a bill of Vitaphone entertainment of the proportions of this coming along weekly in a tremendous picture theatre, was one of the lobby comments.'[2] The first Vitaphone show had whetted the appetite: this one served a warning. Not on the artists. They were still licking their lips over the royalties they might draw for Vitaphone film appearances; though their optimism was tempered by a cold shower of Warner Brothers' economic realism a short time afterwards, when it was announced that Al Jolson, who usually got 10,000 dollars plus royalties for every recording he made on the Brunswick label, had settled for a flat 5,000 dollars and no royalties at all for his Vitaphone recordings. The real warning was served on the vaudeville managers: they were already being blamed for letting this new phase of show business slip out of their hands and into the grasp of 'the picture people'.

If one looks at the Vitaphone programme more closely, it suggests how these short items, filmed head on, and for the most part without close-ups, were serving as pilot films for the sensational debut of talking pictures that was only months away. They showed, as Harry M. Geduld has put it, that 'talk was, almost imperceptibly, creeping into what had been conceived by the Warners as a medium for recorded music.'[3] 'The music – that's the big plus about this,' Harry Warner had said. It wasn't going to be so much longer. George Jessel's whispering wisecracks didn't register too well; but the two Howards in a skit called 'Between the Acts at the Opera' offered proof that a 'talking act' could click. *Variety* reported in a second review of the film six months later – when a certain perspective was possible and the Vitaphone programme was finally being presented not as a 'speciality event', but in continuous performance – '(The Howards') several minutes of dialogue was as clear as their personal delivery and carried throughout the house. Even Willie's low-toned wisecracking got over.'[4] The same reviewer then conveyed a presentiment of the first real star of the coming talkies. He described the Al Jolson sketch. '(Against) a log-cabin background, in cork (black-face) and overalls, the mammy-master sent over three numbers in bell-like fashion. Opening with "The Red, Red Robin", followed by "April Showers", and ending with "Rockabye Baby with a Dixie Melody", Jolson copped the honors of the unit.' It's unlikely that this huge personal success was lost on Warner Brothers. In May (or June) 1926, they had bought the rights to Samuel Raphaelson's sentimental play *The Jazz Singer*, intending it as a screen vehicle for the entertainer who was then starring in it on Broadway – George Jessel. It would of course have been a silent film had it been made then; and at that time Warners had no inkling that sound was so close. But now the second Vitaphone programme proved that Jolson was a bigger hit with the public than

[2] Ibid., 13 October 1926.   [3] Harry M. Geduld, op. cit., p. 147.
[4] *Variety*, 23 March 1927.

Jessel when both could be heard singing on the screen. Warners, incidentally, paid 50,000 dollars for the screen rights to *The Jazz Singer*; and undoubtedly would have had to pay much more had they purchased it when the talkies arrived. It was not an inconsiderable sum, however, for a company which historians have commonly believed to be near bankruptcy at the time. Short of ready cash, they may have been, though able to draw hefty credits from their bankers, Goldman, Sachs, to acquire the Vitagraph Studios and fund Vitaphone. But I can find no evidence to suggest that Warners grasped at the talkies because they were in desperate straits and near financial collapse. If this had been so, they would never have got the huge loans needed to launch Vitaphone.

For a brief, heady period, from mid-1926 till the end of 1927, vaudeville 'names' were courted with competitive urgency by both Vitaphone sound pictures and the ever-expanding radio networks. It was still a good time to be a stage entertainer in America. At the beginning of September 1926 the trade papers carried a report, 'Radio's New Amusement', to the effect that 'radio as an important ally to show business is anticipated on a bigger and never-before-heard-of scale this fall.'[5] The Radio Corporation of America, founded in 1919, was bent on promoting a more popular type of radio artist. The concert-hall image had been stressed hitherto and variety performers were almost incidental contributors. Now, like Vitaphone, the radio interests were aiming right at the masses. The National Broadcasting Company was incorporated as an RCA subsidiary in September 1926. Two months later RCA paid A.T. & T. a million dollars for the latter's WEAF chain of stations in order to link them to the WJZ network and boost the consumer market for the radio sets it manufactured and the rush was on to use headline entertainers to sell hardware. Radio, under A.T. & T., had begun selling advertising time in 1923. Macy's was one of the first stores to boost its wares this way – Gimbel's naturally followed suit. As the advertising rates rose, despite the envious charges of companies which only made hardware and didn't sell time that radio was being 'debased', so did the money available to fund popular entertainment and bring it into the American home.

NBC's chain of twenty-five or so stations could charge six hundred dollars a minute for advertising: it was forecasting an annual revenue of fifteen million dollars on the sale of time alone. Eddie Cantor was paid the then record-setting fee of one hundred dollars a minute for a broadcast in November 1926: he was even allowed to slip in a commercial for his new film *Kid Boots*. Not much less was being paid to Will Rogers and Mary Garden, at this time radio's best-known 'regulars'. Radio was able to pay an orchestra as much for an hour's broadcasting time as it could get for a week's engagement in a hotel ballroom. By December 1926, an even more intriguing prospect opened

[5] Ibid., 1 September 1926.

up. 'Radio artists may be seen over television', said the trade papers. General Electric was making television pilot tests at Schenectady, New York, and *Variety*, like most newspapers somewhat uncertain how the very latest novelty should be described, reported that 'listeners-in are expected to see performers at the mike over long distances'. There was even a report of phonograph records that could produce pictures: a practical foreshadowing of the videodiscs of the electronics age forty or fifty years later. Vitaphone, radio, television: it seemed as if a whole new future had magically dawned for the vaudeville entertainer.

Demand, of course, generated wariness. It began to sink in to vaudeville artists during the fall of 1926 that sound movies could be harmful to them as well as enriching. There was a well-established tradition of music-hall artists playing at the picture houses in towns that did not include a theatre; and *they* were the first to realise that if they made a few Vitaphone shorts, however much they varied their act from film to film there was a real risk of their being in competition with themselves on the screen. Others under contract to phonograph interests, like the Victor Talking Machine Co., which was co-operating at the time with Warners in 'canning' their artists for Vitaphone, began complaining of the film-makers' cost-cutting tactics – which is to say that they held out for more money. The American Society of Composers, Authors and Publishers (ASCAP) had decided as far back as 1922 that radio stations should pay royalties on records played: now it grew so alarmed at the widespread propositioning of artists by radio and film people that it condemned it as 'promiscuous' and said it would do no one any good. In the short term, this was true; but in the even shorter term, few of those who were approached managed to resist seduction.

Variety began regular reviews of Vitaphone short subjects with its issue of 23 March 1927; and by the end of March, NBC flourished its power to go after 'names', and get them, by issuing two well-publicised contracts. One was for 50,000 dollars to be paid to George Olsen, the band leader, for personal services exclusive of his orchestra; the other was for 119,000 dollars to include the salaries of twenty-two musicians and singers whose combined talents were deemed suitable for broadcasting both light music and grand opera. This was topped in mid-June 1927, by a spectacular offer to Paul Whiteman and his orchestra. He signed up with the Old Gold cigarette company to promote its products as well as his own New York restaurant in weekly broadcasts from the place for a fee pitched between 4,000–5,000 dollars an hour. When Whiteman and the band played on a New York stage, he got a 'mere' 10,500 dollars a week. The radio fee confirmed the immense pulling power that the relatively new medium was now exerting on stage entertainers – and on their prices.

Thus by 1927, song, music, monologue or cross-talk act on the radio or in the Vitaphone shorts was bringing sound where there had hitherto been desultory chat in the domestic living-room or mood music from the house musicians in the cinemas – perhaps also a miniature stage show in the larger halls before the silent feature was shown. People were first thrilled by the novelty, then very quickly came to expect it. Where movies were concerned, the 'audible' attraction did not as yet extend to a full-length feature; but it must have been apparent very soon that the feature film could not afford to remain silent, or, at any rate, without voice. The public's expectations, sharpened by Vitaphone and their own radio sets, would soon have considered non-talking movies anachronistic, even archaic. There was a logic plucked from the ether or a wax disc which insisted that movies, too, find their voice. Radio was also affecting cinema attendance, at least in the smaller towns. Business was down to twenty to thirty per cent on the night of 15 November 1926, when the WEAF network relayed a well-publicised 'Big Broadcast'. Just to fight back, the cinemas would have to use the human voice as part of their entertainment. But business generally was bad in 1926–27; so if the voices came with the films, and apparently *in* the films, it might be a cheaper method of combating radio than hiring live performers.

The attitude of the other film companies to Warner Brothers' phenomenal success was a mixture of caution and frustration. They were closely and enviously monitoring the public's reaction as it swelled the Vitaphone box-office: but their problem was that any attempt to tap the audience for sound films with their own Vitaphone productions would mean contributing indirectly to Warners' swelling profits. For the Warners–Western Electric agreement reserved to each company the right to license other producers to use the Vitaphone system for studio production and cinema presentation. The outsiders would be adding to the affluence of an outfit that only a few months earlier they had been viewing with amused sympathy or lofty indifference. Perhaps no other element did so much to delay the general adoption of sound movies, once their potential had been scented, than this ingrained reluctance among the movie moguls to enrich a competitor.

An understanding of the terms Vitaphone exacted for the use of its process will show the economic power it came increasingly to wield – even though the Warner company itself was still in the second rank of film producers. In the first few months of excitement and Stock Market fluctuation (and, it was now openly alleged, manipulation) little concerted effort had been made to market Vitaphone. But as soon as it was seen to be a money-making hit, exceeding even the most boastful claims Warners had made for it, the Vitaphone company, located in the Fisk Building at 250 West 57th Street, began a drive in December 1926 to sell the device to allies or rivals. Again the pressure came from Western Electric, the manufacturing and sales end of A.T. & T. Just as they had done in radio, the hardware sales led the entertainment revolution. Oddly enough, though Western Electric was in partnership with a film company, it knew next to nothing about moving pictures. A year later, when the proud MGM had finally decided to 'go sound', a young engineer, Douglas Shearer, brother of Norma the film actress, was sent along to Bell Laboratories to learn how it was done. He discovered that 'Western Electric didn't know what making a movie was. They thought you just made a movie by sticking films end to end and that made a picture.'[6] And this was the company now set on revolutionising the film industry and, through Vitaphone, dictating very stiff terms for doing so! Abe Warner spelled these out for the trade in April 1927 when a tactical decision had been taken to sell Vitaphone devices to picture houses outside the prime sites in the big cities; since business was in decline countrywide, it was felt the response would be quicker from the average exhibitor, rather than the big man with more to lose in prestige and perhaps not quite so desperate to 'try anything'. Installing Vita-phone projection and amplifying equipment, Abe Warner said, would cost between 15,000 and 25,000 dollars: this included a fee of 2,000 dollars to Bell Laboratory engineers. The price varied in ratio to the individual cinema's location, its reputation for good business, its size, construction and acoustics. The cost of equipping the 6,500-seat super-cinema, the Roxy, on Broadway, which had opted for Vitaphone, would be 25,000 dollars because of the enormous amplification problems. All the money paid for equipment went to Western Electric, not to Vitaphone; the latter's sole income was derived from leasing films and the accompanying sound discs. Thus if the box-office didn't flourish, neither would Vitaphone. Then came the crunch. The initial installation was for five years only – at the end of which the apparatus reverted to Western Electric. Thus cinemas were left virtual hostages to those who owned an essential part of their means of livelihood and yet were not themselves engaged in producing films.

Moreover, if an improved apparatus were installed, the same terms applied; and while an exhibitor could move his Vitaphone equipment from a cinema that did disappointing business to one with better prospects, he had to pay the full cost of re-installation. Deferred payments were possible, Abe added, as a sweetener; on a 16,000 dollars job, for example, 2,000 dollars on ordering, 2,000 dollars on installation, and the balance over twelve months (but no more than eighteen, if mercy had to be asked by the exhibitor). Vitaphone also made a 'privilege' charge of ten cents a seat per week. 'For the privilege of playing Vitaphone,' Abe added laconically, anticipating the obvious query. Part of this revenue was supposed to go to keep the apparatus in good trim. For an average 2,000-seat cinema, therefore, the bill would be 450 dollars for renting three Vitaphone films each week, plus 200 dollars 'privilege' seat charge. Any exhibitor who found the business he did was not the equal of the bill he had to meet could go to the New York Arbitration Board; but he must undertake to play Vitaphone films for no fewer than forty weeks a year. 'This leaves a balance of twelve weeks,'

[6] Douglas Shearer quoted in *The Real Tinsel*, ed. by Bernard Rosenberg and Harry Silverstein (The Macmillan Co., 1970), p. 382.

Abe Warner added, showing his generous side, 'during which there will be no charge levied if the house should be closed due to unfavourable weather.' Some of the listening exhibitors might have added under their breath '. . . or bankruptcy'. Vitaphone, he concluded, had capital of five million dollars and an additional million dollars had been spent on producing the vaudeville and concert-artist films as well as the synchronised music discs for such otherwise silent movies as *Don Juan* and *The Better 'Ole*.

Now these were tough terms. They reflect how relatively bad cinema business was at that time, as well as the huge novelty value of Vitaphone. They certainly brought it home to theatre owners just how sweeping the sound revolution was going to be in terms of their individual finances. But Vitaphone must have been encouraged to drive hard bargains by the awakening noises they could detect in their competitors' camp. No one really knew what, if anything, Vitaphone would amount to at this early date. All the trade knew for certain was that Warner Brothers, good showmen as they were, had scored a massive public success which stood them in better stead for exploiting their novelty than the individual entrepreneurs in the past who had gone individually to the movie companies and tried to sell a device that would cause more confusion than anything else. But the film industry's jittery watchfulness towards anyone lucky, smart or plain crooked enough to steal a march on it was now coming into play and serving to make other companies scout around for ways of emulating Warners without having to surrender to them too obviously.

The 'Big Five' of the film world (at this time MGM, Universal, Paramount, First National and Producers' Distributing Corporation) had already met in secret session in December 1926 and agreed on a defensive strategy – none of them would adopt sound pictures until they all did and, if and when they did adopt it, they would all use the same device. They resolved, piously, it would not be the one Warners were using. This was a devious manoeuvre. But even more devious had been the tactics adopted a month or so earlier by one of the 'Big Five', Adolph Zukor, head of Famous Players-Lasky, the production wing of the Paramount distribution-company. Not for nothing was the diminutive Zukor nicknamed 'Creepy'. As early as October 1926 he had secretly begun courting Warner Brothers, using as his 'dowry' the guaranteed exhibition of Warner-Vitaphone pictures, silent and sound, through the six hundred prime-sited cinemas owned or controlled by his associated Publix company. Tempting bait. It would have made it possible for Warners to bid for the sixty per cent stock interest in Vitaphone held by Walter J. Rich, the entrepreneur they had had to 'take along for the ride' when they had acquired the process: it was worth between two and three million dollars. When the deal fell through – Warners characteristically raised the price to the point when Zukor baulked – the Paramount chief declared huffily that, come what may, he would very soon have a sound device of his own. Which seemed all too likely. For already there were five sound devices, including Vitaphone, in more or less practical form on the market: soon there would be some fifty, and within a year over two hundred! General Electric and RCA were pioneering one of them, though it would be September 1927 before it was demonstrated. Others were of more obscure and legally perilous origin. If there was any one man who looked the most likely to succeed in blocking Warners' lead, it was another one of the 'Big Five' – William Fox, President of the Fox Film Corporation.

Fox was the classic buccaneer, an impresario whose reach always exceeded his grasp – until, as will be related in its place, he overreached himself and crashed ruinously. He had a passion that mounted to manic proportions for acquisition and expansion: and quite apart from huge corporate assets, a personal fortune, valued at thirty million dollars in 1927, gave him ample means to indulge his passion. Fox had sunk a reported one hundred thousand dollars in Lee De Forest's Phonofilm system, the one with the optical sound track: then he fell out with the inventor over a German sound patent which the acquisitive Fox had picked up without having a use for and on which he was to spend years in trying to prove it antedated De Forest's system. (The courts decided against him in 1935: but by that time events had taken him out of the game.) This immensely tangled situation had a couple more knots tied in it by two other inventors, Theodore W. Case and his assistant Earl I. Sponable. They had been developing an optical sound system almost identical with De Forest's – all three inventors knew each other, but that is as much as has been reliably established. Early in 1926, Case and Sponable inveigled the ever curious Fox into viewing their invention – and he was as bowled over as Sam Warner had been when *he* had actually *heard* a pianist in the Vitaphone demonstration short unbuttoning his gloves before sitting down to the keyboard. Only this time it was a canary singing on the screen that sent Fox scurrying into the projection box to see if a ventriloquist (or a canary) were concealed there. Just to make certain, he ordered a repeat screening at his mansion, Fox Hall, whose private cinema thus probably became the first in America to be wired for sound. On 23 July 1926, just two weeks before the Vitaphone première, Fox bought patent rights to the Case-Sponable system, which he renamed Movietone, set up the Fox-Case laboratories to refine and promote it and started Sponable directing tests of 'name' performers, Harry Lauder among them. The canny Scot stopped in the middle of singing 'Roamin' in the Gloamin'' to announce 'This is a taist', lest the film be used commercially without his permission. Glendon Allvine, Fox's publicity chief for many years, reports that Adolph Zukor saw some of these test films late in 1926, but went away saying he wasn't impressed. His production chief, Jesse Lasky, disagreed: he was enthusiastic about the possibilities they opened up. 'Zukor the businessman (was) intent on preserving the *status quo* and Lasky the partner with creative imagination . . . saw the dramatic potential.'[7] This succinctly sums up the schism that sound pictures were slowly opening as Hollywood had to make up its mind whether to buy in or stay put.

As well as swallowing rival corporations, Fox could swallow his pride – and did so at the beginning of 1927 when it was publicly announced that, contrary to all the 'Big Five's' grim resolves, a deal existed and he and Vitaphone had signed mutually useful agreements, each licensing the other to use his respective sound system. Generosity was not part of Fox's nature: he had done the deal with Vitaphone to get the use of the amplifying system owned by Western Electric who had sub-licensed it to Vitaphone. But besides satisfaction in seeing a 'major' like Fox having to come to their door, Warners must have been relieved – for now that an essential part of their sound system was to be used by Fox, they were in less danger from the 'Big Five' or from any other sound system that the excluded studios might develop or adopt.

Fox didn't rush things, however. Though he got the first Movietone programme on to the New York screen in January 1927 all it consisted of was a number of songs sung by the Spanish entertainer Requel Meller. But the belief that he had his eye on 'something' other than Vitaphone-type stage shows is suggested by a report in April 1927 that he was developing a talking newsreel. The Movietone engineers were reported to be making tests to pick up street noises. 'Not long ago a military ceremony was "shot" for Movietone . . . successful unto the capture of the strains of the band, tramp of feet, commands of the officers, and the handling of rifles during the manual of arms.'[8] What lay behind this, Fox wouldn't reveal until he was ready – which was a few weeks later. Meantime, he fell back on what he knew definitely sold films – 'names'. Using Warners' successful blueprint, he went out to create what he called 'talking picture favorites' – the very phrase conveyed where the emphasis was now shifting – who could be used to put the stamp of popularity and quality on sound films, just as they were currently doing in increasing numbers on radio programmes. Fox had one significant new approach: what would count in sound films, he believed, was not simply good recording quality but a personality suited to the screen. Hence his early insistence on screen-testing 'names' for their visual impact and then, and only then, if they registered as personalities, signing them to exclusive performing contracts which granted them either flat payments of 10,000 dollars or royalty payments up to that amount. This precaution is sure evidence of how it was becoming appreciated that there was more to the novelty of sound than simply 'sound'. *Variety* put it succinctly, if none too grammatically, when it underlined the dawning consciousness of the new medium by reporting, 'Both Vitaphone and Movietone are taking their cues from the first

[7] *The Greatest Fox of Them All*, by Glendon Allvine (Lyle Stuart Inc, New York, 1969), p. 74.
[8] *Variety*, 20 April 1927.

Vitaphone performances, with "names" who may have "canned" well, but not screened as good. Since the entertainment is as much a motion picture as a sound reproduction, *if not more so*, extra attention to make-up and personality becomes imperative.'[9] Fox's instructions, in February 1927, to have Vitaphone installed in his theatres gave the process a great fillip: soon the devices were going in at the rate of twelve a week. But as the Vitaphone film programmes spread into the larger towns, each of them having a month or two's run along with the main silent (or synchronised) feature, the public were becoming more critical. The novelty appeal tended to vanish very fast: this was to be characteristic of almost every advance in talking pictures over the next year or so, and the disenchantment or outright criticism in turn played its part in spurring the film-makers on to fresh and, they hoped, better experiments.

Vitaphone's third programme, premièred on 3 February 1927, at the Selwyn Theater, New York, was a sort of 'holding' show, an attempt to combine the appeal of the earlier shows by splicing grand opera into musical comedy. It was an awkward compromise, though the sound showed great improvement. But by 19 March 1927, when a new show took over at the Colony from the one that had accompanied *The Better 'Ole* feature, it is clear that the appeal was being definitely angled at the neighbourhood houses and 'the sticks'. The sixty-five minutes were crammed with popular names, including Al Jolson's. Yet the New York audience were to receive it 'with remarkable composure, not to say indifference'. *Variety*'s reviewer commented, 'An hour of mechanical sound production . . . is a pretty severe experience. There is something of colorless quality about the mechanical device that wears after so long a stretch, not because the reproduction is lacking in human quality, for it has extraordinary exactitude and human shading. It must be that the mere knowledge that the entertainment is a reproduction has the effect of erecting an altogether imaginary feeling of mechanical flatness, such as one gets from a player (automatic) piano.'[10]

The presentation of the items was now thought uninventive, even though John Barclay, the baritone, opened his number in a dressing room, *talking* to camera while putting on Mephistopheles make-up for a *Faust* aria, then switching into redskin costume ('Pale Moon') and finally into Tommy Atkins's khakis ('Danny Deever'). Something for everyone, indeed! But Warners obviously anticipated a euphoric reception for the film, as they had built an inordinate number of 'bows' into the performances – and some of the artists on the screen were left acknowledging gratefully the complete silence of the live audience. A sign of how tricky it still was to separate the sound film from the variety stage. Even the great Gigli's act was spoiled by this piece of theatricality in a new Vitaphone bill at the Colony on 2 April 1927. 'As Gigli ends his *Cavalleria* solo to a little applause, he walks upstage to join the ensemble,

[9] Ibid., 11 May 1927.   [10] Ibid., 23 March 1927.

this creating what is nothing more than a wait. As the audience is wondering what it's about, or (what) the trouble (is), Gigli turns and walks to the footlights to take a bow, to no applause and only giggles by that time.'[11] 'Where is the comedy?' the same reviewer asked, demanding more lightness of tone. Technical imperfections in the recently wired cinemas were also getting Vitaphone off to a sense of anticlimax in some places. 'George Jessel appeared in bad form,' *Variety*'s Pittsburgh correspondent noted. 'His voice was anything but the Jessel voice known to Pittsburghers. At times it was even difficult to understand what he was saying.'[12] One soon senses a note of desperation intruding into Vitaphone's policy. The Colony's new bill on 23 April 1927, featured a dancing bull and a Black Bottom-ing horse which showed its tail to the camera. 'Animals hardly qualify for Vitaphone,' *Variety* sniffed.

The truth was that by late spring 1927, 'the newest wrinkle in moviedom' was starting to look distinctly tired. The euphoria of the initial audiences had evaporated. The applause once so generously given to the performing images was now considered redundant or even faintly comic if the artists insisted on it. People were finding the camera's relatively immobile position, shooting most of the acts head on with only an occasional jerky panning shot, had become tedious. Even in America's hinterland, the enthusiasm radiating from an entertainment capital like New York, making the locals eager to share the experience that was judged 'better than vaudeville', was proving counter-productive once the local theatre had been wired for sound and they *could* see and hear what were sometimes badly reproduced numbers.

At just this moment, when public attention appeared to be faltering, William Fox produced a much-needed new sensation. His second Movietone programme of shorts opened on 2 May 1927, at New York's super-colossal Roxy Theater, whose original owner, Sam Rothapfel, (popularly known as 'Roxy') found his financial position had deteriorated so swiftly after its opening on 11 March that ten days later he was glad to make a forced sale for twelve million dollars to William Fox. But it was not size that impressed the audience: it was the sound, the *natural* sound of a platoon of West Point cadets marching with their band and going through their drill manual. So that was what Fox had been filming so secretly! Even this was nothing to the sensation that closed the bill which was in support of the silent feature *Yankee Clipper*: a two-minute recording of Lindbergh taking off on his record-setting Transatlantic flight. 'The roar of the motor when it starts,' said one report, 'and the following mechanical stutterings and stammerings as the engine begins to drag its load thrilled everybody in the house.'[13]

An enlarged edition of this Movietone programme supported the synchronised feature *Seventh Heaven* at the Harris Theater on 25 May 1927. As well as the two news events, there were now three musical items:

[11] Ibid., 6 April 1927.   [12] Ibid., 6 April 1927.
[13] Ibid., 1 June 1927.

Gertrude Lawrence, Requel Meller and Ben Bernie and his band, all of whom Fox had sound- and sight-tested before signing to exclusive contracts. In spite of Bernie's agile wisecrack, 'Good afternoon, ladies and gentlemen, or is this an evening performance?' their thunder was stolen by the verisimilitude of the outdoor events. The performers were now regarded by *Variety*'s reviewer as 'incidental': a view in striking contrast to the exclamations of wonderment at the original Vitaphone première nine months earlier. What Fox had done to scoop attention was add sound to a six-minute newsreel event, or an 'interest short' like the West Point cadets, and thus inject a sense of drama into sound pictures. He had also shown that Movietone could be used outdoors, whereas Vitaphone, with its cumbersome disc-recording, was still an indoor event. On 14 June 1927, again at the Roxy, Movietone showed Washington D.C. giving Lindbergh a hero's welcome home. The feature film was hardly noticed: but world attention focused on the sound shorts, which included Mussolini making a brief speech, barely intelligible in English or Italian but definitely showing a real live dictator *talking*. By October 1927 Fox had begun a regular sound newsreel.

It is from the early summer of 1927 on that one senses the tempo of the talkie revolution perceptibly speeding up. Competition between the two pioneers, Warners and Fox, was beginning in earnest. And very soon there was an important change in the relationship between Vitaphone and Warners. The film company bought out Walter J. Rich and thus became the main controllers of Vitaphone. At the same time Warners, while undertaking to produce enough films to keep pace with Vitaphone installations, surrendered to Western Electric's specially created subsidiary, Electrical Research Products, Inc. (ERPI), the right to license other producers who wanted to use Vitaphone or Movietone and collect royalties from them. This *détente* did more than clear the air: it cleared the way for all the other studios who had jibbed at adding to Warners profits to conclude their own agreements with Western Electric.

In the same month of May 1927 news broke of an event that eclipsed even Fox's stunning demonstration of what sound could do for actual events. In a front-page banner headline *Variety* announced: 'Full-Length Talking Pictures'. Now that Vitaphone's novelty value had waned, Warners were out to restore their pre-eminence by shooting a feature film in which the sound wouldn't simply be a synchronised musical score with a few novelty special effects: it would be dramatically integrated into the action. Furthermore, the film wouldn't be shot in the company's Manhattan Opera House studio, which had been grinding out six or seven song, musical and comedy acts weekly, but back home on the thirteen-acre Hollywood lot, just as soon as a sound-proof stage could be built. No title was yet made public; but George Jessel was mentioned as the likely star. As things turned out, the film was indeed a breakthrough of historic proportions for sound – shattering forever the era of silent movies. But George Jessel wasn't destined to be part of it.

Perhaps the most famous film poster in the world: certainly one of the best designed. Note that there is no mention made of Jolson 'talking'. Appropriately enough, 'word of mouth' publicity was what spread the revolutionary impact that this irrepressible ad-libber made on the screen in 1927.

'You ain't heard nothin' yet.'

'Is it any wonder I always felt bitter?' George Jessel used to ask years later. 'It was my part and partly my story. I tell you, I felt sick.' However, he was generous enough to say of Al Jolson's performance in *The Jazz Singer*, 'He was better at it than I would have been!'

No one could doubt that Al Jolson in the 1920s was at the height of his career as a vaudeville artist who specialised in doing 'blackface' Mammy routines. His earning power was colossal, his drawing power infallible. Robert Benchley even thought there was something 'supernatural' at the root of Jolson's power over an audience. His hyperthyroid 'love affair' with them, from the instant he came on stage, made it feel

> as if an electric current had been run along the wires under the seats where the hats are stuck. The house comes to a tumultuous attention. He speaks, rolls his eyes, compresses his lips, and it is all over. You are a member of the Al Jolson Association. He trembles his under-lip and your heart breaks with a loud snap. He sings a banal song and you totter out to send a night letter to your mother. Such a giving off of vitality, personality, charm and whatever all those words are, results from a Jolson performance. We got enough vitamins out of being present that night to ride our bicycle at top speed all the way to Scarsdale, and we had enough left to shingle the roof before going to bed.[1]

Jolson's nation-wide popularity was such that Calvin Coolidge personally invited the entertainer to help him launch his 1924 re-election campaign by singing 'Keep Cool With Coolidge' at a White House breakfast. The Brunswick records company not only agreed to pay him the vast fee of 10,000 dollars a side to record on their label, but

---

[1] *Life*, 13 January 1925

showed their gratitude for the favour he had done them in taking their money by electing him to their board of directors. His marvellous ease in manipulating people's emotions, turning, as *The New York Times* critic once said, 'the base metals of vulgarity and sentimentality into pure gold', undoubtedly owed something to a tribal histrionic ability. Knowing he had a particular appeal to Jewish customers, he would slip into his act the odd Yiddish word or phrase. An irrepressible and irreverent anecdotist, he did not scruple to add to the book of any show he was starring in some pithy ethnic ad-lib. His tongue wagged fast and uncontrollably. He was a ruthless loner, too. One Jolson trick was to stop the orchestra dead, advance to the footlights and, with the house lights turned up, ask the audience if it was he they wanted, or the rest of the cast. Of course the cry went up, 'Al, Al, Al,' so he dismissed everyone else on stage and did reprises and tried out new numbers, often protracting the show's running time by half-an-hour. It made him feel the audience was closer to him: it made the stage, quite literally, all his. His search for perfection was unremitting; but vanity was also one of his over-exercised traits, and any hint of competition in the vicinity, any rival for the limelight, drove him to extremes. His feud with Eddie Cantor led to a famous clash in Chicago, when Cantor while suffering from a crippling attack of pleurisy was doing *Kid Boots* in one theatre and Jolson, almost voiceless from laryngitis, was disobeying doctor's orders and refusing to withdraw from his show, *Bombo*, in a neighbouring theatre. Jolson waited till Cantor collapsed before he rang down the curtain – then collapsed himself. By mid-1927, Jolson was in Los Angeles being paid 3,500 dollars weekly, plus half the net profit made by touring in the musical *Big Boy* in which he played a happy blackface jockey. The show played forty-three weeks in towns and cities through-out America, using a special train to transport its cast, and grossed 1,419,000 dollars. Jolson stood to collect around 350,000 dollars.

Now such figures deserve quoting, for they confirm that in no sense was Al Jolson made into a star by talking pictures. He already was a star, the biggest in America, before he agreed to appear in *The Jazz Singer*. The figures also show why he was not Jack Warner's first choice as the lead in the film version of the play about a cantor's son who runs away from home and becomes a Broadway star instead of a pillar of the synagogue. Jolson was just too expensive for Warners to consider (at this point anyway) paying him his usual fee or – even more unthinkable – cutting him into the profits. Moreoever, although the play was loosely based on Jolson's own life-story, it had become associated with its stage star, George Jessel: it was *his* vehicle. Jessel had already appeared in several Vitaphone shorts and seemed the natural choice. He readily signed a declaration of intent and was to be paid 2,000 dollars a week.

What happened then is still a matter of divergent speculation; but it seems clear that Jessel, or his manager, had second thoughts about the songs that were to be integrated into the action. Songs meant making phonograph discs to accompany the picture; Jessel felt he should get an additional fee for this. He also pointed out that as Vitaphone was a separate corporation from Warner Brothers, there was a risk of the discs being sold separately – perhaps he should get royalties, too. In any case he was not so sure about singing in the picture: he had thought it was going to be essentially a silent movie with a synchronised music score. As such, it would have been a useful trailer for the stage version of *The Jazz Singer* which he looked forward to touring in for another year or two. The idea of turning his singing voice over to movie-makers was akin to robbing himself of his stage exclusivity. All in all, it was a bad deal – unless he were paid more money. It is at this point that versions of the story begin to differ. Jack Warner says in his autobiography that he was willing to meet Jessel's demand for an extra 10,000 dollars until the singer demanded his promise in writing and an offended Warner abruptly terminated negotiations. But there is a second account of what happened, which holds that Jessel suddenly began making demands that had more to do with faith than cash. Though not by any means a strictly orthodox Jew, Jessel took his religion seriously – more so, anyhow, than Al Jolson, whom he sometimes criticised for not being Jewish enough. To Jessel's proprietorial way of thinking, *The Jazz Singer* was a shibboleth of the Jewish ability to make it big in show business without severing the links with Judaic obligations. The stage play ended with young Jakie Rabinowitz giving up the footlights to become a cantor like his father; but the film version scripted by Alfred A. Cohn had substituted an ending that was more flattering to show business than Semitic tradition. Young 'Jack Robin', the hero's stage name, certainly sings 'Kol Nidre' at his father's death bed, but the film ends with him donning blackface make-up and singing 'Mammy' to his overcome mother in the front row. Jessel intensely disliked the new ending – which Warners had insisted on, lest the film prove 'too Jewish' for the mass audience. Furthermore, Jessel demanded that Warners employ a Jewish director and insisted that whoever played the mother and the cantor father be Jewish as well. When Warners told him that Alan Crosland would direct and that Warner Oland, who was Swedish, and Eugenie Besserer, who was Irish, would be his screen parents, Jessel said he wanted none of it.

This account of how George Jessel thus lost a measurable immortality, not to say a sizeable bit of money, appeared in *Variety* on 29 June 1927, in its 'Inside Films' section, a column usually reserved for items that for one reason or another could not be easily substantiated or openly attributed. It may have been Jessel's face-saving apologia as he now saw Warners proceeding without him to film the stage show he had made his own; but from what we know about Jessel's ethnic tetchiness, the story has a ring of probability.

Whatever the truth of the matter, negotiations were broken off with Jessel in mid-May, in spite of the fact that a lot of publicity material about his appearing in *The Jazz Singer* had already been prepared.

Warners re-opened talks with possible replacements. They tested Eddie Cantor; but it was Al Jolson they settled on, meeting his fee of 75,000 dollars as another of those 'last gambles' which had so far bought them out of debt with Vitaphone, though not yet into the security of huge profits. Some accounts state that Jolson had to agree to being paid partly in film company stock. This is untrue. He later denied it, though as Warners' stock had by then soared sky high it may have been a rueful denial. The fact is he was paid one-third down in cash and the rest at 5,250 dollars a week. As the film took about four months to shoot, Jolson was paid in full well before production ended in the last week of September 1927. As the première took place at the Warner Theater, Broadway, just a week later, on 6 October 1927, it is evident that the film-makers wanted to waste no time in getting their money back. It had cost half a million dollars, an enormous sum in those days for a non-spectacle production.

The Jazz Singer was not Al Jolson's first attempt at films. D. W. Griffith had persuaded him after numerous rebuffs to star in a silent film in 1923. It was called *Mammy's Boy* (sometimes also known as *His Darker Self*) and Jolson was to play a young lawyer who masquerades as a black in order to solve a murder: a neat way of exploiting his fame as a blackface vaudeville artist. But being unable to crack audible gags, ad-lib lines or even give voice to lachrymose songs in those pre-talkie days, an impatient Jolson quickly became disenchanted with his own movie debut: he felt nothing of himself was coming across; his own bossy temperament clashed with Griffith's imperious manner; and after seeing the rushes, which made him think he looked 'like a zebra', he abruptly left the unfinished film to 'recover from the shock' by taking an extended vacation in Europe. Griffith's suit for breach of verbal contract did not come to a head until September 1926, when the director, who was claiming damages of half a million dollars, was awarded a paltry 2,627.50 dollars.

What made Jolson revise his view of the movies after this inauspicious start? Undoubtedly it was the seductive new element Warners promised to add to them – sound. Now at last he could be heard! Silence had screwed down his vocal personality: sound would let it explode out of the bottle. The Vitaphone shorts he made were in a very real sense the pilot films that supplied him with confidence and whetted his easily aroused appetite for starring in a longer sound movie. He realised what a tantalisingly wide audience his voice could now be carried to in the new medium. In April 1927 he had even tackled radio, singing Irving Berlin's 'What Does It Matter?' on an NBC appeal for the victims of a flood disaster, and had received a very good Press for his debut. His vanity was thus in excellent condition when, at the end of August, he stepped on to the new sound-proofed stage at Warner Brothers' studio on Sunset Boulevard to begin the singing sequences for the first full-length Vitaphone feature. All other work throughout the studio had been suspended and the whole production staff crowded on to the set to hear him. Jolson liked nothing better than an audience: the fact that it was made up of film folk held no terrors for him. 'Besides their pay cheques,' he later cracked, 'they got four dollars worth of show thrown in.'

The sound stage on which Jolson now prepared to give voice to the musical numbers – and interpolate an ad-lib that would go down in history – was an altogether novel structure in Hollywood – or, indeed, the world. Reports differ on the precise dimensions of the stage: Harry M. Geduld says it was roughly 75 feet wide by 100 feet long, other sources say it was much bigger, 90 feet by 150 feet. Floor and walls were covered with 'Cellutexture' to aid sound-proofing. All doors were felt-lined and tight-fitting. Visitors to the set found an unexpected object outside the door: it was a notice saying 'Silence'. Light bulbs flashed to admit them, or deny them entry when shooting was in progress. The casual caller and the studio executive 'just dropping in' were the first casualties of the new discipline that sound brought to Hollywood. On one side of the stage, about fifteen feet up the wall, was a glass-fronted gallery, doubly sound-proofed, which was the nerve-centre of the system. This was the monitor room. Here sat an operator who could see and hear the action down below and regulate the sound so that the right tone and volume were recorded. The monitor booth was connected to a 'playback room' where it was possible to play back to the director and the actors the sound of the scene they had just finished playing. Every scene shot, therefore, meant a trip to the playback room to judge the result and, if need be, then go back and improve on it. Even more than usual, it was 'stop-start film-making'. The monitor man used a phone to communicate with the director and declare a 'take' satisfactory or 'N.G.' – no good. The camera booths had acquired a little more mobility since the Manhattan Opera House period, but they were still very restricted: nothing like the fluent camera-work of silent films was remotely possible. And it wouldn't become possible, either, till the microphone achieved the old mobility of the silent-era camera. At present it was a fixed unit: players came to it, or stood near it, wherever its camouflaged presence happened to be. Frank Murphy, Vitaphone's chief electrician, had now permanently discontinued the noisy, crackling carbon arc-lamps and installed incandescent globes, diamond-faceted with special reflectors, suspended over the players and bathing them in a sauna-like atmosphere of stifling heat but silent illumination. Sound syn-chronisation required the film to go through the camera at a faster speed than the sixteen frames per second of the silent days: twenty-four frames per second became the norm. And this in turn meant much more sensitive film stock had to be used. . . . It would prove that problems spawned problems *ad infinitum* in these early days of sound.

As far as the players were concerned, the psychological changes were even harder to endure than the technical ones. In spite of the name, 'silence' had been the last quality to be found on a film set during the shooting of a silent film. The trademark of the silent era in Hollywood studios had been a casual, audible bustle of work. Musicians might be playing mood music to put the players in the right frame of mind for their mime or sometimes, in the case of comedy, to give a rough tempo to the scene. Directors frequently talked their artists through the scene, intimating the emotions they wanted them to show, doing a spontaneous 'commentary' on their playing which often accounted for the astonishingly 'plastic' quality of emotional response in the best performances of the pre-talkie era. The lamps sputtered and the cameras cranked, and most players found these 'work noises' more comforting than distracting. All round them, too, grips, carpenters and the still un-unionised hobble-de-hoy of 'little people' got on with their own work or swapped small-talk. Almost every corner of the communal set could be used for some bit of the production: so long as people were out of sight, no one had to worry about being within earshot.

Two rather perceptive authors, Jan and Cora Gordon, who visited Hollywood in the 1928–29 period to report on the movie scene and do sketches and paintings of its colourful aspects, have left one of the most vivid, first-hand impressions of what it was like at this transition point. They visited Josef von Sternberg who was then directing his last silent movie, *The Docks of New York*; and though this was almost two years after the production of *The Jazz Singer*, and they had to suffer an autocrat in the director's chair instead of the sort of director who coaxed emotions out of his stars, something of the easy, relaxed, good-humoured, communal atmosphere of silent days lingered on.

> From the darkness behind the big sun-arcs a violin wailed and a harmonium grunted like a passionate duet between a musical hyena and a melodious wart-hog. The director allowed a few moments for this stimulus to work on the feelings of his actors, then through the megaphone, bellowed 'Go!' The actors sprang into motion. But von Sternberg was not satisfied. He bellowed 'Stop' through the megaphone, and, turning the instrument towards the musicians, shouted, 'That tune's no good. Stir us up a bit. Put more battle spirit into it. Gee, nobody feels like fighting to a damned waltz!'[2]

Now it's unlikely that this ebullient atmosphere had entirely vanished from the Vitaphone set in 1927. For one thing, Jolson's exuberant personality precipitated a bustling communality all round him. For another, the song-and-music sequences of *The Jazz Singer* needed the noise of an audience. Most important, the film was only to be a part-sound production: most of its sequences were to be shot silent – i.e. in the relaxed babble of studio workmates – with silent film sub-titles conveying the minimum dialogue necessary for carrying the story from

[2] *Star-Dust in Hollywood*, by Jan and Cora Gordon (George G. Harrap & Co., London, 1930), p. 78.

point to point. However, the new restrictions on movement and volubility were highly discomfiting: at least they were to film actors used to the old ways. But Jolson was not a film actor, yet. He was so self-centred and inexperienced in Hollywood ways that he could make light of restrictions that were to paralyse many a veteran star of the silents. In fact, he made fun of them. 'Say,' he told a reporter, Francis Gilmore, who visited the set, 'the other day I sang for an hour straight. I thought the camera was grinding all the time, but afterwards they told me they had only needed twenty feet of film. But they hadn't stopped me because it was lunch time and they liked to hear me sing.'[3] This does not suggest a man in the slightest degree put out of his way of going by sound.

What subsequent parts of the same interview vividly convey is the quality that was to make Jolson's performance outstanding. Francis Gilmore didn't interview the star so much as transcribe what he said. Possibly he was unable to get a word in, and didn't really need to. The shorthand reporter's pencil, keeping swift pace with Jolson's manic monologue, admirably conveys the cocksureness of a man who knows he is the star of the show from the start and is determined to do things his way.

> The first scene they says to me, 'Now Al, you've got to show by your expression that you've been away from home fifteen years after your father (that was a rabbi) had turned you out because you wanted to go on the stage instead of being a cantor. That's all. Except maybe you might suggest you've been a great hit on Broadway and got money in the bank.' Well, I played the scene as emotional as I knew how. I even tore my hat in two, and it was real emotion, too – right from the stummick. Then that night I got to thinking. I said to myself, 'Al, if you had a Mammy' – which I haven't – 'and hadn't seen her for fifteen years, would you waste your time looking round the dear old sitting-room and having emotions over the pictures and furniture, or would you rush right out to the kitchen where you could hear her scraping a cake bowl and open your arms wide and grab her and yell "MAMMY"?' So the next day I told them that the scene had got to be taken over again and they said, 'You're crazy! It looks great in the rushes.' But I made it over again anyhow and everybody on the set was crying when I got through. Miss Besserer, who plays my Mammy, was sobbing so hard she leaned her head against the wall and cried twenty minutes straight. I says to her, 'You mustn't give it all at once, ma'am. There's the scene coming where the old man dies. You've got to feel worse then, and if you give it all, then you won't have anything left.'

The *chutzpah* of advising fellow artists, far more experienced in movie-making than he was then, to hold something back while he himself was giving everything he had – this is the authentic Al Jolson. It

[3] *Motion Picture Classic*, November 1927. Italics on p. 36 are the interviewer's.

was also an early warning signal, for those who could read it, that he liked giving direction better than taking it. Despite his phenomenal successes, Jolson was never to be the star of a really big-scale Busby Berkeley-type musical, probably just because few people were willing (or able) to cope with an outsize ego whose owner wished to take charge of everything and everyone.

For the moment, however, Jolson's tear ducts were put at the service of the new-fangled medium, and the dam overflowed on command. He had to be not only full-throated, but also wholehearted. 'Why didn't I speak the words instead of singing them?' he asked, echoing his interviewer's at last successful attempt at an interruption.

> I couldn't *feel* them if I did that. You saw me crying, didn't you? Well, between each shot I got to go out behind the set and get goofy, sort of wallop my stummick up and down, see? So's I can cry. Then when I've been crying an hour like my heart was broke, and I'm all in, the director says, 'Once more, please. And this time put some *feeling* into it.'

Is it at all surprising that such a temperamental artist should burst out with the impulsive and impromptu remark that became world-famous: 'Wait a minute, wait a minute. You ain't heard nothin' yet.'? Yet in the often inaccurate mythology that has grown up around what seems like a semi-prescient comment on the talkies, no mention is usually made of the fact that filmgoers in 1927 would have *expected* this very remark from Jolson. These words had already the mark of a Jolson catch-phrase. They were his stage trademark: he used them often, as a typical bit of boastfulness to intimate that whatever act had preceded him on stage, he could top it. He had been using the quip from his earliest vaudeville days, though the most notorious occasion on which he uttered it wasn't in the Winter Garden, or on any other music-hall stage, but at the Metropolitan Opera House, on Armistice Night, 1918, at a fund-raising concert for veterans. The great Caruso had just sung 'Vesti La Giubba', and before the applause for the world-famous tenor had died away out bounced Jolson. 'Folks,' he announced, 'you ain't heard nothin' yet.' The remark was breath-taking in its *lèse-majesté*; but the audience loved Jolson's native cockiness – and so, incidentally, did Caruso.

The lines occur in *The Jazz Singer* during the ragtime restaurant sequence where Jolson, as the famous entertainer Jack Robin, is spotted by his fellow diners eating bacon and eggs – another symptom of his break with orthodox Jewry – and cajoled into singing 'Dirty Hands, Dirty Face', the first of several of the film's thematic songs stressing sons and mothers and the love between them. As his listeners applaud wildly, Jolson cries out his celebrated promise – then launches straight into the "Toot, Toot, Tootsie' number. The story goes (and probably it's true) that the spoken words were recorded only because the microphone preparing to pick up the 'Toot, Toot, Tootsie' number was 'open' a sign perhaps, of how the film's musical numbers had to take their cue from Jolson's excitable and variable timing. But it is certainly true that as soon as the rushes were screened, the producers recognised their value as an authentic piece of Jolson's act, and kept them in rather than erase them from the recording or cut them from the film. There are only two sequences in the film which use synchronised speech: this was one of them. The other does not possess the landmark value of 'You ain't heard nothin' yet', but it's considerably more important in the way people reacted to ordinary, naturalistic talk in a film. It is the singer's emotion-charged reunion with his doting mother. Silent titles give it the build-up and imply Jack Robin's rolling crescendo of success: 'New York'. . . . 'Broadway'. . . . 'HOME'. . . 'MOTHER!' As the son sits at the living-room piano, preparing to play his mother a number from the show, the dialogue between them is a shamefully calculated mix of schmaltz and ethnic humour. 'You haven't changed a bit in all these years,' she cries. 'That I should live to see my baby again!' And then, when he gives her a brooch, 'Diamonds . . . You didn't do anything wrong, did you, Jackie?' The dialogue picks up again after he's played her 'Blue Skies'. 'Mama darlin' – if I'm a success in this show, well, we're gonna move from here. . . . Oh yes, we are. . . . We're gonna move up in the Bronx. A lot of nice green grass up there. A whole lot of people you know. There's the Ginsbergs, the Guttenbergs and the Goldbergs. Oh, a lot of bergs. I dunno them all. And I'm gonna buy you a nice, black silk dress, Mama. You see, Mrs Friedman, the butcher's wife, she'll be jealous of you.' And so on, for a minute or two, until the vows of filial affection stop short just this side of the Oedipal danger line.

Now although hindsight puts the accent of interest on the 'You ain't heard nothin' yet' line, the fact is that virtually no reviewer of the film did. None singled it out for the revolutionary breakthrough it was supposed to be at the time. After all, why should they? The Vitaphone variety items had familiarised them with patter like this; they had already heard Jolson's voice in the vaudeville shorts; in any case, it was his catch-line. They might have commented if it *hadn't* been in the film! The passages that did draw comment, stirring interest and awakening critics to Vitaphone's possibilities, are the ones quoted above – between Jolson and Eugenie Besserer. 'He is of course breathtaking when he sings,' a reviewer wrote in *Moving Picture World*, a periodical aimed mainly at exhibitors, 'and one of the most delightful bits in the photoplay is an episode of gentle repartee between (him) and Eugenie Besserer'.[4] The *Times* critic commented on an aspect of sound that was to plague the early talkies. 'The dialogue is not so effective, for it does not always catch the nuances of speech or inflection of the voice . . . (which is) usually just the same whether the image of the singer is close to the camera or far away. There are . . . times when one would expect the Vitaphoned portion to be either more subdued or stopped as the

[4] *Moving Picture World*, 22 October 1927.

camera swings to other scenes.'[5] What the reviewer was uttering, albeit in a slightly puzzled manner, was a desire for the greater realism that in a short time would be the chief drawing-card of the talkies. James Agate drew the right conclusion, though possibly for the wrong reason, when he wrote of the same scene between mother and son. 'Al Jolson forced his voice upon the ear . . . gave us illusion coupled with admiration that a machine could do so well. Eugenie Besserer . . . was content to mumble, and here the illusion was perfect and unmannered. Every flesh-and-blood actor knows that he must not speak as an actor, the essence of theatrical illusion being that the actor is overheard. The same applies to films, the essence of film illusion being that the film actor shall be overheard.'[6] The fact is, however, that Eugenie Besserer was simply poorly recorded: the microphone was aimed at Jolson, to record his 'Blue Skies' number. In any case, her motherly interpolations wouldn't have carried the sock-it-to-'em impact of her vaudeville-singer son. Nevertheless, the effect she makes is indisputably more naturalistic; and this was the hardest problem confronting silent-era actors essaying sound for the first time.

But it is to Jolson's driving energy that *The Jazz Singer* owes its contemporary impact and a lot of its subsequent durability. Heavy-lidded, dark-eyebrowed, a skull-cap of hair, a lean, streaky, ever-eager expression on his face and a body that never seems content to be at rest, he punches his personality over with a resonance that must have played havoc with the recording apparatus in the early days of shooting. '*The Jazz Singer* proves that talking pictures are considerably more than a lively possibility; they are close to an accomplished fact,' wrote Robert E. Sherwood, after seeing the performance. 'Al Jolson as an actor is only fair. But when Al Jolson starts to sing . . . well, bring on your super-spectacles, your million-dollar thrills, your long-shots of Calvary against the setting sun, your close-up of a glycerine tear on Norma Talmadge's cheek – I'll trade them all for one instant of any ham song that Al cares to put on.'[7]

What Jolson's performance confirmed was the new dimension that sound could add to even an established star of show business. May McAvoy, who plays his girl-friend in the film, sums it up in one silent-film title when she says, 'There are lots of jazz singers, but you have a tear in your voice.' The power of lachrymose feeling charges three of the most potent themes that any film has been built around: Jewish tradition, show-business sentiment and mother love. All are combined in a story that is irredeemably mawkish, yet crudely effective. Ghetto attitudes and back-stage free-and-easiness collide in a way that, in 1927, must have caused a familiar wrench to thousands of America's new

[5] *The New York Times*, 7 October 1927.
[6] *Around Cinemas*, by James Agate (Home & Van Thal, London, 1946), p. 28.
[7] Robert E. Sherwood in *The Silent Drama*, 27 October 1927, p. 124.

Jewish immigrants. In a very real sense, *The Jazz Singer* is about the making of an American as well as an entertainer. 'Would you be the first Rabinowitz in five generations to fail your God?' asks the rabbinical friend of the singer's father who calls on him in his dressing room. Jolson replies: 'We in show business have a religion, you know – the show must go on.' Sacred and lay shibboleths, Judaism and American fervour, father-worship and mother-love: these are elements that the story reconciles with an unselfconscious directness which survives the overloaded sentimentality better than it has any right to do. Even Jolson crying on his mother's shoulder borrows a stoicism from the long traditions of Jewish suffering. 'If I'm a success in this show . . . we're gonna move from here,' must have touched a kindred response in the desire of 'new' Americans to 'make it' in the land of opportunity. And the link with mother, taking her along, too, with the success story, must have been all the more potent because it could now be *heard* coming like a vow from the lips of her son. The combination of old and new traditions is maintained right up to the end, with the cantorial music of 'Kol Nidre' being succeeded by the vaudeville punch of 'My Mammy'. The irreverent thought occurs that the only trick the film-makers missed was having Jolson sing 'Kol Nidre' in blackface, thus achieving an unbeatable overlay of racial sentiment.

Mordaunt Hall in the *Times* reported that at the première 'Jolson's personal vocal effects were received with rousing applause.' When the film ended, he appeared on stage, to a 'tumultuous ovation', as *Variety* reported, and said, predictably, that he was so happy he could not stop his tears flowing. The audience's only regret, the *Times* said, was not being able to stop the film for encores. All the same, as Harry M. Geduld has said, 'the original audience were excited not by a *dramatic* use of recorded dialogue, but by synchronised speech being used *naturally* in contrast to "performed" songs and the convention of the silent drama'.[8] The ad-libbing that Jolson went in for in the scene with his mother was the innovative element: it did not try to re-create the form of a vaudeville act, it made the film look and sound like everyday life.

Between shooting his last scenes and appearing at the New York première, Jolson veered between aggressive self-confidence ('It ought to be a good picture') and fatalistic resignation in case *hubris* brought its own punishment ('But I don't know. I'm scared. That's straight.'). One result of appearing in the movies was that for the first time he took to doing his stage act in picture houses, almost as a live trailer for the coming movie. He brought his talents to a whole new audience – the one that, if all went well, would take themselves off to see *The Jazz Singer*. *Variety*'s issue of 12 September 1927 carried a by-lined article by Jolson – by-lines of any description, even those of staff writers, were rare in that periodical then as now – in which he came out with some good populist sentiments about the folk who patronised picture houses. 'I find the

8 Harry M. Geduld, op. cit., p. 185.

audiences here . . . more wholesome and more appreciative than those who put their four dollars over the ticket ledge (in the legitimate theatres).' Appreciative they certainly were. For one week's engagement at the Metropolitan cinema, Los Angeles, Jolson drew 57,286 dollars gross, and was personally paid the biggest net sum earned anywhere by a single turn, 17,500 dollars. No fewer than forty-one film industry notables participated in a contest to guess what his gross would be: that's how powerful Al Jolson was in 1927! Showmen believed he could earn between 600,000 and 1,000,000 dollars just by touring the picture palaces; Harold B. Franklin, controller of William Fox's West Coast chain of cinemas, and the author of one of the earliest and best books on the talkies, offered him 20,000 dollars weekly. Jolson refused it. He also turned down post-première engagements in New York, Boston, Philadelphia and Chicago, all places where he knew his film would soon be playing, lest he found he was in competition with himself.

With all these excellent omens, it is not surprising that *The Jazz Singer* was a success. What no one anticipated, though, was the unprecedented degree of its success. It put Warner Brothers securely 'in the money', as one of their *Gold Diggers* numbers would soon have it. There were only three brothers now: on the very eve of the film's première, Sam Warner died in Los Angeles of a brain abscess complicated by pneumonia. Within two weeks another sudden death shook the film industry, that of Marcus Loew, head of Loew's Inc., which owned one of the largest cinema chains as well as MGM studios. He was commemorated by a whole front page of *Variety* that was left blank but for the announcement of the mogul's demise, followed by over 100 pages of tastefully displayed funeral tributes. No wonder his brother moguls felt the ground move beneath them: Loew's death and the arrival of sound were the shocks of which earthquakes were made.

As *The Jazz Singer* opened outside New York, exhibitors across the nation opened their trade papers to be apprised of its drawing power. What the movie contributed to sound on the screen was not really a novelty value – Vitaphone's vaudeville shorts had already exploited this. It was the confidence factor. The reassurance that sound was more, much more than a passing attraction – that it could be permanent and profitable. Exhibitors already knew that 'there is a measurable difference between synchronisation, to replace the pianist or violinist in the small theaters, and talking films, Orchestra synchronisations will, without a doubt, find a permanent welcome in the smaller theaters throughout the country. The proposed talking films (Warners had announced in November 1927 that they were going to lens twelve talkies) represent another field.'[9] Where neighbourhood cinemas had been up against a vaudeville house, the Vitaphone variety shorts had helped them hold their own. But where an exhibitor had been forced to invest, say, 20,000 dollars in having his house wired for sound, his

[9] *Variety*, 4 January 1928.

return was slower – and his source of supply had to be guaranteed. He couldn't afford to regard sound simply as a novelty: he had to be assured that it was a staple part of entertainment. Until *The Jazz Singer* came along, exhibitors were still far from being persuaded that this was so. The huge success of that film could not have left them long in doubt: its box-office grosses were the galvanic coil that passed a kind of visionary thrill through the whole industry. Other studios and cinema chains witnessed the fortune that Warners were making out of it, with the relatively few outlets that played their product at this date. A silent version of the film had been prepared and it went into the cinemas not equipped for sound, where the takings were sometimes deviously boosted by playing Jolson recordings behind the screen. But the receipts of these places were well below those cinemas playing the sound version. In the first week of January 1928 Warners took a full-page advertisement in *Variety* and ran the famous black-and-white graphic of the solarised 'Mammy' singer, arms outstretched, mouth agape, as if in astonishment at the accompanying boast: 'Warner Brothers Supreme Triumph'. Playing to 1,000,000 People a Week'. The lesson was blindingly clear: the great dramatic draw was the human voice – not only singing, *but talking*.

'They will speak lines throughout!'

Though *The Jazz Singer* opened to capacity business in New York and several other cities before the end of 1927, it didn't start breaking sensationally across the country in the one hundred-odd cinemas already wired for sound until the first few weeks of 1928. The 'telegraphese' of box-office reports catches the cinema trade's lip-licking reaction to the phenomenon: '25,000 dollars in Two Weeks. Held Over' – Milwaukee; 'Biggest Thing Last Week' – Baltimore; 'Singing Jolson Sell-Out' – Philadelphia; 'Wonder of the Week' – Portland. A bare two weeks after its Broadway première, Warners announced that all their 1927–28 production, some twenty-six films in all, would have Vitaphone music synchronisation. One also senses the envious stir created among the Hollywood majors as they watched their rival's success. 'Actual "Talking" Pictures Line Up As Screen Possibility Shortly', a *Variety* headline announced on 23 November 1927, reporting that Warners were even then 'dialog-ing' a highly dramatic court-room scene in a coming release. A week later, as already mentioned, the same company declared it intended to shoot twelve talkies in addition to the twenty-six silent films in the coming season. This impulsiveness itself showed how swiftly 'talk' had become an imperative part of a movie as the public reaction to Jolson's excitable patter became impressively apparent.

One of these talkies was to be *The Lion and the Mouse*, a domestic melodrama starring Lionel Barrymore, May McAvoy and Buster Collier, all of whom 'will speak lines throughout'. Another would be an underworld story entitled *Tenderloin*, starring Conrad Nagel and Dolores Costello, which would have 'speaking interludes', though not too many, 'otherwise Vitaphone would cease to be a novelty'. This is an interesting caveat: it shows the uncertainty already present about how much dialogue a movie should have – and also an apprehension about how patient the audience might be once the novelty of hearing speaking voices on the screen had worn off. Early in February 1928, Warners' rivals also heard rumours that a five-reel story of Broadway life, tentatively titled *The Roaring Forties*, was to be made on a closed set: and it was to be an 'all-talking' production! There seemed no holding Warners – and, apart from Fox, no one else in Hollywood had yet got off the mark.

Actually, at this very moment Warners' studios were lying idle. No production was going on. Some people believed that the confident announcements of their production plans had been made with the aim of killing the rumour that they were about to scoop up their *Jazz Singer* jackpot and pull out of the movie-making business altogether. This paradoxical situation was partly due to the fact that continuity of production in the 1920s was by no means the rule it became once the 'studio system' got into full gear in the 1930s. Movie-making in California was still a spasmodic, jerky, 'seasonal' thing, almost entirely non-unionised, dependent on irregular exhibitor demand, and often using shaky self-financing methods. Another good reason why studios occasionally went idle was that many contracts contained clauses enabling the studio owners to revise their terms, generally to their own advantage, if there was a lull in production. Warners may have been catching their creative breath: perhaps they were also using the 'break clauses' to re-organise their work-force (they had about 600 employees) for what they saw as the Vitaphone revolution.

The rival studios were in different stages of cautiousness, indecision or frustration where sound was concerned. Paramount's head of research, Roy Pomeroy, was experimenting with a device that, if successful, would add sound to the studio's Magnascope process, introduced in 1924, which enlarged the screen image to four times normal size: it had been used with spectacular effect in the roadshow presentation of *Wings*, the First World War aerial drama which had increased its realism by using phonograph discs placed behind the screen and providing machine-gun effects during the dog-fights. William Fox in 1928 was urging his partner, Theodore Case, along the road to a Movietone talking feature. The policy at MGM was still wait and see: it would cost the studio dearly later on. At United Artists, where stars like Chaplin, Fairbanks and Pickford were also company directors, there was no obvious need, and less desire, to rush into sound. But already one reason for the majors' hesitation was disappearing. A rival to the sound devices of Vitaphone and Movietone materialised at the end of September 1927 when General Electric, a subsidiary of the Radio Corporation of America, demonstrated its Kinegraphone (soon re-named the Photophone) at a theatre in Schenectady, New York. The programme was like an early Vitaphone bill: a spoken introduction by the theatre owner, then a series of musical turns, including a banjo quartet and a vocal quintet ('The voices sound powerfully from the loudspeakers, though a bit "throaty" at times.'). Photophone used a 'belt and braces' approach, combining sound-on-film *and* synchronous disc systems, and claimed its sound was 'superior'. Vitaphone counter-attacked a week later with a demo of its own in the same town. Competition hotted up still further in January 1928, when RCA acquired the theatre chains of B. F. Keith and Orpheum as well as the film production company with the tame name of Film Booking Offices and merged them to form a new company called RKO (Radio-Keith-Orpheum). This meant that RKO could use the Photophone sound system and go into talkie production right away – in theory, anyhow, though like other film companies its full talkie debut was held back by the problem of equipping the silent films it had completed, but not released, with talkie sequences so that they would not look so dated. This process of rejuvenation became known as 'goat-glanding'.

The general manager of RCA, the aggressive David Sarnoff, the ex-Marconi radio operator who had become a national hero at the time of the Titanic disaster, revealed that he had been experimenting in adding voices in place of silent-film dialogue titles to no less prestigious a production than MGM's passionate romantic drama *Flesh and the Devil*, made the year before and starring John Gilbert and Greta Garbo. Sarnoff announced that Photophone would be leased to any studio that wanted it: an important selling factor. For, as mentioned, members of the Motion Picture Producers and Distributors of America had pledged themselves not to go into individual sound production until they had all agreed. They had felt Vitaphone's asking price was too high; the Movietone secrets were locked away from them in the Fox–Case Laboratories. Now that a cheaper sound device was on the market, the association members no longer regarded themselves as bound by their agreement. (In the event, the majors opted for the other two systems: but the existence of the so-called 'cheaper, better' Photophone helped them dissolve their pledge to each other: and on such self-interest is progress made in the movie industry.)

If they needed any other spur than their members' readiness to steal a march on each other, *The Jazz Singer*'s profits supplied it. By the end of 1928, filmgoers would have paid over 1,500,000 dollars to see it; and it would eventually make over twice this sum. As an editorial in *Motion Picture* put it, 'This is the final answer to all arguments about the practicability and acceptability of the talkies. They have been done and they have been liked.'[1] But at the start of 1928, there was still a lot to be done – the question was, 'What?' Many people in the industry could see the advantage of sound for a movie with musical numbers starring the greatest entertainer in the land. But *talk* was still the great unknown. The perfecting of 'effects', adding to stories the realism of natural sounds other than human speech, was being canvassed as the first priority. Of

[1] *Motion Picture*, December 1928.

course it was conceded that 'within the year' films would start appearing which would suddenly switch into dialogue so as to emphasise the action. But there was one big proviso. 'Inability to secure players who can both talk and screen well is always a possible deterrent or check on the industry going completely over to the talk pictures.'[2] This is one of the earliest hints at the cataclysmic impact the talkies were going to make on the Hollywood stars within a few months. But as 1928 began, these privileged beings viewed the talkies with the distant curiosity of liverymen in earlier decades who had heard of the coming of the horseless carriage. Yes, interesting . . . but until the master had actually bought one, why worry?

Over 42,000 people were then employed full-time or casually in Hollywood: and the industry accounted for eighty-two per cent of the world's film entertainment. The foreign circulation of American-made features accounted for forty per cent of the films' total gross: these were, of course, *silent* features able to communicate with audiences everywhere. In the film capital there were nine major studios (Fox, MGM, Paramount, United Artists, First National, Pathé, Universal, Producers Distributing Corp., and Warners) and fifteen smaller outfits (Columbia, FBO, Christie, Sennett, Tiffany–Stahl, Educational, as well as minor comedy producers and independents). A conservative estimate put the value of the studios at sixty-five million dollars. About 18,000 extras were registered as available for work: Central Casting Office had just opened, in an effort to bring order to the chaotic nature of freelance employment, and had 16,500 names on its books, including 70 stars, 100 featured players and 2000 'persons regarded as actors'. Along with other workers, there were some 75,000 people in film production in America, 200,000 in distribution and 110,000 in exhibition. Except for the top handful of stars, craftsmen and studio executives, wages on the Coast were not extravagant. It is a mistake to imagine that many people enjoyed the well-publicised rates of reward available to the lucky, talented or ruthless few. The casual character of the work, and the absence of trade unions to fight for higher pay and better conditions, naturally kept the labour market depressed – and the 'glamour' of the movies made people accept less while they daily lived in hope of more. Talent or some other kind of uniqueness was the stuff on which dreams were made; and payrolls generally reflected the over-abundant supply of ready labour. Stars averaged 2,500 dollars a week, featured players 750 dollars, studio executives 700 dollars: small-ish sums compared with what the topmost talents of all could earn: 5,000 dollars for Emil Jannings, the sensational import from Germany; 6,000 dollars for Pola Negri; 8,000 dollars for Adolphe Menjou, and a very select band of stars who were paid fees per picture such as Colleen Moore who got 125,000 dollars a feature; Gloria Swanson who had been offered 900,000 dollars

[2] *Variety*, 23 November 1927.

for three pictures a year by Paramount, plus half the net profits, and who had turned it down to go completely independent; or Tom Mix, the cowboy star who received the highest fees on the range in 1928, estimated at a million dollars a year: as for people like Chaplin, Fairbanks and Pickford, there was no knowing what they earned since they owned their own talents so completely.

In 1928 there was no uniform pay structure between the studios: one bargained for what one could get. Although insecurity was therefore endemic, and no one was slow to take advantage of anyone else, there was still a freelancing freedom that would certainly never again be repeated until the dislocation caused by television in the 1950s began breaking down the ironclad contract system that the studios had established in the 1930s – with the talkies as one of their strongest weapons.

The entire motion picture industry at this time represented an investment of two thousand five hundred million dollars; by far the greater bulk of it comprised the theatre chains owned by the major producer-distributors. Paramount operated five hundred houses worth four hundred million dollars; First National in association with the Stanley theatre chain had three hundred and fifty houses worth three hundred and fifty million. MGM, through its owner Loew's Inc., had about three hundred worth three hundred million dollars; and Fox, Universal, Pathé and United Artists accounted for another four hundred theatres valued at four hundred and fifty million dollars. As one can see, this left Warners, the only company making the running in the talkies at this time, with few theatres it could call its own and dependent on the deals it could do with other theatre owners. As it turned out, there was no better way of letting your competitors know how sensational the talkies were than to have *your* money passing through *their* box-offices. In all of the United States in 1928 there were about twenty thousand places showing pictures, producing a gross annual revenue of three hundred and sixty million dollars, although many of these were small or dilapidated theatres, not much advanced from their nickelodeon beginnings in back streets, amusement arcades and fairgrounds.

This was the economic scene that the talkies were now to turn upside down. As usual, the bankers were the earliest to see the opportunities. The increasing investment in film companies by Wall Street, the ever more frequent mergers and take-overs soon to be pursued by film tycoons backed by huge bank loans, is the best indicator of the ruthless power scramble that was beginning in 1928. Over the previous two years the banks had been buying into the film industry to the extent of five hundred million dollars. Vitaphone's sensational debut stimulated investment sharply, and gave the financial powers a sufficiently large interest in movie companies to put in their own 'efficiency men' charged with bringing Wall Street accounting methods to what they clearly regarded as the enormous wastefulness of film people. For example, though Hollywood then had about 120 directors, figures showed that only half of them were in regular work; though about 4000 'name' actors were available for work each day, the average number used was only 1,200. Financiers could only blench at this conspicuous waste. Thus the production downturn at the end of 1927 felt by nearly every major studio, and reflected in their share prices, was put down to the shakeout demanded for economy reasons by the new paymasters. Sound would only increase the ability of the latter to crack the whip over the artists, when the film companies at last faced the almost inconceivable fact that the talkies necessitated the wholesale reconstruction of their twenty-five-year-old industry, from flesh-and-blood down to bricks-and-mortar, and all in months, not years.

This moment of awesome illumination, though, had not yet come. Warners were closest to it; and even they were hedging their bets, with a production roster that was still two-to-one in favour of non-dialogue pictures. But the need to distinguish between the true silent picture and the other varieties of sound picture was becoming more urgent weekly.

Variety on 18 January 1928 ran two reviews side-by-side of the same picture, *The Fortune Hunter*, an eighty-minute slapstick farce set in a drug store and starring Syd Chaplin. One version had synchronised music, but no songs or dialogue, and it was viewed in Warners' screening room; the other, twelve minutes shorter, was silent, and it was viewed at the Hippodrome Theater with organ accompaniment. The nod of approval was clearly given to the Vitaphone version. Factors other than art or box-office were nudging the talkies into public acceptance as a normal rather than an exceptional event. A fleet of trucks projecting talking pictures was used in the California federal elections in December 1927: the candidates delivered brief campaign speeches from portable screens. And by the following March the advertising agencies having by now established themselves in radio – J. Walter Thompson and Batton, Barton, Durstein and Osborne had already added 'radio showmen' to their staffs to handle the accounts – were hungrily eyeing talkie pictures as the next potential source of revenue. One can only guess at the pressure which the agencies brought on the local cinemas to get themselves wired for sound: it was estimated that talking equipment in a mere one thousand cinemas could reach fifteen million people weekly with the audible message from the manufacturers of consumer goods. About 8,850,000 dollars would be spent on advertising in 1928, more than double the 1927 budget; and significantly the products that had most money spent on selling them were radios and phonographs, the very devices that increased people's awareness of sound entertainment.

An unexpected blessing for the new medium came from George Bernard Shaw, though, as usual with Shaw, it was not entirely free of self-interest. He hoped, he said, in February 1928, that 'Movietone will supersede the present plan of dragging lecturers around the States from one town to another and shaking hands with them, finally returning them to their homes in a badly damaged condition.'

If one had to decide when the American film industry really woke up to the inevitability of sound, as distinct from its demonstrated practicality and speculative profitability, one would have to choose the period between the first week of March and the last week of April 1928.

On 7 March 1928 Warners announced 'A Talking Picture that will be The Talk of New York. TENDERLOIN. You will see and you *will* hear. Dolores Costello in *Tenderloin* with Conrad Nagel talking on the Vitaphone.' Almost simultaneously they produced another innovation – a fifteen-minute talking trailer which contained a scene from *Tenderloin* with narration by Conrad Nagel. The film opened at the Warner Theater on 14 March 1928 at the very same time as preparations were in hand, just up the road at the Roxy, to re-present *The Jazz Singer* which had at that date been seen in its sound and silent versions in 235 theatres across the nation. The town did indeed seem to belong to Warners.

Tenderloin, running eighty-five minutes and directed by Michael Curtiz, had an importance in the history of sound as virtually the first conscious try at character-talking on the screen. *Variety* acknowledged the novelty by running two reviews of it in the same issue, one after seeing the film with a 'hard-boiled' first-night audience containing many show-business celebrities, the other a screening on the third night with the ordinary paying public. The two reviews were a necessary precaution; for, talk or no talk, *Tenderloin* was scarcely an experience for the sophisticated. In fact it was a crude underworld melodrama: a nice girl from cabaret mixed up with a crook, a bank robbery, suspicion falling on her, her lover's penitence and resolve to go straight, and his sweetheart's belief in him. The première audience missed none of the ineptitudes – and laughed. It was the first example of what became a commonplace response to talkies in which the vocal characterisation seemed either inadequate or in some way excessive to audiences who had come along expecting novelty, but did not yet know how to account for the film's technical or dramatic shortcomings except by laughing at them. Some of the laughter on this occasion undoubtedly came from the sceptical and the prejudiced; for people were now beginning to discriminate between the novelty of audible talk and the *quality* of what was said – as well as the competence of *how* it was recorded. Others were simply embarrassed by what was a new situation for cinema-goers – eavesdropping on voices confiding disembodied intimacies to each other. The private nature of silent-filmgoing was being broken. Now one's own neighbours were hearing what one could hear oneself! A self-consciousness was present, as well as a feeling of novelty.

Actually, there was not all that much novelty. *Tenderloin* had only four dialogue sequences, lasting in all between twelve and fifteen minutes; and by the third night two of these had been cut out of the film and erased from the Vitaphone wax discs. One went because its dialogue was judged by the audiences as just too inane. But the other disappeared because the New York censors ordered it. It was a scene where the heroine was trapped in a farmhouse by one of the villains who allows his aroused passions to make him forget he has come looking for the loot. Mordaunt Hall in the *Times* described the scene:

> The 'Professor' (a lame, but immensely powerful man) enters the room, locks the door, puts the key in his pocket and then looks at Rose who is in her prettiest negligee with her fair hair showered over her shoulders. The 'Professor' thunders that he knows all about women and he virtually tells Rose that it is a case of the money or her life. Rose shrinks with fear and the 'Professor' approaches her with a respect for all the old nickelodeon lines.[3]

Now it was probably here that the hapless Miss Costello as Rose lisped a line that instantly became a catch-phrase among movie-goers of the day, a catch-phrase repeated like a mynah bird's as the 'in' joke of the moment. 'Merthy, merthy, have you no thither of your own?' she implored her threatening captor. Hall concluded:

> It looks very much as if the title-writer had supplied the words to the actions. . . . At any rate, the spectators were moved to loud mirth during the spoken episodes of this lurid film.

The film censor, however, was moved by something else in this visually innocuous and risible scene – namely an uneasy presentiment of the threat to the girl that the realism of sound now presented. For the very first time talk was judged to be more suggestive than silence. It was an intimation that the new talkies were to be subject to the same censorship stringency imposed by the Hays Office as the silents were already.

Other dialogue sequences in *Tenderloin* were judged less than satisfactory, but for other reasons than censorship. The first talkie sequence was a third-degree scene at police headquarters, with the ring of men browbeating the girl suspect. Dolores Costello's voice was weak and thin, lacking volume as well as force. *Variety*'s reviewer, identified *Variety*-style by part of his surname as 'Mori', shrewdly detected something else wrong as well: 'Miss Costello's main fault in talking is the lack of sympathy between her emotional expression and speech.'[4] This was to be one of the most dislocating experiences for silent players making their talkie debuts. They had been used to giving their performance in mime; now dialogue was compelling them to give another one with their voices. Getting the two to fit comfortably together on the screen would not become easy or natural until there had been enough acting done in the talkies to provide players with examples to study – or avoid. The quality of the spoken voice, deemed all-important in the early months of the revolution, turned out to be less

[3] *The New York Times*, 15 March 1928.   [4] *Variety*, 21 March 1928.

49

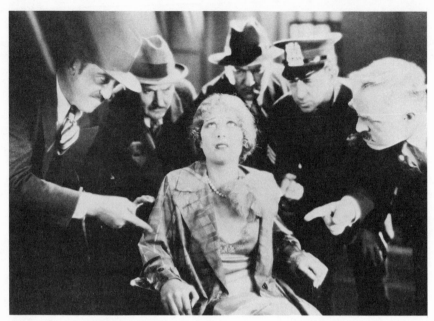

Above, Dolores Costello is given the third-degree at police headquarters in *Tenderloin*
(1928). It was tough going when you were surrounded by five men as well as a
microphone, and the fact 'that she falters at times when speaking cannot be unexpected',
Variety's kindly reviewer concluded. Warner Brothers were less forgiving and included
no scene with her talking in the trailer for their film. *Below*, 'Little question that
Barrymore's voice holds this one up,' a trade-paper reviewer said about *The Lion and the
Mouse* (1928). He singled out in particular the scene between father and son (Lionel
Barrymore, Buster Collier).

crucial than the technique of slipping from mime to vocalising. But this was too sophisticated an idea for these early months. Even *Variety*'s reviewer erred when he said, taking as his evidence the two best actors in *Tenderloin*, that 'vocally the talking picture will draw its appeal from the trained voices of the stage: here notably from Mitchell Lewis and Conrad Nagel, both stage-trained.' This assumption, although it was pardonable, was to be among the most false and costly that the film companies would make when they organised talent raids on the Broadway stage in search of 'trained' voices.

Another feature of the film that disturbed the reviewer was the way the recorded music stopped as the talk started, then picked up again when the conversation finished. The trouble was that no one in Vitaphone knew how to blend the separate tracks of music and sound on the wax discs. The apparatus for doing so did not yet exist. Speaking later of these early days, Douglas Shearer said, 'We had no equipment to do . . . transfers or cut-backs or for combining music under the dialogue. We had to develop all that equipment at MGM'. To have had the music continue under the voices in *Tenderloin* would have needed the Vitaphone Symphony Orchestra concealed on the sound stage and playing away while the lines were uttered – and the balancing this would have required was well beyond the monitor man's capacities at that time. *Variety*'s man hazarded three conclusions. One was that men's voices registered better than women's in the talkies: an opinion that was soon to become almost an article of faith. Maybe it helped explain why Dolores Costello did not figure at all in the talking trailer. Secondly, dialogue meant for comic effect and telegraphing its intention to filmgoers registered best of all: the hit of the film was judged to be a song-and-dance man from vaudeville, Georgie Stone, who played a comic sidekick and used his vocal tones to good effect. Thirdly, deprived of the Vitaphone, *Tenderloin* was rated as only 'a good small-town picture'. 'The direction . . . suggests that (Michael Curtiz) was not given a free hand. . . . Perhaps a dozen or more of the Warner people were watching and suggesting during this experiment. It may be believed that a picture director realises but little more of what may be required so far for a talking picture than the actors in it.' 'Mori' ended his review with a chilling comment: 'And for that matter, who does in this day and age? Perhaps Western Electric's engineers would be the best directors of talkers.'[5] Meant sarcastically, perhaps, this came true a few months later, when 'talkie panic' hit Hollywood and the services of former telephone engineers and radio mechanics were at a premium for the know-how and authority they could wield on the sound stages.

The same reviewer also made a prediction that was more seriously intended, and just as accurate. 'Unless the novelty of the screen talking is strong enough to overcome the picture itself, the talking picture appears

[5] For several years *Variety*'s house-style referred to the new medium as 'the talkers'. I can find 'talkies' used only once or twice before 1930 in its columns.

to be a matter of the voice and the calibre of the dialogue to be employed, together with the situation involving both. . . . Stripped of its mechanicals, *Tenderloin* is a very ordinary crook meller.' This may have been so: but the public were not as cool towards it as the critics, or indeed editorial writers like Walter Lippmann. It was generally believed that it was Lippmann who wrote the unsigned editorial in his paper, the *New York World*, which declared that 'while the movies do talk, as advertised, they haven't anything to say.'

> This, it would seem, might have been expected. The average movie deals with things that have no relation to words at all: it is quite inessential to know what the characters are saying to each other. For example, take a fist fight. This furnishes the climax of a great many movies. Yet what is added to the effect by letting you hear what the belligerents are saying? What they are saying, as a judge once remarked in excluding profane testimony, can be taken for granted. To hear the grunts, groans and damns is only to be distracted from the much more entertaining business of watching the uppercuts to the jaw.[6]

Though the writer is taking an extreme case for polemical purposes, he was expressing an early view of something that soon became more widespread and acceptable: the sheer dislocating effect that talkies were going to have on the rapt attention of a generation of silent-era filmgoers. Already present in this editorial is a nostalgic vibration that many soon began to share for an art form that was to vanish with a suddenness beyond belief, never to return. The article continued:

> The field for the talkie movie, aside from its obvious usefulness in news pictures, is to help do away with the sub-title. But it has a job on its hands here. For the sub-title, originally regarded as the big defect of the movies, has been developed into an art in itself. It is often half the picture. But in becoming so important, it has acquired a tradition of its own. It has learned to evoke what the theatrical profession calls 'eye laughs'; that is, the kind of humor that is funny when you see it, but not good when you hear it. If the talking movie could develop another kind of sub-title which would be effective when spoken and which would furnish a running comment on the story, that would eliminate the interruptions which obtain at present and would justify itself very handsomely.

A week or so before this editorial, Jesse Lasky, head of Paramount production and a man who preserved an equivocal attitude to sound for quite some time after movies had definitely adopted it, said he believed dialogue was impractical. Sub-titles would do the job more economically. (It didn't escape anyone's attention, of course, that Paramount had not yet committed itself to sound and, like most of the

[6] *New York World*, 23 March 1928.

other majors, had a backlog of unreleased silent films.) If the talkies did catch on, Lasky warned darkly, studios would have to be entirely rebuilt. 'Either concrete or brick instead of the present flimsy structures will have to be used.' Emperors had found Rome brick, and left it marble: but there was no similar rush among movie tycoons to upgrade the plywood empire of Hollywood. This was an attitude typical of nearly all the other moguls at this date: they alternately bit their nails with envy at Warners, but counted the cost of copying them with consternation.

Only William Fox was getting sound films going at the same pace as the Warner brothers. He had been expanding fast: a symptom of his accelerating megalomania. He had bought two large theatre chains in California and Minnesota – and was ready to go after virtually any others that took his fancy. In February 1928, he was moving production out of his Hollywood studios, whose real estate value now exceeded their worth as a movie lot, to a 180-acre ranch in the hills where he was planning to erect ten stages and three 'specials' for films 'with Movietone talking characters'. In fact he was to release no fewer than fifteen sound movies in 1928, beginning on 13 February with one of John Ford's early and greatest successes, *Four Sons*, which had a synchronised music score, sound effects and a theme song, 'Little Mother'. Fox had cut the cost of adding music tracks to essentially silent features like this one from 19,000 dollars to about 10,000 dollars a picture. Scoring, rehearsing and recording took on average fifteen hours instead of twenty-four. The tempo was speeding up.

Early in March 1928 Welford Beaton, then editor of a quixotic, opinionated and often personally vitriolic periodical, *Film Spectator*, which was published in Hollywood, watched a two-hour demonstration of Fox's Movietone system. It left this by no means easily impressed man with the conviction that 'the talking picture is here'. Well, at least the sound-effect picture was here. 'We see a naked boy dive into the ole swimmin' hole and hear him exclaim, "Oh, gee!" We see the papal choir in the Vatican grounds and hear it sing. We hear a rooster crow, and the band playing when the guard at Buckingham Palace is changed.'[7] A week or so earlier, Beaton had complained of the 'flatness' of scenes in a silent film shot on location at a football game. Now to hear sounds backing up the Army *v* Navy match in the Fox film was 'stirring'. 'I heard the bands play and the rooters sing, and watched the cheer leaders dance in front of the blocks of their hilarious supporters.' He concluded: 'Nothing is sacrificed when we add sound, but something will be missing when we omit it.' For good measure he opined that 'screen art will not be held back by the fact that an actress lisps'.

Now this last sardonic observation may be a reference to Dolores Costello's unfortunate 'merthy, merthy' line in *Tenderloin*, which Beaton could have seen in Hollywood just before its New York première; but he was an inveterate 'preview' man and, despite occasional bans operated

[7] *Film Spectator*, 17 March 1928.

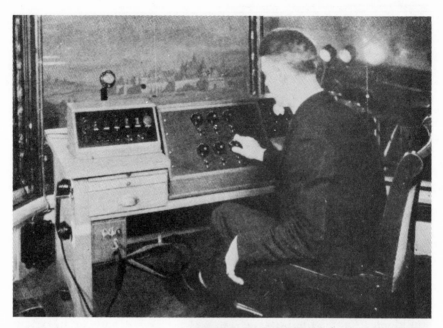

Above, The 'monitor man' at his mixing table in a Hollywood sound studio early in 1929, 'pulling up and toning down the voices of the stars'.

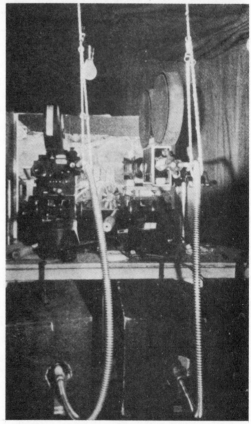

Right, The camera booth from the inside looking out.

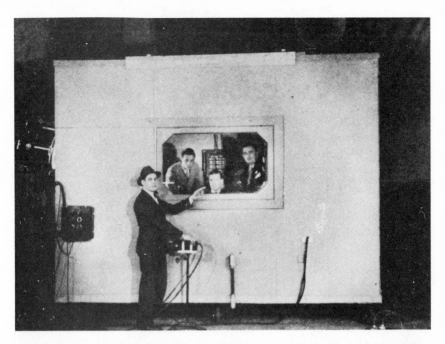

Above, A portable monitor booth in Paramount's Astoria Studios on Long Island. The horn on top enabled the monitor to converse with the director on the set. The director could reply by using the green or red lights on the 'signal box' in front. *Below*, The sound recording room of a Hollywood studio where perfect synchronisation was often the frustrated aim.

against him by movie moguls angered by the caustic personal tone his magazine took towards them, he appears to have enjoyed easy access to most of the studios where he sometimes acted as 'script doctor', taking pleasure in telling the film people how to do their business and using what pay he got to finance the periodical in which he astringently criticised that business. It is thus perfectly possible that he was referring to another film, then unreleased, which he had previewed and which co-starred the lisping Miss Costello. This film has an importance beyond its now largely forgotten title. It was one that actually brought the sound revolution home to Hollywood's front doorstep. It was called *Glorious Betsy*.

Sound at this time, as far as most of the film colony's residents were concerned, was something that was stuck on to films in far-away New York. The big sound premières – Vitaphone, *Don Juan*, *The Jazz Singer*, *Tenderloin* – had all happened on the East Coast, too. The Hollywood folk, physically remote from such events, felt a comforting insulation. It still took over three days to cross the American continent by train; regular passenger services by air had begun in mid-1927, but cost a daunting fifteen cents a mile. Opinion about the talkies that filtered back to the Coast was therefore late, frequently second-hand, or coloured by the bearer's own apprehensions. The progress of a talkie towards Hollywood was even more retarded by the sporadic wiring of the theatres in which it could be shown. Movies, like people, travelled more slowly in those days: sound movies, more slowly still. Many Hollywood people only got to see and hear their first talkie on 26 April 1928, when Warner Brothers' Vitaphone production of *Glorious Betsy* was premièred there on the very same date that it opened in New York. It had begun, like most of the early talkies, as a completely silent film. Conrad Nagel, who had been loaned to Warners by MGM, attributes the decision to add sound to it to the snowballing success of *The Jazz Singer*. 'We were working on our picture when Jack Warner came running on to the set with Darryl Zanuck, who was then in charge of production. Warner said to us, 'Darryl's got a great idea. You've heard about *The Jazz Singer*. Darryl wants to put some talking scenes into this picture.' As a result we finished the picture and then put some talking scenes into it.'[8] Nagel added, 'The night it opened (at Warners' new Hollywood theatre), my God, all Hollywood was there to see it.'

Among them was the film director William C. de Mille, who has left a memorable account of the night.

I shall never forget the moment when André de Segurola (the Metropolitan Opera singer), playing the part of a military officer, stood in the middle of the picture to address the people around him. 'Ladies and gentlemen,' he said. *He said!* A thrill ran through the

[8] Rosenberg and Silverstein, op. cit., pp. 183–4.

house. The screen had spoken at last: an operation had been performed and the man, dumb from infancy, could talk.[9]

The story of a love affair between Napoleon's brother Jerome and a belle of Baltimore, the film was Alan Crosland's first intentional attempt at a part-talkie – *The Jazz Singer*, it's fair to say, had been more Jolson's intention. But as William C. de Mille and the audience listened, they felt the initial thrill subsiding. 'We felt constricted movement in the characters as they were forced to manoeuvre in order to face an implacably fixed microphone. Poor Dolores Costello's excellent voice came out at times as a deep rich baritone, while Conrad Nagel thundered in a sub-human bass, like immortal love declaiming through the Holland Tunnel. When they whispered together confidentially, the resulting sounds took me back to the old woodshed of my boyhood where the hired man wielded a mean saw. The rustle of Dolores' silk dress suggested the fevered panting of a yard engine. The letters "s" and "f" in their speech sounded like tearing silk.' Nevertheless, de Mille concluded,

> As I realised the future possibilities of what I was seeing, I felt a nervous quiver run through me. . . . The nervous tension and sense of excitement . . . was to last all through the first two hectic years of 'sound'.[10]

It is interesting to compare this response to the film with that of the East Coast where sound was by now no novelty. 'Mori', who reviewed the film for *Variety* a week later, appears quite *blasé* by now: worse, he has even got impatient. 'Speaking lines, even when delivered well, do not impress because none added anything of special interest, like useless lines in a stage play, and wouldn't be missed if eliminated.'[11] This was one of the earliest signs that a talkie could have too much talk – and remember that *Glorious Betsy* was only a *part*-talkie! Even Mordaunt Hall, conceding that *Glorious Betsy* was 'a vast improvement on *Tenderloin*', turned pernickety. 'There might, it is true, have been an attempt to have a suggestion of French pronunciation in Conrad Nagel's utterances (as Jerome). . . . He might also have refrained from saying "Betsy" three times in the last episode, for you felt then that silence would have been golden. On the other hand,' Hall added, relenting, 'Miss Costello's subdued utterance of "My tomorrow has come" was decidedly effective.'[12]

Tenderloin and *Glorious Betsy* drew very mixed opinions from the critics, and de Mille reports his Hollywood compatriots left the latter's première snorting, 'So these were talking pictures – the public would never take to them.' But of course the public *did*. *Tenderloin* opened to the public's 'healthy attention' with 17,500 dollars in its first week in New York; in Chicago it was 'A Real Hit'; in Washington D.C., *Variety*

[9] William C. de Mille, op. cit., p. 269.   [10] Ibid., pp. 270–1.
[11] *Variety*, 2 May 1928.   [12] *The New York Times*, 27 April 1928.

reported that it 'Leads *The Jazz Singer*' in receipts. *Glorious Betsy* beat the notices to become another amazing crowd-puller. Even if the lines on the players' lips were poorly recorded or dramatically inept, the lines of people outside the cinemas eager to hear them were what counted. All the more, since business generally had been badly off, fifty per cent down in places, during the early months of the year. Universal had had a five or six week closure; even Fox was working at only two-thirds' capacity, and it was the busiest studio on the Coast. By the end of March, half the studios in Hollywood were temporarily idle; and for the first time in the memory of many the habitual rhythm of the movies was significantly faltering over longer stretches of the year than usual. It hardly needed Warners' exceptional run of success to persuade people that now, if ever, was the time to 'try something new'. Just three weeks after *Glorious Betsy*'s opening, on 15 May 1928, three of the majors, Paramount, United Artists and MGM, signed up with Electrical Research Products Inc. (ERPI), Western Electric's marketing subsidiary, for the installation of Movietone's optical-sound and sound-on-disc systems in their studios, and Western Electric amplifiers in their cinemas. First National had already done a similar deal: other majors were expected to follow. ERPI apparently took this initiative without even obtaining Warners' consent to equipping its rivals with the means of competition. As a marketing company it was better placed to sell and install equipment than a film company, and more impatient to get going. An impatience now matched at the other studios as the public clamour for the talkies became irresistible.

Over three hundred cinemas had been wired for sound by mid-1928, and three hundred more contracts were being fulfilled. It was estimated that one thousand would have the new marvel in them by the end of the year. The original pioneers were especially bullish. William Fox lavished 2,500 dollars on a talking trailer which went on show on 23 May 1928, and featured stars and directors waxing enthusiastic about the up-coming talkies. And as he sailed for Europe, to sound out the Vitaphone possibilities there, Major Albert Warner boasted that his company would soon be scoring another 'first'. It was even then negotiating for the 'Vitaphon-ing' of Broadway's hit plays and musicals – and it would use the original casts. All of the twenty-six Warner–Vitaphone features planned or in production would now have talking sequences. He went on: 'The demand for legitimate (stage) players for talking pictures will be considerable. It will also be necessary to acquire writers with a knowledge of the theatre for the construction of effective speaking lines. An art with which Hollywood title writers are not on good terms.'[13] Quite obviously, the lessons of the early talkies were being quickly learnt. What no one foresaw as the new sound era now opened for all Hollywood was that mistakes were about to be made with even greater rapidity and at much, much more expense.

[13] *Variety*, 28 March 1928.

5
'The actors are saying that you make them feel nervous.'

Lionel Barrymore in 1928 was no longer one of MGM's most valuable stars: he had grown lame, querulous and corpulent. The studio made no objection when Warners came seeking him to play a part in their new Vitaphone production, *The Lion and the Mouse*. In fact it was not Barrymore's lingering reputation as a leading man of the silent screen that attracted director Lloyd Bacon to him: it was the experience he had amassed long before that, as a stage actor. It was felt that someone with a trained stage voice was essential for the role of the ruthless financier in the film, whose son defies his orders and marries the daughter of the judge ruined by papa. As may be guessed, the plot itself was more than somewhat *passé*: the stage play it was based on came replete with Victorian melodrama and 'heavy' scenes. Not the sort of thing, one would have thought, to attract a Jazz Age audience looking to the screen for *risqué* thrills and plausible sophistication. And yet Welford Beaton declared,

> After *The Lion and the Mouse* is generally released and shown in the hundred theaters already equipped for Vitaphone, we will have no more important silent pictures. They will be as dead as the dodo. Instead of producing revenue for three years (the silent pictures now completed) will be put on the shelf within one year to make room on the screens for pictures that reproduce dialogue and music.[1]

Clearly an overstatement: but bearing the excited *pronunciamento* of a man who had come hot from witnessing, at a private screening, what he regarded as the breakthrough for the talkies. This film is in fact the first one that really lets us sense the problems and the potential of the new medium which were now becoming monthly (and soon weekly) reality

[1] *Film Spectator*, 28 April 1928.

59

for Hollywood. Reactions to it are thus very important: even reviewers dismissing it as art or deploring it as entertainment ('As drama it is very dull') generally added that 'movie-goers who want to hear [sic] what the future holds for them had better go'.[2]

The intention had been to shoot most of it as a silent film, with one Vitaphoned sequence near the start. But as soon as this had been done, it made all the rest of the film look dated: so about a dozen more talking scenes were included throughout at irregular intervals. Like most of the crucial developments in the talkie era, accident and afterthought were the determining factors: foresight very, very rarely played a part. The film opened in Los Angeles on 26 May, in New York on 15 June; and two lengthy reviews in *Variety* enable us to gauge in valuable detail just how the sixty-five-minute movie (sixty-nine minutes in New York) struck the critics of a trade paper who were sometimes much sharper and more precise in setting down what they observed for the guidance of their showmen readers than writers for the independent film periodicals who were simply out to entertain the uninstructed.

Variety's anonymous reviewer in Los Angeles painstakingly took a seat at the rear of the balcony 'to compare the film with the stage' and found 'this newcomer does not pass the test with credit'. Sound and lip-movements were out of sync in close-ups. May McAvoy, as the fiancée, had a voice 'which hardly carried to the back of the house, giving the impression that it was insufficiently robust. Yet in a later sequence it came back clear and strong.' Acoustics may have been the cause of this: but it could also have been due to faulty communication between the film's director and the sound controller in the monitor box. At any rate, it had been corrected for the New York opening. One comment is striking, for it anticipated a feature that was a general source of bafflement to early talkie audiences. The reviewer expected the volume of the voices to change as the speakers moved from close-up to long-shot. But it did not. One senses in this comment an audience's difficulty in adjusting expectations derived from real life to the still novel conventions of talking cinema. In a way it was a re-appearance of those primitive expectations held by the very first cinema audiences who half-expected the train on the screen to continue its momentum into the auditorium. The vocal discrepancy in *The Lion and the Mouse* was due to the need to keep players a constant – i.e. measurable – distance from the fixed microphone, no matter where the camera might be at the time. Where the film had dialogue scenes, the talk in most cases came in a single close-up, rarely in a two-shot, and no more than once or twice when three people were in the shot. The sheer lack of room around the microphone explains this. It suggests, though, that we should revise our ideas about the detriment caused to the early talkies by the relatively immobile cameras. Though the cameras still had to be encased in sound-proof cabins, they were in fact far more mobile than the

[2] *Motion Picture Magazine*, September 1928.

60

microphones. The cameras could and did move with the action, though they moved slowly and expensively. Different set-ups with such cumbersome equipment took time. And time in film-making, then as now, was money. Thus the first effect of talkies was immediately to reduce the number of interesting camera 'angles', adding to the static quality of the film. Moreover, sound movies had to shoot with film moving at a faster speed, for reasons already mentioned; so the shooting speed of the camera tended to slow down the players' responses still further. Actors had to become used to speaking and moving more swiftly than they had done in the silent films; and this may help account for the hectic pace set in some of the later talkies by players and crew who had learnt their lesson. The staccato rhythm of the early 1930s is as much the result of adjustment to the techniques of sound as it is to the tempo of a hardboiled, swift-moving new era. But even allowing for these retarding effects on the speed and variety of shots in the early talkies, the microphone was more to blame than the camera. Until it was put on a mobile boom, and could thus discreetly follow the players, everyone in the shot had to *stand* by it or around it. It was the real cause of the tableau-esque effects which soon made the old silent films seem absolutely bubbling over with *élan* and vitality.

Variety's reviewer noted one major miscalculation in the construction of *The Lion and the Mouse*. Its first talkie sequence came two minutes into the film: it showed Barrymore ponderously 'planting' the story in a conversation with his yes-man secretary. During the ensuing dozen silent sequences, the audience was left in suspense, wondering when the film would 'get its voice back'. There were in all about thirty-one minutes of dialogue, with a thirty-eight-minute gap in the middle plugged with synchronised music: the last twenty-three minutes were solid talk. This was delivered abnormally slowly: a feature of early talkie acting where the man in the monitor cabin, seeking an even, clearly modulated voice, overruled the film director on the floor who probably desired more pace and emotional expression. There was a heavy concentration on picking up ev-ery syl-lab-le, which led to retarded delivery. Where the movie really came to life, in most critics' opinion, was in the brisk scene between Barrymore and Buster Collier, as his son, the dialogue being better written, with more pace, and the sarcastic chiding of the parent drawing spirited ripostes from the defiant boy. Some thought Barrymore had written his own dialogue; for he sounded completely at home with it. Even listening to his resonant voice sending a telegram, *Variety*'s 'Mori' declared, 'could make a telephone dramatic on a raft'; while Mordaunt Hall reported that 'only Barrymore managed to continue the character's interest through the silent scenes'.[3] The other players, Hall noted, with the significant exception of Barrymore's contemporary and one-time stage crony, Alec Francis, playing the judge, 'in their desire to "utter" . . . forgot to pay enough

[3] *The New York Times*, 16 June 1928.

attention to the psychology of the scene, so that there was a throwback to the days of melodrama'. Other reviewers, writing for snappier publications than the *Times*, were blunter. 'May McAvoy and Buster Collier', said one, 'had better enroll in the first class of voice culture they can find.'[4] In such a cutting remark one can sense the seed of the most expensive delusion that the talkies fostered: the notion that the most desirable voice for the speaking screen was the cultured one. Once this idea seized the front offices of the film studios, where the power to make or break careers was lodged, the tycoons utterly forgot the truth of a remark that John Barrymore made to Mordaunt Hall when the *Times* critic was making a fact-finding tour of Hollywood in July 1928. 'President Jefferson', remarked Barrymore with feeling, 'said that fine voices killed more good actors than whisky.' But even Hall had commented, after seeing *The Lion and the Mouse*, that ordinary screen players noted only for an agreeable presence would obviously have to go through a course of stage training before they could deliver competent Vitaphone performances. The misunderstanding that vocal naturalism did not depend on clear or refined enunciation took deep and early root in Hollywood; and poorly recorded, ineptly written films like this one helped spread the subsequent terror that a few months' breathing-space for reflection and experiment would have spared everyone.

But time was the one thing the movies could not afford; and experimentation generally meant, in practical terms, someone else's bad film which you had seen the night before or the one you yourself had made the month before. The stock company of players and crew now being haphazardly built up by Warners with each new talkie were among the first to undergo the rigours and fears of the new technique that was obviously not quite 'stage', but in ways they did not yet fully comprehend was not quite cinema, either. Sound and talk were dominant: visual quality had suddenly become secondary. There was also the strange sensation of getting used to the sound of one's own voice. That person on the screen, hitherto silent, now developed unsuspected characteristics, some of them highly unsettling: he or she drawled, hesitated, hissed, lisped, or occasionally declaimed as if seeking to reach the back rows of a theatre. Enforced silence in the studio increased the self-consciousness, so that sometimes an old-fashioned camera would be cranked by hand during the rehearsals to provide the companionable whirr of audible work. Rubber shoe-heels became *de rigueur* for players and technicians. 'As welcome as a sneeze on a sound stage' became the in-joke around Hollywood at this time. Three-sided sets, which were often standard in silent movie-making, were suddenly discovered to induce 'hollow' voices. A battery of terms invented by callous technicians characterised players whom the microphone didn't favour: one could be a 'blooper' (blasting on the recording device), a 'sizzler' (hissing effects), a 'sucker' (whispers), a

---

[4] *Motion Picture Magazine*, September 1928.

'growler' (gutturals), or suffer from 'corduroy voice' (one that wavered, now loud, now soft, the very bane of the monitor room).

Jan and Cora Gordon who have given us a graphic account of silent-era filming, already quoted, also recorded their impressions of how the talkies had changed the entire mood on the set. Hitherto the Gordons had felt they were being roped into a small carnival: now they felt distinctly unwelcome as they were 'smuggled' on to a sound set.

> Here was none of the bustle and jollity that (had) ruled. . . . It seemed a ceremony almost religious, church-like in a sense of awe that oozed from the operators. I could never imagine the script girl here perched on the director's knee. The influence of 'Silence' seemed to have turned even the stage-hands into ghosts; the director spoke his instructions in a lowered voice, not a megaphone on the premises. No gay music burst out to stimulate the stars to an emotional brilliance; they must suck it all from their emotional entrails; the silence became so intense that we might almost have heard the music of the spheres instead; the yellow 'inkey' lights did not murmur with a cheerful sizzle; the 'juicers' stood frozen in rigid attitudes; not a joint creaked.[5]

The visitors soon noted that shooting 'sound' made scenes last far longer: sub-titles had been economy measures in the silent movies. Silent scenes had been a mosaic of feelings, allowed to run only as long as was needed to make themselves 'felt'. Once words began to express those feelings, the shots had to be held till the player finished speaking. (There was no such thing as a 'reaction shot' at this date: the camera shot only the people doing the speaking and, as yet, had no eye for the people doing the listening.)

What the Gordons felt was the new atmosphere of subconscious dislike of the new medium: it hit them like a smack in the face. In spite of the fact that they tried to appear inconspicuous – they felt more intruders than visitors – the annoyance of the actors, possibly frustrated by takes which the sound monitor declared useless, settled on the Gordons. 'The actors are saying that you make them feel nervous', a publicity man told them, and they were quietly hustled out.

Perplexity and anxiety was the growing mood in Hollywood in May and June 1928. No one could offer anyone words of genuine reassurance. There was an almost total dearth of technical experts. Although sound engineers employed by radio and telephone companies were being desperately wooed to come out to the Coast, many were reluctant to leave steady employment in their present jobs for what they felt would be only a passing novelty! So the craftsmen already on the spot – perhaps in more senses than one – began meeting in seminars for the mutual exchange of information, which usually meant rumour and opinion. These were held under the auspices of the Academy of Motion

[5] Jan and Cora Gordon, op. cit., pp. 278–81.

Picture Arts and Sciences, a body set up on 4 May 1927, by leading film people to promote the artistry, craft and status of the cinema – and also, some were to allege, to ward off any aggressive intrusion into film-making by the labour unions. (Equity had been defeated in the same year in its attempt to unionise Hollywood players.) The American Society of Cinematographers had pioneered the kind of 'bush telegraph' that the talkies now made Hollywood's essential and indeed sole means of communication in 1928. At the start of the year there had been only six cameramen with a working knowledge of the new incandescent illumination used for the talkies; six months later, thanks to the ASC 'schools', there were one hundred and fifty.

In the first week of May, therefore, the writers' branch of the Academy met in session to voice their fears and gain what limited assurances could be offered by people who had actually worked on sound movies and were now giving themselves the airs of veterans returning from a far-off war front with decorations (or scars, as appropriate). It is fascinating to read the accounts of such meetings with today's hindsight: one feels, almost tangibly, the obfuscating cloud of ignorance, second-guessing and downright doomsday prophesying that accompanied the move into sound.

Roy Pomeroy, then in charge of all Paramount's experiment and research, told the writers that one whole year would be essential to photograph a sound picture properly, accompanied by a complete dialogue track. 'In the matter of speech between two characters,' he warned, 'it is necessary to permit an appreciable lapse of time between the end of the remarks of one and the beginning of the other's, so that the audience may follow the change and have an opportunity to realise the shift in speakers.'[6] It was implied that characters could never be photographed from the back while they were talking – for how were filmgoers to know who was speaking? Pomeroy also referred to the clumsiness of projectionists who might eliminate essential sound-track dialogue as they changed reels. If the film were silent, the loss of a few frames would not matter; with talkies, it would sound like a bad case of the stutters. Another thing still baffling him was adjusting the volume of the sound as the camera moved from long-shots to close-ups. One of Warners' writers, Anthony Coldeway, described as 'seeming to know more about writing for the talking subjects than any of the others', said that 'in making Vitaphone features it was the policy to outline the story with dialogue in the first couple of sequences, depending upon action to carry through the tale from that point, with an occasional spoken title to build up the story'. This need to unfold the story quickly limited the type of theme being chosen at the moment. The 'sound' script, he said, was first written without dialogue: if approved in that form the title writers from the silent movies then took over and did the dialogue. The need for dialogue, Coldeway concluded, would mean that the supervisor

[6] *Variety*, 9 May 1928.

(producer) 'must do all his homework before the picture is shot'. As writers generally held their 'supervisors' in low esteem, this caused 'hearty laughter' and was probably the most welcome thing any of them heard that evening.

One (unnamed) woman writer forecast that dialogue was going to reduce the size of the audience for the talkies, since poorer people could not be expected to comprehend dialogue meant for middle-class filmgoers. (It's apparent that an analogy is being drawn here with the 'sophisticated' theatre.) What almost everyone agreed on was that sound would destroy the lucrative overseas market – at that time almost half of a film's gross revenues. If any language other than English was desired, the company would have to employ directors and cast (and writers) other than the original ones: would that reduce everyone's pay? Donald Crisp, actor and director, said that the talkie director must be prepared to rehearse his cast as if they were doing a stage show: production would take four times longer than in silent days.

The gloom deepened the following week when technicians and directors ('the meg. men') held a seminar to rue their respective fates. Pomeroy (the Job's comforter on such occasions) told the sound technicians that while the volume of speaking voices could be controlled during the production, it was not yet possible to change the volume while printing the film's sound track. Faces brightened slightly when he announced, with pride, that he had solved one problem. The optical sound track necessarily reduced the size of the frames on the negative by taking up some of the space; but now it was possible to record the sound on a separate piece of film which was synchronised with the one carrying the visual as it passed through the projector. But the way Pomeroy's mind approached the talkies showed the banal side of the technician's inventiveness when he said, 'It will be more economical to photograph successful plays with dialogue than . . . straight pictures. This is due to the smaller number of sets to be photographed compared with necessary locations in the case of a picture.'[7] Compare this with what the directors said at their seminar a few days later and one can see how sound was already, even before most of the studios had got a talkie into production, beginning to split Hollywood into separate encampments depending on whether one's principal concern was art or cost. William C. de Mille asked, 'Will not the solution lie . . . in increasing the action so that the natural use of language will be reduced?' Edward Sloman forecast, 'There will be a dearth of speech and lots of business.' Nathan Levinser reported, on the basis of one experience with Vitaphone, that 'today the lines are cast four or five days in advance of the photography, instead of, as in the beginning, just a few hours earlier'.

And here Alan Crosland revealed the unpublicised use of 'doubling' (or, as would be said now, 'dubbing') during his film *The Jazz Singer*. Warner Oland, who couldn't sing, had played Jolson's cantor father. A

[7] Ibid., 16 May 1928.

real cantor had been stationed 'in the wings' – i.e. off-camera – and Oland's lips had had to move in sync with the chanting. 'It was not entirely satisfactory,' Crosland added. Ever the upbeat contributor to these seminars, and possibly still feeling the tingle of excitement started by *Glorious Betsy*, de Mille heartened the throng by predicting,

> In as much as the introduction of American films into Europe has resulted in Europeans wearing American hats and shoes and almost everything else, so we may be sure that in a couple of generations from now, all Europeans will be speaking English so that they may continue to see and understand American films.[8]

Hollywood's role as 'America's overseas empire' has seldom been as confidently stated before or since.

If the Hollywood folk, emulating earlier pioneers, were drawing the wagons into a circle for self-protection, another band of film people were already taking defensive action. Among the first to be affected by the technical change-over to sound were the projectionists. It was they, whose consciousness had been raised by pressure from the salesmen to wire the cinemas, who demonstrated the new, aggressive effect that the revolution would have on the casual nature of the industry. To project talkies satisfactorily now required far greater skills than to show silent movies: skills in synchronising sound discs, supervising the optical tracks, checking on amplification and acoustics, rescuing the situation if anything went wrong with the horrid, audible suddenness of sound breaking down. Three men, instead of just one or two, were now required in a projection booth: four were needed for a full Vitaphone show with discs. By mid-1928, with only a few sound features in release, projectionists were already demanding fifteen to twenty dollars more a week than for showing silents. The minimum wage scale was then fifty-five dollars a week: two extra men for sound projection, paid at the new rates, would bring the cinema's minimum weekly wages bill for them to over two hundred dollars. In first-run cinemas working a shift system, six men regularly employed at, say, ninety-five dollars a week would have to be supplemented by three extra men working at the one hundred and ten dollars a week which their union now demanded for handling sound: a weekly wages bill of nearly eight hundred dollars, a yearly one of over forty thousand dollars. In California itself, projectionists were unusually vociferous, demanding a minimum of ninety-five dollars a week, two men per shift, a minimum of two shifts a day, and a six-day week. While Hollywood could only draw on rumours of how sound would affect their craft members, projectionists in the field were made instantly militant because of the very precise instructions which showed how the talkies would change their way of going. Moreover, these instructions were given to them directly by their own union organisers

[8] Ibid., 16 May 1928.

66

who attended the ERPI training schools, then passed on their instruction to the projectionists in the cinemas. The union was thus alerted to change far more dramatically than the guilds in the film capital. They saw the threat: equally important, they saw their opportunity.

It was this sudden jump in the wages bill for those in the projection boxes which stripped the theatre owners of their desire, never mind their power, to go on using live musicians 'out front' to accompany the film with mood music or provide an overture and interlude for the performance. Once the house orchestra had been done away with, silent films just had to go, too, for no one was left to 'accompany' them. The disappearance of the house musician was startling in its rapidity, heartbreaking in the sheer numbers. New York's Strand Theater announced that, starting 2 June 1928, it would replace its stage acts with Vitaphone shorts; its regular house orchestra for accompanying the movies would be cut from forty to under twenty players. The U.S. Bureau of Labor Statistics has estimated that in 1928 some 20,000 musicians were in the employ of movie theatres across the country: during the next two years alone, fifty per cent of them were sacked. There were already ten 'talking houses' on Broadway in June 1928 and 3,200 musicians employed in theatres in that city; by 1931, Broadway was all-talking and well over half the musicians were out of work – and likely to stay that way as the Depression bit deeply into the hearts and pockets of America.

The agonising reaction among musicians and variety acts, who had so lately seen the talkies as a great new source of employment, contrasts vividly with the euphoria now developing among all the other Hollywood chieftains who were about to go into sound pictures: or almost all. Nicholas Schenck, head of Loew's Inc., which owned MGM, announced that fifteen to twenty per cent of all up-coming productions would be 'Movietoned'. Jesse Lasky at Paramount declared his 'firm conviction that (the sound and talking picture) is here to stay' and, despite technical imperfections now evident in the haste to meet popular demand, he had 'not the slightest doubt . . . that it will improve. At the same time, I don't think that the silent picture will disappear from the screen.'[9] (Lasky still had a shelf of silent productions awaiting release.) Sam Goldwyn, cautiously welcoming sound, feared that 'so many inadequate talking subjects will be issued that people will eventually long for the peace and quiet to which they have been accustomed with the silent features'.[10] But Goldwyn, too, had cause to pause. His 1927 silent hit, *The Winning of Barbara Worth*, had made Ronald Colman and Vilma Banky, two of his contract players, into a potent romantic team. He had finished two more films starring them, and had no quick desire to have to break up the team when the time came for the public to be acquainted with Miss Banky's strong Hungarian accent. United Artists'

[9] *The New York Times*, 29 July 1928.   [10] Ibid., 5 August 1928.

president, Joseph M. Schenck (who was Nicholas's brother), was dead against sound. 'Talking doesn't belong in pictures,' he decreed. Perhaps he recalled the ill-omened debut of the famous film people on radio a few months earlier. But the fact was that this company drew little of its revenues from productions made by its illustrious shareholders like Pickford, Chaplin and Fairbanks, all of them by now slow if celebrated workers. It relied on distributing films by independent movie-makers, who were just the people without the financial means to go into sound, even if they desired to do so.

But while movie chiefs spoke thus 'for the record', out of self-interest or prudence, there is no doubt from the preparations the studios were now feverishly making that they accepted the talkies as a fact and looked forward to them as a new fortune. The public would have speedily resolved their doubt, anyhow. The long stretches of dialogue in *The Lion and the Mouse*, and especially Lionel Barrymore's sensitive 'vocalising' of the stern papa whose heart is softened, proved enormously popular. But even it was eclipsed a few weeks later by the next sensation, *The Lights of New York* (8 July 1928).

Actually it would have been understandable if this film had proved a set-back for the talkies. As well as being boosted as 'the first of the all-talking pictures', it was clearly one of the worst. Hardly surprising, considering its origins. Not only had it not been conceived as an all-talkie, but also it had not even started life as a feature-length film. The story is that it 'just growed' out of one of the Vitaphone short subjects. Its director, Bryan Foy, who had been made supervisor (producer) of these shorts, preferred talking sketches to musical acts or opera singers. *The Lights of New York* (known at one period as *Bright Lights*) ran just fifty-seven minutes and is said to have been shot in under a week at a cost of 75,000 dollars – which had Foy almost dismissed for extravagance. Like so much else about how films of this period got made, this story must be treated with reserve. Accident and improvisation did play crucial roles, as has already been noted, but the genesis of *The Lights of New York* is probably more ordinary. As early as August 1927, Vitaphone had signed two scenarists specially to work on 'gags, drama and unusual effects'. They were Murray Roth, a comedy writer for Fox, and Grant Clarke, a well-known author and movie title-writer. A trade paper announcement said '(they) are now hard at work on a unique subject which promises to be something new in the realm of Vitaphone presentation. Bryan Foy will direct.'[11] This does not sound like an unpremeditated movie. *The Lights of New York* was Foy's first feature-length assignment, and Murray Roth wrote it with Hugh Herbert providing the dialogue.

Viewed today it turns out a commonplace gangster film, unbelievably naïve, especially for an era that had direct acquaintance with the 'public enemies', and there is only one sequence in which the contemporary

[11] *Moving Picture World*, 20 August 1927.

reviewers detected any originality – the placing of a murdered man's body in a barber's chair so as to mislead the police. Its theme is sentimental and heavily moralising. An opening title announces it as 'A story of Main Street and Broadway . . . Main Street – 45 minutes from Broadway – but a thousand miles away.' In other words, for all the topicality of a reference to 'last night's newspaper', it deals in the age-old contrast between small-town virtues and big-city temptations. Two, far too trusting, barbers in a sleepy old hotel are cajoled into moving to New York where bootleggers use their shop as a 'front'. The fiancée of one of them, a night-club dancer on 'the Giddy White Way', is falsely accused of shooting her boss, the club-owner and chief bootlegger. But all ends happily, morally and mushily, with the lovers freed from police custody and heading back to the country where, as a detective who is obviously one of New York's more poetic finds puts it, 'there's trees and flowers and mountains. . . . Leave the Roaring Forties to roar without you.'

Twenty-two of the twenty-four sequences in the film contained dialogue, 'every character speaking, more or less', as *Variety* put it; the dialogue instead of the sub-title for the first time really carried the story. The acting is for the most part wooden, totemesque, lodged in one spot, except in the night-club scenes. *The New York Times*, categorising the picture rather kindly as 'experimental', added that when the music and dancing begin 'it zooms upwards'. *Variety* said that 'the only evidence of careful direction to be found is in a cabaret scene where a door opens and the music sounds louder. Then when it closes again, the music goes dim.'[12] In those early days, this was accounted quite an advance for sound! But contemporary opinions like these are not altogether fair. Foy clearly realised how the immobile microphone limited his actors, so he shot a robbery scene entirely in highly mobile shadows, synchronised music and sound effects to give it pace and drama. But working against him all the time is the monotonous tonal quality of the speech. No cast member, *Variety* reported, ominously, 'is starred or featured in the programme or Press sheet. . . . Nearly all are vaudeville players who talk as best they may in lieu of legits (stage-trained players) or picture actors who can't talk.' (This isn't correct, though, as Eugene Palette, who played one of the barbers, had a stage background, while Cullen Landis as the hero and Wheeler Oakman as the gang boss had appeared in numerous silents.) Even so, no mercy was shown to Helene Costello, as the heroine, who was deemed to be 'a total loss. For talkers, she had better go to school right away.' Harry M. Geduld, however, awards the prize for the worst delivery of dialogue to Mary Carr as the heroine's mother: 'her misguided notion of rendering lines . . . was to say them at a speed equivalent to that of the most painfully slow reader of silent film titles'.[13] This tranquillised quality contrasts bizarrely with the story of gunmen, conmen, chorus girls and bootleggers and it must obviously be

[12] *Variety*, 11 June 1928.   [13] Harry M. Geduld, op. cit., p. 206.

Above, Lights of New York (1928) began life as a musical short and somehow gathered a story about the underworld as it went along. The film cost 75,000 dollars and grossed over a million. *Below,* Josephine Dunn, Joan Crawford and Anita Page were *Our Dancing Daughters* (1928), a drama of the Jazz Age and its flappers which gained nothing in particular from having sound effects added to it which one reviewer described as 'love songs, stentorian cheering and, at the end, a chorus of shrieks'.

due to Foy's desire to follow the decrees of the sound engineers for whom a monotone delivery with no conversational fluctuations was the ideal recording voice. 'The Broadway look,' said *Variety*, 'the double-crossings, the crooks, the "Take him for a ride", the dances and the dames and the mush stuff and the terrible voices will still interest audiences when the terrific quantity of commercial publicity being given the talkies before they are actually seen makes curiosity pep up for something different on the screen.' This different 'something' certainly included the parts of the dialogue peppered with underworld slang such as was sure to be imitated by 'decent folk' who saw the film, thus ensuring it valuable 'word of mouth' success.

Typical of this was the dialogue between the gang boss and an underling: '. . . the dicks will be here at ten o'clock.' – 'Uh-huh?' – '*But they must not find Eddie!*' – 'What do you want us to do?' – 'I want you guys to make him disappear.' – 'Disappear?' – 'Certainly. If they don't find him, it will clinch everything for us. Don't you understand. . . ?' – 'You mean – ?' – 'TAKE HIM FOR . . . A RIDE.' – 'Oh . . . !' 'Take him for a ride' became as celebrated a part of popular speech as 'Make him an offer he can't refuse' did in more recent times. On such slight novelties an inordinate amount of fame can rest: it was the case here. Public response was instantaneous and unwaning. '(The film) drew unusual crowds to the Strand on Monday afternoon. At the end of every show the audience broke into spontaneous applause.'[14] This 'love at first sound' affair between the public and the early talkies was a great shock to many professional film-makers who knew, better than the public did, just how crude and retrograde the new device was rendering their established art. *The Lights of New York* was a set-back in virtually every department, except the one that had not existed when similar genre subjects, like von Sternberg's *Underworld*, had been shot the year before. To most film-makers, it was heartbreaking to watch, and even worse to listen to – though not to all.

One exception was Edmund Goulding, the British stage actor who had gone to Hollywood, turned screenwriter and, in the same year as *The Lights of New York*, directed Garbo and Gilbert in *Love*. He had been selected by Paramount to make a sound test for *Burlesque* which that company planned as its first talkie: and the fruits of his study were exposed in an enthusiastic full-page by-lined article in *Variety* which reveals a Wordsworthian vision of sound doing everything from fostering democracy to promoting better race relations. 'This theater of the future will completely picture human life.' It was quite obviously difficult even for someone as eminent as Goulding to separate the new techniques of the screen from the old ones of the stage. 'The producer will select a story,' he wrote.

The sound picture scenarist will adapt it. When the director is

[14] *Exhibitors Herald and Moving Picture World*, 14 July 1928.

assigned, he will engage a cast and rehearsals will begin. At the end of a week or more, the producer accompanied by his engineers and studio technicians will witness a rehearsal in a specially designed small theater. He will hear the dialogue, watch the action in much the same way as a stage producer now watches his final rehearsals. He will see the picture before it gets to the plant (studio). He will criticise, change, and express himself generally, to return again to another rehearsal when his directions have been carried out. Meantime, the engineers and technicians of the studio will work from a prompt copy of the script made during rehearsals by the scenario writer from the director's mechanical design and prepare sets with metronomes set in positions indicated, etc. Thus when the producer, satisfied with his dress rehearsal, sends his director and company to the plant to manufacture a commodity known as a motion picture, he can be reasonably certain that nothing but a technical accident can delay the expensive schedule of the actual making.[15]

This was a blueprint for perfection all right! Albeit a mechanical perfection. But elsewhere in his article, Goulding's attempt to come to grips with the new medium suggests, in a more sympathetic manner than the hard-nosed pronouncements of businessmen like Zukor and Schenck, all the confused excitement, the muddled aspirations of the actual film-makers.

The camera will move forward and back according to mood. It will move in a spirit of enquiry. Only when it wants to hear what is said will it move up for its sound close-up. The drama will proceed accompanied by all the vague, unconscious sounds of life, from the song of the bird to the wash of the waves and the sigh of the wind. Nature's obligation to her own drama. The roaring mob in the street will be heard and not cut to. The distant choir in the church will chant the entrance of the star. Pantomime will be carried to its ultimate, as it is now (or should be) in the silent picture, and only when dialogue is indispensable to the story's progress will it be heard. This will not complicate; it will simplify. Short sentences will characterise the new dialogue. The new director will be more de Maupassant than Dickens – terse, tense, succinct. . . . Only when talking motion-picture projection has been developed to a perfection not yet attained will the quality and tone of the voice, its graded richness and tonal picturesqueness, be of interest to the public. The girl who, in a close-up, can sing a soft lullaby to her baby and whisper – 'Good night, my darling' – in such a way that the camera might be listening to her through a key-hole – she will be the new star.

Well this was the ideal, in some minds at the time. But most minds in

[15] *Variety*, 13 June 1928.

the film industry were preoccupied with intimations of doom rather than intonations of harmony. What the new stars might achieve was of less immediate importance than what some of the old stars felt they were going to lose.

6

'Eet is all foolishness! Eet is a fad!'

.

It was in the summer months of 1928 that the stars began voicing their opinions about the increasingly dreaded device that was shortly going to force them to voice their lines. Once they saw the fabric of their working life being literally torn down to make room for the new and hostile sound stages, they could not ignore developments any longer. The sheer physical upheaval helped induce the psychological shock. For most studios sound did not mean adaptation but wholesale replacement. Glass and plywood came down and the California sunshine that had been one of the lures for the early pioneers was shut out by thick walls of brick and concrete. All wood used had to be kiln-dried, to get rid of resin which generated electric static. Doors were of intimidating thickness and rubber-sealed. In the very early days the main stages on some lots were surrounded by a twenty-foot moat to eliminate surface vibrations. When there was no time to bury sound cables, they were left exposed, visible threats of a cure for declining audiences that many felt to be worse than the disease.

By midsummer, too, the stars had something else to unsettle them: the taunting of the fan magazines. Their coverage of Hollywood up to then largely meant silent films, for they served movie-goers who were still largely a nation of sub-title readers. One can trace the accelerating rate at which cinemas were being wired for sound by the increased space these magazines start giving to 'the celluloud screen'. Apart from Welford Beaton's *Film Spectator*, a magazine edited from Hollywood by an industry 'insider', their coverage of the talkies at this time was scant, unprophetic and eerily uninvolved, almost as if they were in collusion with the movie magnates (apart from Fox and the Warners) to regard the phenomenon as a novelty soon doomed to vanish. *Photoplay*, the premier periodical, still reflected a slavishly fan view of Hollywood typified by such articles as 'The Married Life of Doug and Mary' or 'Why Can't They Stay Married?' or 'Intimate Visits to the Homes of Film Magnates'. Not till the issue of August 1928 (which was, in fact, sent to press in June, since *Photoplay* had a three-month deadline) did its magisterial editor, James R. Quirk, grudgingly mention 'the so-called talking pictures' and admit that 'though sceptical of them for a time, *Photoplay* believes they will change the map of the entire motion picture within two years'. By September he had initiated a special 'Sound Pictures' review section; and no doubt his prophetic powers were strengthened by the rash of talkie-inspired advertising that began appearing of which 'You Too Can Be a Talking Picture Star' (by cutting a disc) was typical. *Motion Picture Classic*, a slightly weightier publication, was just as tardy about recognising sound, though in June 1928, its publisher, George Kent Shuler, printed an editorial suspiciously like the one already quoted from the *New York World* in which he shrewdly remarked that, 'once the intimacy of the voice is known by the fan, then a new and different slant is taken of the star'. Shuler's stable-mate publication, *Motion Picture* ('The Screen Magazine of Authority'), waited till October 1928 before pitching into the talkies and their likely effects on those objects of curiosity and envy, the stars.

It was the perfect situation for the love-hate relationship between fans and their idols; and in the next few months the magazines brought little for the latter's comfort. The *schadenfreude* conveyed in con-descending editorials or gloating features revealed the magazines' jubilation at the new vulnerability of the pampered and privileged few. Cedric Belfrage, an English-born critic, a radical and a Hollywood correspondent (all attributes that put an edge on his sarcasm) sped one of the earliest and sharpest knives into the palpitating heart of the movie colony.

> A small group of kind-hearted Hollywood souls, deeply touched by the facial and bodily contortions into which the stars have had to go, owing to their inability to speak at personal appearances on the stage, has for some time been trying to raise interest in a fund to bring the light of language to the studio fraternity. Nothing, however, could apparently be done to give them the benefits of conversation with their fellow men. They preferred to go on as they had always done, talking among themselves in their strange native sound-language. And now the wheel of circumstance has taken the matter out of their hands. The talking picture has arrived.[1]

That was also the tone of a hundred other snide jeremiads, overtly delighted that obligation of talking was going to expose to public view (and hearing) the reality of the uncouth, uncultured or merely tongue-tied stars which the silent-screen had so generously concealed. The

[1] *Motion Picture*, October 1928.

impression given was that practically anyone in Hollywood who knew that 'woid' was pronounced 'word' was sitting on velvet.

Stars now bombarded by the latent sadism of the very magazines that had sucked up to them for interviewing and access privileges felt even more helpless because reliable information about the talkies was as thin on the ground as actors who had actually had experience of them. Public reaction to the stars' 'Big Broadcast' a few months earlier had been inconclusive at best, at worst hostile. Up to now, no film star of the first magnitude had 'taiked' in a feature. Jolson, despite his ad-libs, was a singing star; Barrymore's stage experience had been an insurance policy not available to many other Hollywood names. Yes, Conrad Nagel had proved he did not have 'mike nerves'. When talkies were now being cast, the automatic command was 'Get Nagel – he can talk'. MGM increased his salary to 2,500 dollars a week in August as a result of his success – and lent him out to other studios for 30,000 dollars – which effectively put him into the rank of the 5,000-dollar-a-week star. Sound had thus done him a world of good by refreshing his wilting career: but what damage might it not do to a flourishing one?

Actors who knew they had poor voices trembled at the prospect. Even those with stage experience were often shocked to hear their voices for the first time on home Dictaphones. Until the major studios had their sound facilities working there were few possibilities in Hollywood of doing fully-fledged voice tests. Conrad Nagel, however, was already assisting Warner Brothers by passing judgement on their contract artists as they 'auditioned' – a new word in the film colony – for the Vitaphone talkies. Superstars like Fairbanks, Pickford, Swanson and Dolores Del Rio could bide their time; many of them were their own producers. Other stars and contract artists in thrall to a studio saw their 'day of utterance' drawing nigh as the sound stages rose around them.

In some cases pride was swallowed and vaudeville agents began reporting a flood of requests from silent-picture players anxious to get stage experience before the talkie deluge descended on them. 'The big shots of the silent racket are willing to take apples to dive into vaudeville for a few weeks between pictures.' Vaudeville performers were also seen to be putting on peppier stage acts, lest talent agents were out front searching for acceptable screen voices. The stars most exposed to this cruel speculation were the highly-priced artists so recently imported from Europe. Emil Jannings was said to be taking English lessons. Pola Negri put on a bold face and declared in broken English, 'Eet is all foolishness. Eet is a fad, a curiosity. I do not think of it at all. Bah!' Greta Garbo had gone home to Sweden for a visit: not coincidentally, some said. Others felt *they* might have to go home for good. Vilma Banky, Nils Asther, Lya de Putti, Lupe Velez and Olga Baclanova, to name just a few, were hardly soothed when Conrad Nagel appeared at an AMPAS actors' seminar bearing all the smug marks of a man who had passed the exam and now proposed to teach the class. 'It's nonsense to claim that talking pictures will drive any star from the screen,' he assured his peers. 'The movie camera can make people with casts in their eyes and crooked noses look well. Why shouldn't the sound recorder be able to do as much for voices?'[2]

Beverly Hills preferred to put its money where it hoped its mouth might be trained – into one or other of the seven colleges of voice culture which had sprung up there by July 1928, and were fuelling the gathering panic by high-pressure advertising. They increased to several dozen within months. Elocution teachers who had been making a lean living since 'The Curfew Shall Not Ring Tonight' went out of fashion now fell over themselves to pack a bag and get out to Hollywood. The two most eminent 'voice teachers to the stars' at this time were the wife of director Paul Sloane and Felix Hughes, brother of director Rupert Hughes. Mrs Sloane had quickly gone into partnership with the same André de Segurola whose singing of the 'Marseillaise' in *Glorious Betsy* had made such a deep impression on everyone. She was running what was called 'a big three-ring voice circus', with Carmel Myers and Nancy Carroll as her prize pupils. Mr Hughes, a singing instructor, promised to put what he called 'resonance' in place of twangy Hollywood nasals and *his* prize pupil was one Virginia Bradford, 'the most beautiful natural voice in Hollywood'. It was scarcely balm to the tortured nerves of established stars to know that the future belonged to the likes of Virginia Bradford! A lot of hope was, not surprisingly, being pinned on the belief that voice dubbing would soon be perfected. As mentioned earlier, it had been done with Warner Oland in *The Jazz Singer*. But then Oland had worn a considerable amount of facial hair, which helped the illusion. Did voice dubbing mean resigning oneself to an endless series of bearded roles?

In any case, could a foreign language be successfully dubbed on to English-speaking lips? A reader's letter in *Film Spectator* in May 1928 was already asking, 'How is our poor Abyssinian to enjoy Tom Mix?' And then there was the ethical aspect of dubbing. . . . Informed opinion believed that if the stars were forced to use other people's voices on the screen, then dialogue they had never uttered in the first place could prove censorable and the reputation of the guiltless star be injured. Censorship was already taking more and more interest in dialogue. The Pennsylvania board had actually held up a Vitaphone short, objecting to some of Winnie Lightner's songs – namely 'We Love It', 'God Help a Sailor on a Night Like This', 'That Brand New Model of Mine', and 'You Got a Lot to Learn'. Warners asked the censors to merely pass judgment on the visuals: the censors refused.

At the end of July 1928 New York State began censoring talkies and required film producers to send typescripts of all intended dialogue to the censorship board before production began. Will Hays was urgently despatched on a troubleshooting mission and got this *ukase* suspended – but it was a clear warning of troubles ahead. Dialogue writers con-

[2] *Motion Picture Classic*, September 1928.

sequently got nervous about writing the stuff that would have to pass into a censor's ears as well as before his eyes. Between bouts at the typewriter they were wrestling with other problems contained in a questionnaire sent out by the writers' branch of AMPAS at the end of June 1928. Among much else, it asked: 'Do sound effects add realism to the pictures? Which sound effects seem to you unnatural? Is voice reproduction desirable? If so, must dialogue be written in advance? Can it be successfully interpolated during shooting? What kind of dialogue should be encouraged – wisecracking, naturalistic, melo-dramatic? Should talkies be rehearsed like stage plays?' It was all part of the impatient furore of self-questioning that instead of bringing enlightenment generally deepened the gloom.

It is hardly surprising amidst all the confusion that Hollywood turned to an unlikely source for help in facing the task of speech – to Academia. Two campus professors addressed a well-attended AMPAS seminar under Donald Crisp's chairmanship in mid-September. They told the actors present that their vocal capacities should be determined by tests specially devised 'to eliminate the human element'. Chilling news: but worse followed. The speakers, Dean Immel of the University of Southern California and Professor McDonald of the University of Oregon, spread out wall charts which classified the stars' voices as being 'euphonic, allisophonic, eulexophonic, eurythrophonic or rhythmophonic'. The voice that recorded really well, they said, was called the 'dynaphonic'. It is not known how many requests for a dynaphonic voice entered into the prayers going up nightly from Beverly Hills; but a rather wan smile greeted the joke which inevitably followed this seminar. 'If you hear any funny noises, don't shoot – it may be Lon Chaney.' Alec Francis, emboldened by his own vocal baptism as the judge in *The Lion and the Mouse*, asked if they were not all getting a bit too academic: 'The work of acting is more than a matter of elocution.' Francis X. Bushman, recently Messala in *Ben-Hur*, told of once consulting a voice specialist when he had resolved on making a stage comeback after many years on the screen, and later inviting his tutor to take a part in the play. The result was a total failure, since the man preferred diction to drama. But Bushman proposed that the English stage actor Forbes Robertson, who had said he found out something new about the human voice every day he lived, be brought over to Hollywood to tutor the natives. (In fact a few months later no less a luminary than Mrs Patrick Campbell arrived to coach Norma Shearer, while Broadway's Constance Collier helped Colleen Moore with her diction, and Laura Hope Crews did the same for Gloria Swanson.) After listening glumly to further erudite criticism from the professors, the company applauded William C. de Mille when he remarked,

If David of the Old Testament had been obliged to figure out Newton's law of gravitation and then the laws of centrifugal force governing the stone he was about to hurl, as well as the relative density of the skull he was about to hurl it at, I wonder if he would really have hit Goliath.[3]

De Mille's reaction to the talkies had been swift as well as hard-headed. No sooner had he thrilled at the potential in *Glorious Betsy* than he rushed over to Paramount and applied to learn all he could about the new technique in the sound department under Roy Pomeroy, who had been his own assistant only a year or two earlier. De Mille now told the seminar that 'one of the things I have learnt in my apprenticeship is that no one really knows anything yet'. There was a cheer at this crumb of comfort.

But the next night at the best-attended seminar of the series, the stars were further depressed by hearing that even if they could be taught to speak acceptable English, the current state of many cinema amplifiers would play havoc with their expensively cut vowels and diphthongs. Eight out of ten theatres had defective acoustics, said Verne O. Knudson, associate professor of physics at USC and the chief adviser to MGM Studios. A sound engineer, one Fred Pelton, confirmed that many of those present would soon owe their fate to radio and telephone engineers whom the equipment-makers were even then putting through crash courses in preparation for taking over the studios' sound departments, perhaps even the direction of the pictures. And as if that wasn't bad enough news, the already badly rattled stars were informed that the present maximum of 7,000 cycles wasn't a high enough frequency to permit perfect recording of the troublesome letter 's'. Many left the seminars with sinking hearts. What *could* be done? Write dialogue that eliminated all the letters 's' – or resign oneself to a lifetime of lithping? Such were the gruesome alternatives.

Several playhouses had recently opened in the Hollywood area without creating much of a stir. But over the next few weeks the Community Players (nightly rep.), the Lucerne Club (weekly playlets), Dixie McCoy's (a talent agency casting productions with artists on its own books) and the Academy of Theater Arts (a sort of actors' workshop) all reported the same thing: a spectacular rise in admissions. The radio stations were now fawned on by feature players who had hitherto turned up their noses at the very notion of being 'a voice without a presence'. Now anything that offered a body a chance to air his voice was in demand. Dictaphones were bought by those who could afford them – the sales actually doubled over six months – and actors practised lines in the privacy of their homes, using their servants as 'feeds'. Many had plenty of time for such secret sessions, for the production pause caused by rebuilding the silent stages for sound created temporary redundancy which in turn added to insecurity and in

[3] *Variety*, 19 September 1928.

some cases insolvency. The most affluent stars decided that the best tactic was to show no fear – and live with the newcomer. Harold Lloyd became the first Beverly Hills resident to have his home cinema wired for sound; a few weeks later, in September, Gloria Swanson followed suit and even announced that in her new production, a film called *Queen Kelly*, she would appear talking. She thus became the first of the major stars to declare for sound – though this intended debut was to have consequences of catastrophic proportions.

Suddenly the uninitiated were offered hope by the appearance of a surprising new star of the talking screen. None other than George Bernard Shaw. Shaw had welcomed talkies for reasons already mentioned – and now he followed his own advice by appearing in a Movietone short (25 June 1928) which created a sensation out of all proportion to its running-time, partly due to Shaw's own tongue-in-cheek *chutzpah*. Walking 'on camera', Shaw put on a dictatorial frown that was a blatant imitation of Mussolini's overbearing brow in the newsreels, then threw off this parody of self-importance by announcing that unlike the Fascist leader he would be his 'engaging self'. He proceeded to be it, talking impishly, naturally, articulately, with 'the indubitable charm of his intonation' surprisingly unmarred by any of those treacherous 's' sounds that lay in wait for the established stars of the screen. It was 'the first time that he had ever talked directly and face to face with the American public. What a voice, what a face!'[4] Shaw was then in his seventies. But one columnist advised Sam Goldwyn, when next in London, to sign him up as a leading character actor. That he made his own sound effects did not escape notice, either: the very crunch of his feet on the gravel path in his garden drew comment for its realism, as did the English birdsong. And when Shaw ended by bidding filmgoers, 'Good-day,' and adding, 'or, depending on when you are seeing this, good-night', the immediacy of his personality had an impact on the audience second only to Al Jolson's. It quite eclipsed a rather tepid supporting Fox feature called *The Family Picnic*, billed as 'the first Movietone picture with dialogue', but actually little more than a sketch made on location. Even Movietone's success in doing dialogue out of doors escaped notice, though it was soon to be the next significant advance in the talkies.

One must remember that most of this panic reaction was based on apprehension of what sound had in store for the stars, not actual experience. That was still months away from many featured players, longer still for stars with more to lose who were therefore more hesitant. What those studios which had opted for sound were doing by the middle of 1928 was fitting up the silent films they had already completed with a synchronised score, sound effects or a few timorously voiced dialogue sequences, just enough to let them be billed as talkies. The public were soon immensely confused over the terms 'sound', 'part-talkie', 'all-

[4] *Photoplay*, September 1928.

talkie', etc., and cinemas had to show a specially made information-short to set patrons on the right sound-track. Sound effects had obvious temptations for anyone aiming to freshen up a silent movie: they could be tacked on more easily than human voices. And they cost no salary. Paramount's *Warming Up* (15 July 1928) proved the awkwardness of the result need not (yet) adversely affect business. Originally a silent movie about the trials and tribulations of a raw baseball player, starring Richard Dix and Jean Arthur and directed by Fred Newmeyer, it was given a badly fitting 'overcoat' of sound including 'wild track' dialogue – i.e. generalised talk recorded at random and not issuing from any specific lips – so that it could be advertised as a talkie without drawing a charge of misrepresentation. 'Above the roar of the crowd, you hear a high, sweet voice. What was she trying to say? Is she trying to tell that courageous figure out there that she loves him? . . . That he MUST win? Her voice cries out, and yours too. Together you cheer him on. But whatever the high, sweet thing was trying to convey, its intelligibility was almost nil. *Variety*'s reviewer, one "Con.", judged that "without the south effects which picked up the yells of the crowd in the stands, remarks of players at training camp, the picture is one of the worst duds to come out of the Hollywood factory".[5] Yet he added, 'While the sound recording didn't synchronise with the lip movements, it lifts the thing unbelievably. The excitement of the crowd is in some measure transferred to the audience.' *Warming Up* went on to generate con-siderable box-office heat. Sound, it seemed, for the moment *any* sound, was what people really wanted from the movie industry.

MGM also got off to a shaky start with *White Shadows of the South Seas* (31 July 1928), publicised as the studio's first feature synchronised for dialogue, music and effects. Directed by W. S. Van Dyke, who replaced Robert Flaherty, it dealt with the callous exploitation of a splendid pagan people by white mercenaries. Its visuals still combine epic breadth and tonal delicacy; but even on its release it was agreed that 'sound lessens rather than heightens the illusion'. Wailing noises supposedly emanating from the mourning natives seemed lugubriously detached from the source of their grief; and when Monté Blue cried 'Hello!' to attract attention, the amplification was so poor that the shout sounded like a discreet whisper. The best sequence did not rely on dialogue, but on the somewhat unfocused art of whistling which Blue taught Raquel Torres to do – 'and even here the action and sound do not match up'.[6] But neither in this case, nor in Columbia's two early sound features, *Scarlet Lady* (14 August 1928) and *Submarine* (30 August 1928) made respectively by Alan Crosland, who had been lured away from Warners, and Frank Capra, did poor quality sound diminish the commercial appeal.

Another way of filling the dialogue gap on the sound track – and one

[5] *Variety*, 27 June 1928.
[6] *Motion Picture*, December 1928.

which persisted for many years into the talkie era and is still with us to some degree – was the theme song. It was not in itself a novelty. Quite a number of silent films, even straight stage plays, had had theme songs composed to publicise them. The hope was that the cinema musicians playing the theme music and sometimes accompanied by a song plugger who went the rounds in advance of the film would predispose audiences to see it. It worked both ways. The longer life of a movie ensured more sales of the sheet music. 'Charmaine' from *What Price Glory* and 'Diane' from *Seventh Heaven*, Lew Pollack and Erno Rapee compositions, sold over a million copies of the music. The title song of Dolores Del Rio's *Ramona* was credited with helping the film to a large part of its 1,500,000 dollars gross by the end of 1928. Mediocre songs sometimes exceeded expectations when they became associated with popular pictures. Thus 'I Loved You Then As I Love You Now' topped Irving Berlin's own 'Roses of Yesterday' because it was associated with *Our Dancing Daughters*, an originally silent comedy about Jazz Age flappers which MGM put out at the end of 1928 with what one reviewer called 'several love songs, stentorian cheering and, at the end, a chorus of shrieks'. 'Jeannine, I Dream of Lilac Time' helped enormously in establishing First National's 1928 synchronised romance of the First World War, *Lilac Time*. Other theme songs of 1928, mainly from Fox's early sound releases, were 'Angela Mia' from *Red Dance*, 'Sally of My Dreams' from *Mother Knows Best*, 'Little Mother' from *Four Sons*, 'Mother Machree' from the film of the same title – obviously *The Jazz Singer*'s emphasis on mother love had a lot to answer for. So lucrative were theme songs in the early sound era that writers now got special instructions to make a detour in the story line if a scene could be fitted in that inspired a theme song. Sometimes the songs showed the strain of composition. For Cecil B. DeMille's first sound venture *Dynamite*, the song commanded, 'Dynamite, Dynamite, Blow My Sweet One Back to Me'. And for Norma Talmadge's 1927 silent movie, *Woman Disputed*, a strong, declamatory lyric was written, a line of which went, 'Although you're refuted, Woman Disputed, I love you'.

The value of theme songs made the studios eager to get into music publishing: not just to protect their source of supply, but for all the extra royalties to be squeezed out of sheet-music sales, records, rolls, sound synchronisation discs, etc. William Fox tied himself up with the authors of many of these hits, DeSylva, Brown and Henderson; MGM bought up the Robbins Music Corp.; Warners bought Witmarks Inc.; Erno Rapee, who had done cinema-orchestra scores for films such as *The Iron Horse*, took over management of the Crawford Music Co.; And Paramount started Famous Music Corp. Possession of so many allied musical outlets was one of the reasons why the Hollywood musical flourished early and over-abundantly in the sound era. As so often, the addition of one new element like music pushed frontiers forward elsewhere.

For song-writers and composers at the start of the sound era, the new frontier was Hollywood; but even while they looked West, the Hollywood studios had their own eyes fixed covetously on the East, on New York and Broadway. The scramble for people who could talk for the movies began even before it had been determined whether the film stars already under contract had satisfactory voices. To make a successful talkie, it was believed necessary to be a successful stage player; to direct a successful talkie, it was necessary to direct a successful stage play; to write a successful talkie. . . . Panic at the thought of losing the race for the acquisition of stage talent is the only acceptable explanation for the costly failure to sit down and think rationally about the talkies. The fear that if you hesitated, you were lost – this was what afflicted every front office whose executive minds jumped 3,000 miles to where the talking talent was. Hollywood discovered a new kind of caste among its own residents in those summer months, not based on star ranking but on stage experience.

Actors with speaking experience in the slimmest of minor parts are boldly recalling their stage training, and former legits who have been getting the go-by and cold-shoulder on the lot are now demanding that they be starred in the talkers. Writers are proclaiming their contributions to dialogue in the dim past and those who have no background to hang any such claims on are walking around with worried expressions. Directors are in almost the same boat. Those who graduated from the footlights to the Klieg lights are sitting on top of the world, while the others are waiting fearfully for the influx of stage directors.[7]

No sooner had the studios accepted the inevitability of talkies than they were yearning for cinema to be turned into theatre. They doubted their own powers to do so: a quick survey in July 1928 revealed that of 157 directors under contract to eight major studios, only 76 had previous stage experience; of 286 players, only 146 had 'trained' voices. The film companies were not altogether fools. Good elocution might produce more acceptable speaking voices, but they knew it would not enable their players to use words with the dramatic aptitude of those accustomed to make them carry emotions – the stage-trained players. The stars looked on elocution as their first line of defence; but the ability to project emotion through words, rather than physical gestures, was a finely shaded thing and not likely to be arrived at quickly enough. Hollywood studio chiefs figured they had to take it ready-made: the mistake was that it was ready-made for another art form, namely the stage. The delusion overrode all sensible warnings. Even film executives who perceived the false reasoning – Jesse Lasky said in May 1928, that 'the public would rather hear the voices of the players they know on the screen than actors who are unfamiliar' – were powerless for the moment

[7] *Variety*, 25 July 1928.

to resist the talent raids their companies planned to make on Broadway.

Paramount under Lasky was already publicising some corporate thinking which made for great nervousness among its employees. In the near future, the thinking went, film directors would only supply advice to directors recruited from the stage on camera positioning, sound possibilities and the production's style and tempo. The silent screenwriter would be on hand, but only to advise playwrights from New York on the handicaps and potential of the dialogue. The studio had already hired Robert Milton from the New York stage to be a production executive, and John Cromwell to direct. They would help pick talent for the talkies. Before they had even finished their conversion to sound, Paramount and MGM seemed bent on turning Hollywood on its head by announcing, in July 1928, that they intended to produce talking pictures 'in regular stage-play form' – and this extended to producing them on Broadway first, then filming them. Over at Fox, W. R. Sheehan, the general manager, said his studio would proceed cautiously with stage recruits; but this was regarded as a smokescreen, since William Fox had been one of the earliest Broadway raiders, signing up Fanny Brice, Gertrude Lawrence and Beatrice Lillie. As for the stage folk, it seemed to them they could hardly lose. Hollywood had money beyond the dreams, if not the avarice, of Broadway and could buy what and who it liked.

A top weekly salary on Broadway in 1928–29 was just over 1,000 dollars: Hollywood could double that easily. George Jessel put it with brutal abruptness in an interview in June 1928: 'It's simply a business proposition with me. I want the money. It's not ideals or anything else. I can't honestly tell you that I have entered motion pictures to express a suppressed desire, or to make people happy.'[8] Budd Schulberg, looking back on those days, recalled the cruelty and contumely being heaped on the proud film folk: 'An SOS was beamed to the East, a hurrying-up call for what was then described as real writers, to distinguish them from the continuity boys, the gag men, the ideas men and the rest of the colorful if illiterate silent contingent.'[9]

One writer who responded to the call was John Howard Lawson. He was working on the rehearsal of Upton Sinclair's *Jailbirds* late in 1928 when MGM contacted him – he left at once for Hollywood. To a Marxist like Lawson, a man who was destined to be indicted as one of the original 'Hollywood Ten' in the McCarthy-ite investigation of the film colony nearly twenty years later, the studio's top executives appeared totally uninterested in the social implications of the world of sound then opening up to them. There was fear in the air that audible words were going to disrupt the safe, visual world where silence presented the chance to escape from reality through stylised emotions of dexterously manipulated intensity. He was asked to prepare a sound sequence for

[8] 'Why I alternate on Stage and Screen', by George Jessel, *Theatre Magazine*, June 1928.
[9] 'The Writer in Hollywood', by Budd Schulberg, *Harper's*, October 1959.

Flesh and the Devil. The film was already finished, but it was considered too risky to release it without some measure of sound.

> The difficulty hung like a Sword of Damocles over the first story conference in which I participated: Gilbert and Garbo were not ready to undertake the ordeal of speech. . . . Since the stars could not speak, I prepared a fantastic dream sequence for *Flesh and the Devil* with sounds and voices coming from a void. The director (Clarence Brown) glanced at the script and tossed it aside. But Thalberg read every word, slowly, then spoke with genuine surprise: 'There's an idea in it.' The scene was not used; but my future at MGM was assured.[10]

The film capital's own increasing sophistication at judging each talkie as it appeared, with decreasing intervals between each one and the next, probably played a part in precipitating the rush to find trained – i.e. stage – actors. Some films showed all too clearly how much improvement was needed. *The Perfect Crime* (6 August 1928) was an eighty-three-minute-long murder mystery from Joseph P. Kennedy's Film Booking Offices studio, which had earlier in the year been acquired by RCA. Directed by Bert Glennon, it had been shot silent, then furnished with such clumsy talking sequences that the *Times* reviewer declared it to be 'the sort of thing that would cause even Pippa to stop saying all's right with the world'. Despite Clive Brook in the star role, as a police inspector who 'solves' a crime which apparently was in his own mind all the time, its elucidation defeated nearly all those who reviewed it. 'What it is all about,' wrote the *Times*, 'can be called only an open question. A guess at the solution, however, would be that FBO had a mystery story and in an effort to keep up with the times had synchronised it. That explains the beginning, the courtroom scene, and the end. Nothing can clear up the rest.'[11] The trial sequence's glib opportunism, stuffing 'sound' in at every chance, is well conveyed by *Variety*'s account of it.

> The district attorney (questions) the accused: he responds likewise; also the widow of the murdered man; while the wife of the accused breaks out in exclamations; the judge is heard starting his summation; the foreman of the jury verbally [*sic*] pronounces a verdict; even the baby of the accused man, holding a doll, said in dialogue to her mother, 'Why doesn't papa look at my dolly?' The baby wasn't any worse than the mother, hearing her voice.[12]

Reviews of Warners' second all-talkie, *The Terror* (16 August 1928), were as mixed, but more perceptive, though just as disconcerting for the film-actors' colony. Based on an Edgar Wallace thriller and directed by Roy del Ruth, the film was described as 'the first feature without a sub-title' – even the title of the film and its credits were announced from the

[10] *Film: The Creative Process*, by John Howard Lawson (Hill and Wang, New York, 1964) p. 104.
[11] *The New York Times*, 7 August 1928.   [12] *Variety*, 8 August 1928.

Clive Brook and Irene Rich starred in *The Perfect Crime* (1928), a silent film released as a part-talkie, which probably accounted for its ludicrously confused story line. 'What it is all about', said *The New York Times*, 'can be called only an open question.'

Following her performance in *The Letter* (1929), Paramount's faith in Jeanne Eagels (a forerunner of Jean Harlow's incandescent *femme fatale*) was sufficient to rush her into a screen version of the Broadway hit *Jealousy* (1929). But her 'private' life continued to be of more consuming interest to the public than her talkie career, which in any case ended abruptly in 1929 with her death from drink and drugs.

screen by the shadow of a masked man, The Terror, a mad criminal who hunts the heroine through secret passages and gloomy rooms in the Old Dark House that was tenanted by the usual collection of transient oddballs. No question here of 'what this was all about', though technical deficiencies were picked up by the audiences who were now growing more critical of the novelty of sound. They detected the absence of footsteps where some should have been heard as players climbed an uncarpeted staircase. They complained that too often the players seemed to wait till they were in the centre of a scene before uttering their lines. One of the cast, Edward Everett Horton, who played a silly idiot (later revealed as not so silly after all), has left a heartfelt account of what it was like to make *The Terror* in early Vitaphone conditions.

> We were instructed not to talk until we found ourselves in the centre of the camera. So the scene would go around. 'You see this man?'. . . . Camera turns. . . . 'Yes'. . . . Camera turns. . . . 'You know what happened?'. . . . Camera turns. . . . 'No'. . . . Camera turns. . . . 'Killed'. . . . Camera turns. . . . 'What!'. . . . Camera turns. . . . 'Who did it?'. . . . Of course then they took it all and cut it up and put it together again. We didn't think anything could be better than that. It was the last word in progress.[13]

Despite the dragginess, Horton was singled out for praise: like the few others at this date whose voices had registered well, his career suddenly accelerated and he was in great demand by the end of the year. Others in the cast who were ranked high because of their good delivery were John Miljan and Frank Austin. Miljan, praised for his 'smooth delivery', proved along with Conrad Nagel to be the year's outstanding talkie actor and appeared in no fewer than twelve films in 1928, four all-talkies and eight with dialogue sequences. It showed how hot demand was for a proven talent. Austin scored strongly even though his role in *The Terror* was limited to a few lines. 'His intonation as he merely says, "I am the butler",' said *Variety*, 'sounds as pretentious [*sic:* portentous?] and awe-inspiring as a confession of murder in a silent subtitle.'[14]

Where reviewers castigated *The Terror* it was generally on the ground that most of the cast were dismayingly unable to project their lines with dramatic effectiveness. 'Each time (Joseph Girard, as a Scotland Yard inspector) opens his mouth to say a word,' wrote Mordaunt Hall, 'one almost dreads the consequences. His is a voice to make the guilty quake. On the other hand May McAvoy's voice is shy and shrinking, a lisping peep contrasted with the bellowing of Mr Girard.'[15] Hall in fact believed May McAvoy had had someone else doing the screaming in the film for her, as her lusty cries didn't match up with 'her own modest attempts at speech'. Poor Miss McAvoy! She even caught it hot and strong from James Agate when the film reached London. Her silent miming, he said,

[13] Rosenberg and Silverstein, op. cit., pp. 227–8.   [14] *Variety*, 8 August 1928.
[15] *The New York Times*, 17 August 1928.

he could watch for hours: 'but five minutes of that accent would drive me into the street, for the salutary precautionary reason that ten minutes of it would drive me into Bedlam'.[16]

The reaction of Agate and other British critics to the first talkies to reach London was much more acid than their American opposite numbers'. They awaited them with scepticism, unsoftened by the advance publicity and uninvolved in the American excitement of being on the spot where it was all happening – and when they arrived, they fell on them savagely. Their attitude in general was condescending, at worst xenophobic. Now that the American accent could actually be heard, the awfulness of a future filled with such nasal intonations was all too clear to them. *The Jazz Singer*, which opened in London in September 1928, was given the benefit of the doubt: after all, this was Al Jolson. But no mercy was shown *The Terror*, which opened a few weeks later. Reporting under a London dateline on 'Talkers in Britain' in *The New York Times* on 18 November 1928, John MacCormac said, 'if it is the best the all-dialogue film-makers can do, it would appear that the problem contains its own solution. That solution is *felo de se*.' The film was criticised for its Americanisms, its anachronisms, it solecisms – 'Hollywood might have remembered there are no "Captains" So-and-So at Scotland Yard.' The American accent, generously held not to be 'really irritating to English ears', was found to be considerably so when it was on the lips of *soi-disant* English detectives. 'How', MacCormac asked, 'would a New York audience like to hear a Western cowboy address another in this fashion; "I say, old chap, lend me a bob to buy some fags."?' The film's technical deficiencies – dialogue 'dull and banal' or 'laborious and facetious' – coupled with the cast's dragging delivery and petrified stances added up to a verdict that *The Terror* was 'interminable twaddle without either illusion or enchantment. . . . (It) had done the cause of talking pictures in this country (Britain) much harm.' But the same writer admitted to a vestige of hope. He had recently witnessed a Movietone talking short made in England, though processed in America, which featured Lloyd George at his country house. The Liberal statesman gave a talk on agriculture, which went down better with this critic than anything in *The Terror*.

In the light of these reviews it is easy to see why *The Terror* should have been so severely faulted. It was in the main for vocal performances which had the abstracted concentration of recitationists who feared their memories might go before the words came. It is also easy to understand why the solution was so tempting – turn to Broadway players whose minds could take time off from the words to concentrate on the emotions. The stage's allure was to prove more of a wrecker's light than a harbour's beacon, but it even affected the sceptical Welford Beaton who had praised *The Terror* for making no attempt to alter the volume of the voices between close-up and medium shots: 'The first duty of a

---

[16] James Agate, op. cit., pp. 29–30.

sound picture is to bring every voice with equal distinctness to the last seat in a theater.'[17] *Variety*'s reviewer was also ominously fulsome in his praise of talking pictures for making a commercial film out of a stage flop. 'While it is evident that the picture is surefire' – and it was, being Warners' most lucrative talkie since *The Jazz Singer* – 'it is just as obvious that the same words, the very same actions, wouldn't hold up on the Broadway stage for more than four weeks. Through the medium of talking pictures, it is here shown possible to lend greater power to the surplus dialogue and the most inauspicious action. Situations that would fail to hold a stage (audience) are full of tense, eager interest on the screen.'

Such opinions expressed so trenchantly in the industry's leading trade paper added impetus to the tendency to look to Broadway for a new generation of talkie talents. And that was only the start of it. Other forces were encouraging a far more radical break with the past – nothing less, it seemed, than the wholesale transfer of Hollywood production from the West Coast to the East.

[17] *Film Spectator*, 1 September 1928.

7

'The I-told-you-so's are smiling.'

It was dawning on the Hollywood studios by mid-summer, 1928, that as well as becoming a sort of 'Open City' for the imminent influx of talents from Broadway, they themselves might have to surrender much of their autonomy to new production centres in the East. It was only logical to make films where most of the talkie talent was, which meant Broadway and New York. The East, as already mentioned, was still in most cases the destination where reels of voice-less film were shipped, there to meet up with other reels, or discs, containing voices, music or sound effects. The East was also the financial headquarters of the movie companies; and the accounts people at last saw their chance of curbing California's profligacy by keeping an eye on it when it was just down the road. Some companies already had East Coast studios; these were now being frenziedly refurbished for sound; making up time (and profits) lost to Fox and Warners was easier when the equipment-makers as well as the talent were physically closer. Conversion of the studio lots back home in Hollywood was lagging behind the producers' impatience to get started. By the end of May 1928 close on five million dollars had been authorised for converting Hollywood studios to sound. Warners had already three sound stages, Fox and First National two each. But FBO was just getting under way, MGM did not get going till September, by which time Universal's were behind schedule and Pathé's were not complete. In contrast, Paramount's Long Island studio, on which a million dollars had been spent for sound, was expected to start its first production in July; MGM was talking of starting sound shooting at its Cosmopolitan Studios, New York; First National announced it would use the old Biograph stages; Warners, of course, had their Vitaphone studios there still.

Paradoxically, as well as denting Hollywood's self-esteem, such well-founded fears as the phrase 'producing East' implied led to to even more intense efforts in the old established film colony to accelerate the move into sound and so retain as much production there as was possible. At the beginning of June 1928 all twenty-three West Coast studios were active for the first time that year.

But even William Fox, who stuck by his policy of bringing artists West, declared he would in future be casting all major roles from New York centres of supply. His contracts with Broadway talent were particularly harmful to the stage; for the chosen artists, once cast, had to report to Hollywood weeks before actual filming began so that they could be rehearsed 'in scenes', with two directors, from the stage and screen respectively, guiding them through talk and action. This meant they were unavailable to Broadway for much longer stretches of the year than the filming occupied. Fox's 58th Street studio was averaging eighteen screen tests daily, which gives some notion of why the trade papers of screen and stage spoke of the town 'teeming and steaming with rumors . . . all stage writers, actors and directors sense a new field for their talents'. By July 1928 negotiations were well advanced for renting some legitimate Broadway theatres for the rehearsal and filming of the action there and then, without going near a conventional film studio. Such a move was not unwelcome to New York impresarios: they were used to staging 'fill-in' productions to keep their theatres open between the shows that were safer bets. Renting theatres to movie-makers filled the till without any need to fill the seats – though before long it helped decrease the number of shows Broadway presented each season. For the film people it was not always the bargain it seemed. An attempt to shoot one production, *in situ*, in September–October ran into deep trouble. The stage sets photographed flat; the actors were too 'white' against the backdrops; the theatre lights could not muster the candle-power that talkies required. Eventually the producers had to rent a stage from MGM.

The studios were now nearing an end of converting the finished silent movies into sound jobs. Paramount – having added sound to *Wings, The Patriot, The Wedding March* and, as mentioned, *Warming Up* – even took the step of pulling some silent films out of exhibition to give them the new wonder ingredient. *Abie's Irish Rose*, for instance, had been running eight weeks at its New York theatre, with receipts of over 150,000 dollars, when it was withdrawn to be part-dialogued: which meant re-takes for its stars Jean Hersholt and Nancy Carroll. Putting dialogue into Cecil B. DeMille's *The Godless Girl* after silent shooting had finished raised unexpected problems. One of the artists, Linda Basquette, had lost sixteen pounds' weight in the intervening weeks, and had originally had her hair in a 'reformatory' cut; Marie Prevost, who had been dyed blonde for the film, was now a brunette. Neither girl wished to revert to her original state for the talkie scenes. Paramount announced in July 1928, that all its 1929 features would be sound. At the beginning of

October, Warners announced they were discontinuing all silent productions, and, as if to clear the decks, decided to transfer all production of Vitaphone shorts to New York. One reason for this was that it had just about mopped up the vaudeville talent available in Los Angeles. Since that first demonstration of Vitaphone's prowess in 1926, it had produced the astonishing number of over 400 shorts. Some of them now looked as well as sounded their age: New York acts offered more polish and up-to-dateness.

Warners were now speeding their new talkie productions into general release, instead of holding them over at New York showcase theatres. More evidence of the countrywide interest in the talkies – and the rate at which cinemas were being converted to sound. The FBO company had a novel angle to the making of shorts. At its Bronx studios it was shooting sound shorts for use as 'atmospheric' prologues to full-length sound features. A footlights sketch called *Taxi 13* preceded their synchronised feature *Joy Ride* in the cinema bill; *The Scoop*, a newspaper sketch, introduced the part-talkie *Gentlemen of the Press*; and forty-two dancing girls hired from the Everglade Café tap-danced up and down the steps of a cardboard Naval Academy wearing midi-tops, to the tune of a female jazz band, in order to put audiences in the mood for *Annapolis*, an RKO-Pathé feature whose own popular fire power was provided by the theme song 'My Annapolis and You'. These playlets provided good try-out spots for minor Broadway talent; they were a godsend, too, for cinema musicians now being discharged from their jobs almost weekly, since FBO and some other companies had the happy idea of forming them into small orchestral groups to record accompanying music for the shorts.

Another sign of the times was the screen test made by the original Broadway cast of the play *Coquette*, in which Mary Pickford was considering making her talkie debut. Mary had the test run for her – back in Hollywood, of course – and pronounced the cast unsatisfactory in every instance, though she graciously made an exception for Helen Hayes, who was in the role she destined for her own graduation into speech as well as into the maturer roles than the children and young persons she had confined herself to up to then.

Paramount was the first of the majors to get its feature-length sound films under way in the East – with a version of Somerset Maugham's story, *The Letter*, starring the Broadway actress Jeanne Eagels backed up by two other stage-trained talents, Herbert Marshall and Reginald Owen. Jean de Limur, its director, was also stage-trained. Begun in October, the film finished shooting in twenty-nine days, two under schedule. At the same time, Paramount announced that it too would make no more silent films in Hollywood. Any that were needed would be made in the East and be for 'the grind market' – the smaller neighbourhood theatres that played continuous performances. In October, too, there was an unmistakable sign that Hollywood had come to Town – none other than Louis B. Mayer, czar of MGM studios, showed up for talkie auditions at the Astor Theater.

Shooting in New York had its sound problems. Back home in Hollywood, Warners could pay policemen to stand at the intersection of Sunset Boulevard and Bronson Avenue and divert the traffic that would otherwise have rumbled past their sound stages on Bronson. You could not organise New York in the same way. FBO had to cope with the New York Central viaduct at the rear of their studios; production at MGM was frequently halted as a tugboat went up the East River sounding its horn; nearly everyone was troubled by trains thundering by on the 'El'. But at least aircraft did not fly as low as they did in skyscraper-less Hollywood, where the advantages of shooting in the silent reaches of the night were now being seized, with searchlights to warn off noisy and nosy planes. (Barrage balloons replaced the lights in the daytime.)

Other changes were swiftly, painfully, making themselves felt in Hollywood. The huge extra cost of making talkies was now being savagely brought home to the front offices. Costs were already up fifteen per cent since the summer of 1927; eighteen million dollars had been added to the budget allocation for 1928, twelve million dollars of which would be absorbed by studio costs. Economies had become the order of the day. Paramount issued a *ukase* in September 1928 limiting the number of takes a director could order to be printed to two only. A studio spokesman referred to one genius who had deemed twenty-two takes necessary for a scene he was shooting, and ordered thirteen of them printed: such extravagance in the name of 'protecting oneself' was not possible anymore. Needless to say, this confirmed the view of those who had said the talkies would impose much more pre-shooting discipline on directors. 'The I-told-you-so's are smiling,' said one trade paper. But one forecast proved badly off-target. Instead of becoming redundant, the supervisors (producers) used sound to give them new leverage. The story was told of one director of a synchronised movie wanting to substitute a new lyric for the approved one. He had to telephone the supervisor at home and have the player sing the new song over the line. It wasn't good for morale. But then little was.

The sale of raw negative stock soared: it was double that for 1927 and in the three months of December 1927 to February 1928, three times as much raw stock had been sold as in the previous six months. One reason was that films which had previously been shot silent with two cameras were now needing six of these expensive instruments for the talkies. Three of them formed a single unit, for medium, long and close-up shots. Since editing and post-synch-ing had not reached easy feasibility (the lap dissolve, for instance, was not printable till the end of 1928), it was essential to do as much as possible 'in the camera' while shooting was going on. When an export version of a sound movie was desired (for English-speaking territories, naturally), then three more cameras had to be employed, all synchronised at the start of a take. Previously a small item in the budget, raw stock now loomed horrifyingly large: one manufacturer who had previously used a single freight car to bring the stuff to Hollywood, now found two cars *and a boat* were necessary! Freight costs rose, too. New kinds of film stock had to be devised, for sound reduced the demand for raw stock with soft characteristics: the new kind was sold at six-and-a-half cents a foot instead of four. The sale of negative stock for January 1929 was nevertheless fifty per cent above that of the last six months of 1928. Companies using optical sound-track soon discovered that the film could not be waxed, as it had been in silent days, to lessen the wear and tear of the projector. This shortened its life, adding to the cost of making more prints.

Cameramen were now following the militant lead set by sound projectionists. They had previously been classified as 'mechanics'. Now they, too, wanted new status, more pay. The first cameraman no longer simply cranked: he supervised the lighting of the sets, inspected the marks set for players to 'hit' so that their voices would record properly. And he conducted the delicate give-and-take between the photographers and the sound recordists. New pay scales were demanded as a result of the craft's new responsibilities. Even new departments had to be added to some studios, despite the economy order. Fox installed a publicity department in September 1928 specially to promote sound pictures. Looking elsewhere for economies, they eliminated the curious job of the 'gag man' who had followed a film through from inception to shooting, suggesting where comedy touches could be supplied and providing them. It was now said a good director should be able to do this for himself; the gag men riposted that half the humour in comedies was inserted after shooting had begun, and now the director had so much to supervise he was unlikely to be in the mood for jokes. It was calculated that making gag men redundant would save 12,000 dollars a picture. Peanuts, perhaps, but easily sacrificed – though at the expense of further cutting down the old, easy-going improvisation that had added so much to some silent movies. On the other hand, some studios were actually hiring professional gag men to help in timing the audience's reactions to audible comedy. MGM had established a trend by opening a 'sound library' for use in its films. In it were discs containing such items as a wailing baby, wind whistling through the struts of an aeroplane, a sleeping man's snores, and a complete football game recorded at the Los Angeles Coliseum. Evidence of how keenly 'noise effects' were prized at this time is provided by the advertisement for FBO's *Gang War* – 'Gun Fire! Police Sirens! Gangster Jargon! Machine Guns in Action! Bedlam! Bomb Explosions! And Smashing Talk Sequences Culminating in the Reverberations of . . . GANG WAR!' Inflation had also struck the prices being demanded for film rights of current stage hits: the rights for successful plays of recent vintage could not now be obtained for less than 50,000 dollars. One cost cut close to the bone: just to see and hear the daily rushes was costing studios up to 12,000 dollars to wire their own projection rooms for sound!

The attempted economies generally had small effect: they were, after all, small economies, often falling on those least able to protect themselves. The axe was swung at the 'mood musicians' who had kept the players happy in the silent days. Their average weekly wage was 90 dollars. If music were needed now, an RCA phonograph and amplifier cost only 985 dollars and records, renewed weekly, did not bite into more than 40 dollars. MGM estimated that set musicians in 1927 had cost them 52,000 dollars: in 1928, the estimate was a mere 1,500 dollars. Some companies took their economy drive to the extent of eliminating the word 'REGARDS' at the end of telegrams! It was reckoned that as over forty cables were sent out daily from fifteen of the largest studios, the loss of this one word would save 5,000 dollars annually. Outside the studios, economies were as painful but more personal. The shops along Hollywood Boulevard reported in November 1928 that it had been a bad year for them. They had had to give more credit than ever before to actors and others hard hit by the switch to talkies and the subsequent disruption in their work prospects.

Actors generally were in a mutinous mood as the increasing tempo of shooting sound movies forced longer and longer working hours on them. The general practice of film companies in mid-1928 was still to shoot the majority of the film's scenes silent, then recall the cast for the parts that were thought to need dialogue. This frequently meant an indefinite wait between wrapping it up and being recalled. Even worse, pay only began with the actual shooting – and learning the lines and rehearsing them might now take longer than the time spent on the set. Actors took to defiantly filing away the script as soon as they had secured the role and not looking at it again till they reached the studio: they then did their memorising in their employers' time. Not till September 1928 was agreement made with AMPAS giving actors pay for talkie rehearsals and permitting them to seek fresh roles while waiting to be recalled to complete the old ones. Even then, the agreement was not too well honoured. Actors were in no position to complain too loudly. In the interests of economy, characters were being cut out of scripts, even the number of sets used in the average feature had been reduced from twenty or twenty-two to seven or eight. Actors now had to agree not to wear jewellery on the set, lest it jangle, and have their hair oiled, so as to reduce the risk of crackling static. There were few protests.

By November 1928 production was again at a low ebb. The reason this time was studios holding back starting-dates until their films could be *all*-talking. In the twenty-three major studios, only forty-one films were shooting, about half the average number at the same time in 1927. Perhaps the production pause was welcomed by the moguls: their appetites were busy elsewhere. They were trying to swallow each other. A powerful monopolistic thrust was operating during these months, almost the Hollywood old guard's last attempt to take over each other's business. The vast scale of investment in sound had terrified them: now that they had made the leap, the correspondingly vast opportunity of enrichment excited them. The aim was nakedly simple: whoever controlled sound production, and particularly the outlets for the talkies in the cinemas, would control the industry. Mention has already been made of RCA's astute move in early 1928 to form RKO by acquiring a theatre chain and a film studio. This move into production and exhibition by one of the principal manufacturers of talkie equipment severely shocked the old studio hierarchy. An article headed 'Is It a Battle or a Love Feast?' written in October 1928 by David Sarnoff, President of RCA Photophone, provided little mollification. In it he said it was impossible to separate the film studio from the sound laboratory. His company wished to serve both: an avowal that was snidely interpreted as meaning 'serve itself'. Especially sinister was the claim he made that RCA's sound system was interchangeable with all others. 'Just let anyone try,' Western Electric lawyers warned. Thus to give themselves added protection, the other companies tried to swallow each other. Paramount and Fox went after Warners, the wonder company, with Zukor opening the bidding at ten million dollars and Fox riposting with twelve million dollars. Zukor took it up to fifteen million dollars before Harry Warner, who was no doubt pleased to have his rivals' valuation on a company that had posted a loss less than two years previously, decided it was time to cool things – and asked twenty million dollars. Early in September 1928 Warners were under attack again – by their ex-partner, Western Electric, perhaps lured by repossessing part of the old Vitaphone contract which, despite the official separation in May, had left Warners with a perpetual royalty on all cinema licences already issued by the A.T. & T. subsidiary whose desire to get into entertainment paralleled RCA's.

It is hardly surprising if Warners considered that the best means of self-protection was to take the offensive. By late September 1928 they closed a deal to take over First National which had been weakened by the loss of one of its largest theatre chains to Paramount. Jack Warner immediately began a severe economy drive, for First National was an extravagant outfit. He threw a hundred people off the payroll in the first week and warned that First National production budgets must be no bigger than Warners' – at present they were seventy per cent more expensive, though this is more indicative of Warners' rock-bottom costs. First National's 'specials' went up to 300,000 dollars a picture; for the ordinary feature, or 'programmer', the cost was 135,000 to 175,000 dollars. The average Warner movie cost 100,000 dollars – and Jack underlined that good grosses were being obtained for budgets of 50,000 dollars.

Of all the producers who were feeling the pinch, the ones having to pull in their belts tightest were the independents, those without studios or sizeable corporate backing. Just prior to the arrival of sound, these men had been doing well. They had improved the quality of their silent films to the point where they were actually getting prime time on circuits controlled by the majors – particularly as the latter were holding back on their summer releases pending sound synchronisation. But their plight was severe. With sound a 'must' for screen time, they could not afford to make talkies! To rent Vitaphone or Movietone equipment meant a down payment of about 100,000 dollars, expensive weekly maintenance charges, and a royalty on each reel (or part thereof) on which there was dialogue. It might have meant as much as 500 dollars a reel. Few 'indies' had this kind of money. Even if they hired cheaper devices, and by July 1928 some sixty-one were registered at the Washington patent offices, fewer cinemas were wired for these. Even the new Photophone device, backed by such reliable giants as RCA-General Electric, failed abysmally at its try-out at the Rivoli Theater, Broadway, where *King of Kings* was being re-presented as a Photophoned epic on 8 July 1928. The optical sound-track proved too wide for the gate of a projector which had been showing films made on the Western Electric-Movietone system. Even when the latter company gave its consent to the gate being widened, the results were tonally as well as spiritually dismaying, with the baying of the Calvary mob sounding fifty per cent below par. The film had to be hastily reprinted.

Meanwhile, how were the public reacting to more and more talkies, now that they had ceased to be a big-city novelty and were displacing the silent-era picture show in town after town? If public opinion polls and readers' letters to film magazines are reliable, initial curiosity was turning into growing irritation with what even the uncritical fans could see as deficiencies that detracted from the pleasure they received from 'going to the pictures'.

The addition of dialogue did not simply add a dimension to the experience: it replaced an attitude towards it. It shattered the emotional communion between the silent movie and its audience: it was rather like what had been happening on the film sets. Silent movies had enabled the casual customer to drop in, and within a minute or two be locked into the story and characters. Mime-acting made the characters' predicaments easily intelligible; sub-titles gave people emotional cues to follow rather than narrative points to recall. But dialogue altered all this: it demanded attention, it enforced silence on the audiences who had hitherto been able to swap comments on the movie below the music of pianist or pit orchestra. Now one had to shut up, sit up and pay attention to a plot that more and more was conveyed in words, not pictures. The initial wonderment at such verisimilitude as the creak of a cart wheel, a pistol's explosion, the laboured departure of a train, was overtaken by the self-consciousness engendered by dialogue.

Exhibitors began reporting around September 1928 that customers were now 'shopping for sound'. As none of the famous stars had yet been heard talking on the screen, public interest was more than usually concentrated on the film's basic sound properties. Earliest to fall out of favour were the silent films that had had synchronised music added to them. The periodicals began reporting disaffection with them early in the fall of 1928. 'Once the novelty (of synchronisation) had worn off', one house manager reported from the Coast, '(they) will be a drawback and a box-office deterrent, rather than a help.'[1] The rest of this report is worth quoting at length, for it is a cogent statement of wider dissatisfaction among the public.

> This House (in Los Angeles) is now showing its second synchronised film, the announced finale of a famous romantic screen team.[2] Picture is doing business, but the manager says it's the popularity of the team that's the draw, not the sound idea. He reports overhearing many customers express annoyance and distraction because of the canned music and a desire for the human orchestra, of which this house carried a particularly good one, plus resolutions to avoid future synchronised films, with the recurrent expression, 'If that's what sound pictures are like, we don't want any more.' . . . This house has found it necessary, from the start, to cut in on 'canned' music with its own orchestra for short periods, just to relieve the ears of the audiences. It has found that audiences become restless under the monotone of canned music. A typical demonstration of the reaction came on the first day of the showing of the second synchronised film, when the orchestration went sour four times during a single showing. Each time it was only for a second or two, but as the music suddenly slowed and flatted, the audience laughed. Talkers are something else again. Since being wired, this house has had two talking shorts, and each scored. The manager states the difference is striking praise being given the conversational films, while the canned music annoys.

What one detects as 1928 neared its end is certainly nothing like a backlash against the sound film, but a sluggishly running resentment at the usurper beginning to manifest itself, a grumbling dislike at the way it was now seen to be altering an entertainment pattern that had been set in silence for two generations of filmgoers. Small-town opinions expressed this most bluntly. Warner Brothers surprised by some relatively poor returns on sound movies at the Madison Theater, Mansfield, Ohio – and perhaps spurred on by the anxiety of the cinema manager who had invested so heavily in wiring the place – conducted a rough poll by postal enquiry to 500 patrons. Only 73 replied, but ten per cent showed 'violent antagonism' to sound or dialogue and demanded a return to 'unsullied silence'. Like many smallish towns at that time, musical turns were preferred to talking shorts or features; the Vitaphone artists, particularly opera singers, were better liked than the local live vaudeville

[1] *Variety*, 5 September 1928.
[2] Possibly Goldwyn's team of Ronald Colman and Vilma Banky.

shows. But as for dialogue . . . that simply destroyed their illusions. Even in the large cities, the vote was by no means a walkover for talkies. The *Los Angeles Herald* sent out a questionnaire in December 1928. The result favoured talkies, but only by 141 votes to 104. Only 38 respondents wanted to see silent movies ended while 215 wanted them to continue. Against the 57 who liked synchronisation, 197 preferred orchestras; 153 were against part-talkies while only 98 were in favour. Asked if they wanted more talkies, 165 said 'Yes', but 77 thought they were a fad and believed they would pass. Would sound kill the theatre? the poll asked. Some 31 held that it could, but 223 thought the legitimate stage would survive 'the image conversation'.

A frequent cause of complaint was about patrons arriving in the middle of a talkie. Some producers even considered interrupting the action on the screen with 'natural breaks' for latecomers. The absurdity of this was soon evident; but Harold B. Franklin said in his 1929 manual of instructions for theatre-owners that the dialogue picture would enforce prompter public attendance from the start of a picture since 'if the talking motion-picture follows the construction in play-writing, the earlier part of the action . . . will establish the premise for the action that is to come.' He advised making special trailers enforcing silence on patrons before the show began. Warners had already spent 300,000 dollars on each of two publicity campaigns for Vitaphone and in the latter part of 1928 were embarking on a million-dollar campaign to inform and educate people about their talkies. Sound was now flooding in so fast that public reaction was understandably confused. Deceptive cinema advertising began to take up a lot of space in the complaints columns. Some Better Business Bureaux even inserted warning advertisements – 'Sound Doesn't Always Mean Talk'. Soon bizarre percentages began appearing in film billings, indicating the proportion of the running-time taken up by dialogue. It was possible to take one's pick from '63 per cent' or '48 per cent' or even as low as '17 per cent' talking. To the deaf, of course, any percentage of talking was an unmitigated curse.

But movie-goers were experiencing another kind of loss than simply that of silence: the loss of wonder. Characters on the silent screen had no vocal identities: they were assumed to be leading the emotional life that audiences, of greater or lesser sophistication, chose to project on to their mimed feelings. But with the talkies, they were having to declare themselves in speech, define their relationships much more precisely to each other – and, by extension, to the spectator. Being a filmgoer at the talkies offered far less choice in the matter of the emotions. Being a film actor meant losing a measure of kinetic appeal, and some of the near-divinity of the silent image through the homely speech that now formed, in more or less synchronised form, on the characters' lips – but in compensation, players gained a less ambiguous way of impressing their deeds, thoughts and identities on the audience.

Above, Lilac Time (1928) had sychronised music and effects for its First World War story and its theme song, 'Jeannine, I Dream of Lilac Time', became one of the sound era's first hits. Gary Cooper played the aviator who met Colleen More, as Jeannine, by crashing his plane to avoid striking her. *Below,* Boy *talks* to girl . . . Glenn Tryon and Barbara Kent in *Lonesome* (1928), a Coney Island romance in which the ordinary couple who seemed so appealing in their silent state of affection suddenly suffered a descent into ordinariness indeed when they had the banal dialogue on their lips.

The most incisive example of this new psychological adjustment occurs very early in the day, in Paul Fejos's part-talkie, *Lonesome* (2 October 1928). How *Lonesome* found its voice in the first place is an amusing sidelight on the companies' desperate competition to 'go sound'. Universal's sound stages were not going to be ready until October, so the studio borrowed one of the mobile sound trucks which Fox used to shoot Movietone newsreels. The ostensible purpose was to shoot sound tests for Universal's version of the musical *Show Boat*. But inside a frenziedly short time, said to be no more than two weeks by some, and by others to be a mere nine days, the studio deployed their rival's equipment to shoot an eighty-eight-minute feature, *Melody of Love*, starring Walter Pidgeon, Mildred Harris and Tommy Duggan. They used a closed set, brought in the Los Angeles Police Choir, and even cut into the film specially purchased footage from First National's 1927 movie *The Patent Leather Kid*. Ablaze with their success, Universal then whipped sound sequences into three already completed silent movies: *Last Warning*, *It Can Be Done* and *Lonesome*. They were well on their way to 'dialog-ing' a fourth when an angry Fox, getting wind of what was happening, repossessed their sound truck.

Lonesome is about two young people, a factory worker and a switchboard girl, neighbours in the same tenement although they don't know it, who meet by chance and fall in love at first sight, all set against a meticulously realistic background of Coney Island amusement parks and crowded summmer beaches. Up to the moment dialogue breaks out between them, the intelligence and sympathy with which Fejos has presented two 'little people' finding happiness in 'the crowd' has persuaded one to attribute a like degree of intelligence and maturity to them. Suddenly the pair start to speak. And in one distressing instant their sentimentally banal natures become appallingly apparent. 'All my life I wanted a little white house in the country with blue shingles,' says he. 'Pink,' says she. 'Blue,' he insists, 'the colour of your eyes.' The voices are fairly good, Mordaunt Hall wrote, but he added with damaging truth, 'the lines are something like those in a very ordinary musical comedy'.

Sound thus began to sharpen the audiences' social consciousness. Questions were tentatively formulated in these early months about aspects of society that had hitherto passed unnoticed, or, rather, unheard. And the increasing sophistication of the movies, and their audiences, would make it more pertinent than ever to face up to social reality – or elude it. We know from hindsight that the film industry, by and large, chose to elude it – stylising life as the screen reflected it into a set of agreed movie conventions that facilitated profit-making and could be policed by self-censorship. I shall return to this aspect in the final chapter.

But by September–October 1928, film critics as well as audiences were being made more critical of the talkies. Critics were the most articulate group when it came to lamenting the passing of silence; it was already a fashionable pose among the intelligentsia. Welford Beaton, too, was having second thoughts as he heard the trickle of sound increasing to torrential proportions. 'When talking pictures begin to achieve their possibilities as works of art, they will have an air of more repose and quiet than the present silent ones possess. . . . Hollywood will learn that blatantly vulgar and loud pictures will not gross as much as those which possess the quality of artistic repression.'[3] He added with considerable perceptiveness, considering the time he was writing, 'The problem of sound is the judicious use of silence.' What prompted Beaton's strictures was Warners' part-talkie *State Street Sadie* (2 September, 1928), yet another underworld melodrama with Conrad Nagel, Myrna Loy and William Russell as the gangland czar; it was directed by Archie Mayo. Herbert Cruikshank, who reviewed movies in *Motion Picture*, reflected the sharp, carping note now creeping into the critical reception of many new sound movies when he said, 'Folk familiar with Vitaphone are already becoming *blasé* and bored with a production so utterly mediocre as *State Street Sadie*. Of course, any sound film is interesting in these days of the lightning-like development of the new medium. But the day is almost here when there will have to be *pictures* as well as sound to provide the entertainment.'[4] Mordaunt Hall also showed impatience with 'crooks that call each other names, laugh, and say quite a number of "Wa-als", which must be a favourite way for a gangster to begin his interrogation of his underlings. It is said something after the style of a police dog's welcome, who does not quite like a man approaching his master's door.'[5] He contrasted this slangy vernacular with the Edwardian stiltedness remaining in such sub-titles as Conrad Nagel's outburst, 'I, too, have lost someone I loved. The man who killed your father drove my brother to suicide.' Welford Beaton judged the film's conventional tempo in the dialogue sequences to be at least an advance on the monotonous dragginess of *The Terror* though he pointed out, with pernickety pleasure, how off-key some sound effects were – when Myrna Loy rang someone's doorbell, it sounded as if the bell were *outside* the house. *State Street Sadie* did only moderate box-office business and was one of the reasons why Warners conducted their poll among filmgoers in October. Such sharpening criticism spurred those companies just entering the sound market to get the bugs out of their particular system. Even the limited quantity of talkies generated a demand for quality.

The demand began to be satisfied again almost at once. Within weeks of dismissing *State Street Sadie*, Mordaunt Hall wrote of the latest offering, 'As a specimen of the strides made by the talking picture, it is something to create no little wonderment. . . . (It) is in many respects so remarkable that it may change the opinion of countless sceptics concerning talking photoplays.'[6] This was Paramount's first all-talkie,

---

[3] *Film Spectator*, 13 October 1928.   [4] *Motion Picture*, December 1928.
[5] *The New York Times*, 3 September 1928.   [6] Ibid., 17 November 1928.

Above, Norma Shearer and Gwen Lee confide their secrets to each other in *A Lady of Chance* (1928), an MGM silent movie released with 'an audible conversation' in one of its reels. According to contemporary reports, it was barely audible. *Below*, *State Street Sadie* (1928) starred Conrad Nagel, William Russell and Myrna Loy. It was a crook melodrama released as a part-talkie; but the quality of the dialogue was now the thing criticised. However, it set Myrna Loy, who didn't have to do much snarling, on the road to stardom.

Interference (16 November 1928). Lothar Mendes had already directed a silent version which Roy Pomeroy used as a blueprint for his sound version.

It was the peak of Pomeroy's achievement – and immediately preceded his fall from grace and power. His case is interesting, because it showed how a relatively minor technician at this time could use his know-how to achieve pre-eminence over many longer established artistic talents. Pomeroy had been a special effects maestro: he had devised the means of parting the Red Sea in *The Ten Commandments* and writing the celestial 'Thou-shalt-nots' in letters of flame; and largely because no one else wished to volunteer he was sent to make a recce patrol of RCA and Western Electric sound laboratories to learn all about sound. He returned armed with knowledge – and power. His forecasts at the AMPAS seminars were hearkened to with deference, even a director like William C. de Mille came humbly to imbibe his wisdom. To signal his authority he used a special four-note musical horn on the Paramount sound set which squawked out its command every bit as imperatively as Pomeroy's old master Cecil B. DeMille had barked his into the megaphone. To direct the sound sequences in *Interference*, Pomeroy demanded a rise from 250 dollars a week to 2,500 dollars – and got it. At that time he was worth it, for no one else in the studio knew how to shoot sound. But when he then proceeded to claim a rise to 3,500 dollars a week for shooting his next film, he was turned down flat and resigned in a huff. By that time, others knew the secrets. . . .

Interference was designed to be a 'class' occasion even in its presentation. The impresario Daniel Frohman appeared in a talking prologue and made a promise (not undivorced from self-interest) that thanks to the talkies 'no more will our best plays be confined to the few big cities'. This was a strong hint of the kind of film *Interference* was: very much a filmed play, a stage hit about a war veteran who kills his wife's blackmailer – she has remarried, believing herself widowed – and then surrenders to the police, knowing that his incurable heart condition, etc., etc. . . . Possibly the most distinguished cast of any talkie to that date had been assembled: Clive Brook, Evelyn Brent, William Powell, Doris Kenyon. Viewed today, *Interference* appears totally characteristic of what the onrush of talk did to the fluency of the silent screen: it clogged it up. Even in its day, the film had its detractors, significantly enough in the trade papers with a vested interest in following public disaffection with the talkies. 'Earlier in the epoch of the dialogue picture,' *Variety* said, '*Interference* would easily have been a clean-up at the box-office. Now it's dubious. . . .'[7] The critic, admitting the film possessed all the elegance and gorgeous settings that marked Paramount's silent productions, called it 'indifferent entertainment' and blamed just those defects we would seize on today, particularly dialogue as stiffly penned and delivered as, 'I have letters which, if published in the *Morning Bugle*,

[7] *Variety*, 21 November 1928

will ruin your husband's standing as a physician.' But what did appeal to contemporary critics, in the more refined magazines, was its undeniable credentials as the first talkie to be done in 'the drawing-room manner'. All the people in it were cultured, educated: they did not shout, run, fight, fire guns or bootleg hooch. What a relief it was, Mordaunt Hall felt, to hear the ringing of a telephone bell come through completely naturally – 'One even heard a pen scratching its way over the paper as Evelyn Brent wrote a message with her left hand.' The director's finesse was complimented even more warmly when a man at the other end of the telephone – the one that rang so naturally – was heard and not seen. There wasn't even a vulgar theme song. Welford Beaton made a shrewd point when he commended the film for 'retaining the status of conversation as confidential exchange. . . . Their words put over the meaning. Their voices are low-pitched. . . . All the time the film is unreeling we see the figures of the characters moving smoothly through their scenes and hear the low tones of their voices, a slight noise as a door is closed, and a faint tinkle when a phone bell rings.' (Never again perhaps in films would a telephone appear so sedative!) In short, the favourable reviews of a film that did not move talking pictures on very much in artistry, but actually helped clamp dialogue shackles firmly on to them, were due to a reaction against the crude milieux and barked out dialogue that Warners had made characteristic of the talkies.

There were some scenes, though, that advanced the creative use of sound. Hearing Evelyn Brent's disconsolate weeping when William Powell breaks with her, but *seeing* only his face in medium close-up wondering what her next move will be, is one of the earliest examples of sound being separated from the image so as to increase the drama of the visible scene. Up to then, and indeed for quite a time afterwards, audiences were presumed to need the sight of Miss Brent in order to link her with the sound of sobbing. The reaction shot was now charged with a new emotion, impossible in the silent movie. (One contemporary critic actually inferred from this innovation that it would reduce the cost of constructing sets which had not got to be seen for actors who had only got to be heard!) The effect of this scene in *Interference* was precisely anticipated by Pudovkin in *Film Technique*, a book not published in English until the next year, 1929.

I am sure, even, that it is possible to build up a dramatic incident with the recorded sound of a speech and the image of the unspeaking listener where the latter's reaction is the most urgent emotion in the scene. Would a director of any imagination handle a scene in a court of justice where a sentence of death is being passed by filming the judge pronouncing sentence in preference to recording visually the emotions of the condemned?[8]

The silent film of *Interference* was put out at the same time as the talkie

[8] *Film Technique* (Vision Press Ltd., memorial edition, London, 1958), pp. 88–9.

version. Critics who saw both found the mime of the silent film overdone and intrusive: a sign of how quickly the habitual response to the silent movie was waning. We are fortunate in possessing a first-hand account by one of Hollywood's major stars of just how strange an experience it was for him to be working on *Interference*. He is Clive Brook, speaking just before the film's release.

I found that the microphone is more difficult to face than the most hardened audience. . . . My voice sounded unfamiliar to my ears, for it seemed to pass away into nothingness as it left my lips. Every word was oddly muffled; there was no echo, no resonance. Instead of an audience to carry me along on this 'first night' appearance, two ominous, tank-like objects were focused on me. Faces peered at me from the darkness inside these caverns. I caught the reflection of camera-lenses in the plate-glass windows that form the front walls of the tanks. Cameras were grinding, but the sound of their mechanisms had been silenced. It seemed strange not even to receive the customary signal to begin the scene. . . . Now the director cannot even tell us when to start. . . . We must watch a monitor man, who waves his hand for us to begin. . . . I found myself starting off in the declamatory fashion of the stage. I was not thinking in terms of microphone sensitivity or the tremendous amplification of the apparatus. . . . Then, when I had finished, technicians turned on the record they had made. I heard a deep and strange voice come booming out of the loud-speakers. . . . It was not, I told myself, the voice of Clive Brook. It alternately faded into nothingness and then rang out in a thunderous crescendo. Pomeroy smiled at me. 'Was that my voice?' I asked. 'Yes, but you couldn't recognise it, could you? Try it again,' he said, 'and speak just as you would in a small room at home. . . .' Soon I heard the voice in the loudspeakers again. This time it was unmistakably my own. . . . Although it was not loud, somehow it seemed to fill every corner of the huge room. . . . I had learnt my first lesson in microphone recording.[9]

It was praiseworthy of *Interference*'s makers to try and elevate the audible photoplay to the prestigious eminence of the legitimate stage by registering the sounds of cultured people talking in quiet tones. But it was left to a man who was far from backward when it came to facing hardened audiences or solitary microphones to give the talkies, so to speak, their second wind: to create again that feeling of an 'event' which they were fast losing within a year of having first opened their mouth. On 19 September 1928, before a packed audience which had paid eleven dollars top for tickets of gilded pasteboard (which they were allowed to retain as a memento of the event), in his very own New York 'home', the Winter Garden Theater, Al Jolson spread out his arms, threw back his head, opened wide his mouth – and sang again.

[9] *The New York Times*, 11 November 1928.

'The dialogue pushover period can't last forever.'

'After the film had faded from the screen, Mr Jolson was called to the stage. The first words he said were, "What can I say?" To this a thousand voices shouted, "Sing!"'[1]

For once, reticence got the better of Al Jolson: he just talked. He said, not surprisingly really, that *The Singing Fool*, his new film directed by Lloyd Bacon, was a better job than *The Jazz Singer*. It certainly turned out to be more profitable. As the first year of the real talkies neared its end, Jolson was the living justification of what George K. Shuler, *Motion Picture* magazine's publisher, said of

> 'the two pictures (that) are and have been the most sensational screen successes of the last twelve months. It is reported that fans have paid already about a million and a half dollars to see (*The Jazz Singer*); and this, when it is borne in mind it could only be shown effectively in houses equipped for sound, is really astonishing. As for (*The Singing Fool*), it is just now crowding the Winter Garden in New York, the house where Jolson made his first big metropolitan success, to a capacity it has not known save on those occasions when he has appeared there in person. This is the final answer to all arguments about the practicability and the acceptability of the talkies. They have been done and they are liked.'[2]

The Singing Fool appeared most opportunely, just when the novelty of the talkies was flagging, if not actually on the turn, and another huge popular success was needed to secure public acceptance. Jolson was paid 150,000 dollars to make it, a big increase on his earlier fee, though even now he had no participation in the profits. But although it is a more 'sophisticated' effort, it is not as much a part of cinema legend, or indeed

---

[1] *The New York Times*, 20 September 1928.   [2] *Motion Picture*, December 1928.

racial schmaltz, as *The Jazz Singer*, with which it is sometimes confused.[3] Jolson plays a singing waiter whose song-writing talents make him into a vaudeville star until his wife deserts him for a racketeer, taking their son with her. His career slumps, and three-year-old 'sonny boy' dies just when his father is recovering his fame and fortune with the help of a tender-hearted, sentimentally-tipped cigarette girl. Nowhere does the film touch the transfiguring myth of the renegade Jewish son or even the blackface changeling of show-business. Stage-comeback rather than family estrangement is the theme here. Singing to the camera clearly does not suit Jolson as well as performing to a live audience, which always set his adrenalin pumping. The songs, however, which include 'Sonny Boy', 'There's a Rainbow Round My Shoulder' and 'I'm Sitting on Top of the World', became world-hits and Mordaunt Hall expressed the reactions of millions of filmgoers when he wrote, 'One waits after hearing a selection, hoping for another, and one is not in the least disappointed when he promises the night-club a thousand songs.' The singing almost eclipsed the fact that the characters talked.

It was left to *Variety* to remind us that 'Al meets two women in the picture and talks to both of them. Both talk back. . . . Josephine Dunn (as the wife) didn't talk so well, and she looked steely-hearted, even for a blonde. Betty Bronson (as the cigarette girl) talked a little better. . . . There is too much deliberation in the talking roles, excepting that by the three-and-a-half year old Davy Lee (as Sonny)'.[4]

On the strength of this film Davy Lee's fame inside America rocketed to equal that of the child wonder, Jackie Coogan, whom Chaplin had introduced in *The Kid*. The next few years found a veritable rush of children into talking pictures. But Davy Lee's success was not the only reason. More important, the strict Labor Laws which governed the appearance of children in silent films did not (then) cover their employment in talkies; and this acted as an incentive to producers and ambitious mothers alike. Jolson's own reaction to 'the little hoodlum' in his picture was predictably lachrymose.

> B-b-b-boy, I tell you it got me. I was a wreck. I was just breaking my fool heart over that kid. . . . If you cried real tears on the stage, you'd panic 'em. But I cry real ones here, and have to keep on crying 'em for re-takes till I feel like an April shower.[5]

He then gave a highly characteristic account of how the famous ballad 'Sonny Boy' came to be written.

> We were going to use another one. But I dunno. The music was great, but the words – I dunno. I couldn't feel 'em. It said, 'Who's that behind my chair?' And the kid is on my knee, so how can he be behind my chair? I told 'em about it. I said, 'Now listen,' I said, 'I've been

[3] Most recently by Arthur Marx, whose biography of Sam Goldwyn refers to Jolson singing 'Sonny Boy' to a youngster on his lap in *The Jazz Singer*!
[4] *Variety*, 26 September 1928.   [5] *Motion Picture*, 1928.

Above, Fanny Brice, the original of *Funny Girl* (with André de Segurola, the Metropolitan Opera singer), starred in the part-talkie *My Man* (1928). It was intended to make her screen reputation as a female 'Al Jolson', but merely confirmed that unless you *were* Al Jolson the small-town moviegoers might not have heard of you. *Below*, 'Climb upon my knee, sonny boy, Although you're only three, sonny boy.' Father-love replacing mother-love and assisted by little Davy Lee and a Brown, DeSylva and Henderson title song, brought Al Jolson to the peak of his screen career in his second feature *The Singing Fool* (1928).

writin' songs and singin' 'em since I was a punk kid. B-b-b-boy I know!' Last year I didn't know a thing about pictures. I just said, 'Gentlemen,' I said, 'Here I am just like a lil child, do with me as you will, 'cause this is a new racket to me.' But this time I'm speaking up some.

Quips couched in the same racy vernacular are scattered through Jolson's entertaining interview with Herbert Cruikshank and reveal the steely-willed Number One he had become since he had surveyed the profits and popularity of *The Jazz Singer*. 'This year I say, "B-b-b-boys, do I have to be nasty with you fellers and dig down for the old contract?" ' Jolson was quite clearly laying down the law now. For all his Runyon-esque jargon, his gibes about movie producers have a threatening edge to them.

Say, if they stick me in any more café or cabaret scenes, I'm going to grab a boat. I've been in more jernts than Volstead ever padlocked. . . . You know they got a piece of business about a song-writer in the picture, and they got it all wrong. No real song-writer would act that way. A song-writer is the biggest pest in the world and – but anyway I told 'em, I said, 'Say, you need a couple of titles in there to fix up that sequence.' And I gave 'em a couple of titles.

It is not surprising to find C. B. Cochran, the London impresario, saying a bare two years later when he saw Jolson in *Mammy* that 'it was Jolson without a soul'. Welford Beaton had already recorded a curter minority opinion when he saw *The Singing Fool* and berated Jolson for 'his overbearing conceit in almost every note he sings, every word he utters and every movement he makes in his acting'. None of this criticism remotely dented the box-office; and no matter what happened to Jolson's soul, Warners kept the profits. They were growing colossal. In 1928 Warners were to make a profit of 2,044,842 dollars, a remarkable turn-round for a company that had posted a deficit of 1,234,412 dollars in 1927, part of this due to the acquisition of Vitagraph Studios. Greater things were ahead: in 1929 Warners were to show a profit of 17,271,805 dollars – an increase of 845 per cent! But this is anticipating things.

Before the end of 1928 it seemed as if Warners had found a female Al Jolson. They released their part-talkie *My Man* (21 December, 1928), starring Fanny Brice, the original model for the movie *Funny Girl*. She was the *protégée* of Florenz Ziegfeld, whose Follies had made her the best-known vaudeville comedienne in America; and for the film she was asked to do little more than repeat some of her show-stopping numbers in the story of a doomed love – songs like 'I'd Rather Be Blue with You than Happy with Somebody Else', 'Floradora Baby' and, of course, 'My Man'. 'Inasmuch as she does them all characteristically well,' said

Herbert Cruikshank, 'it should interest anyone to see the picture.'[6] All very well, as far as it went, but surely cautious praise after the Jolson ovation. The reason is suggested in the next sentence, and it was one that should have been a distant warning to all those Hollywood talent scouts then appraising the Broadway shows. 'In the film with the star are players better known on the screen. . . . (Such as) . . . prominent among them being Edna Murphy and Richard Tucker.' *My Man* did well enough – but not outstandingly well. Its box-office fell off the farther it got from the towns and cities where Fanny Brice was a known and appreciated quantity. She simply was not the nation's idol, the way Jolson was; and if her fame was inferior to established screen players like Mr Tucker and Miss Murphy, then it was the first faint indication of the balance of popularity in the talkies swinging back to the established screen favourites and away from the interlopers from the stage.

Indeed this was already beginning to happen off-screen before the end of the year. First to feel disenchantment with the 'El Dorado' they had journeyed to were the playwrights and revue-sketch writers who failed to graft their Broadway talents on to Hollywood requirements. The silent scenario writers had been supposed to tutor them; but it is not surprising that the newcomers did not find the residents all that co-operative. Some of the arrivals from the East were so ill-equipped for the job that they believed talking pictures ought to provoke applause, the way smart repartee in stage plays already did. Their efforts were verbose to the point of exhaustion. Time was not on their side. The stage folk had to be put through intensive retraining courses; even then their work was tentative, experimental, frustratingly created and grudgingly judged by studio workers still assigned to the now despised silent pictures or demoted to menial tasks on the sound stage. Bolder souls kept insisting on the logic of retraining the people *already* in the movies to cope with the new art of scripting talkies; and they found an unexpected ally in Jack Warner. Perhaps he had observed the wasteful ways of Broadway-ites struggling with Vitaphone dialogue, for, in October 1928, he told the directors' section of AMPAS that stage directors and writers were 'unnecessary' in the talkies. The best results so far had come from experienced *film* directors and scenarists. Actors, though – Ah, that was a different case! Relishing the panic he could now create as production head of Hollywood's most envied outfit, Warner predicted that screen actors without stage training were for the discard. *Variety* even came up with a fearful percentage for the coming slaughter. Its front-page banner headline on 10 October 1928 declared, '33 PER CENT OF ACTORS ARE OUT'. The story said: 'The number of strictly picture actors available for principal roles will be reduced by 33 per cent when the talker revolution settles down. The clearance will be filled in by players drawn mainly from Broadway. Other necessary talker talent from legit branches will likewise be imported to this end.' The belief that

6 Ibid., March 1929.

only the stage-trained could 'talk' suitably was the last one to die: writers, on the other hand, putting their wits to the test of sound, were vulnerable to the onset of reality much earlier.

By mid-November 1928, about 75 per cent of the writers brought West by Fox for a three-month trial period in the talkie workshops were repacking their cases, paying their bar bills and preparing to catch the train back to New York on 1 December. Of the 25 per cent of the survivors, it was significant that the majority were composers and librettists. Other studios had similar experiences. Musical talents survived and flourished in the Hollywood work ethos. The migration West of songsmiths was so successful that one alleyway between the stages at MGM was nicknamed 'Forty-Fifth Street'. Such melodymakers as Gus Edwards and Buddy DeSylva held auditions there. There, too, were Billy Rose, Arthur Freed and Herb Roth. Sammy Lee, who had staged many Ziegfeld numbers, was now working in Hollywood. Universal imported the youthful Cherniavsky to weave theme songs round the titles of their productions. They thought that one of their productions, *Give and Take*, had him stumped: it was the first production on the new sound stage in November 1928. But inside a few minutes he came up with 'Give a Little Smile, Take a Little Kiss'. Broadway art was vindicated!

In the last few months of 1928 there is growing evidence of a perceptible refinement in talkie techniques. With each new advance, however slight, Hollywood confidence was returning. Lessons were being learnt, even from mistakes. Talk for talk's sake was still overvalued, but critics were now less tolerant of it. Fox's part-talkie *The Air Circus* (2 September 1928), about a high-school kid with a fear of heights training to be an aviator, had dialogue in it, but it mainly consisted of a mother giving a pep-talk to her reluctant boy. 'Interpolating a talking short in the middle of a programmer doesn't make it two dollars,' commented one reviewer acidly. Warner's third all-talkie, *The Home Towners* (23 October 1928), directed by Bryan Foy, was a literal transcription of George M. Cohan's disaster-proof farce about a small-town hick's chronic mistrust of the big-city slicker. The cast in large measure came from 'the boards'. (Singling out one Robert McWade, a rash reviewer predicted 'his success is assured right now'.) The interior scenes still revealed clumsy grouping round the concealed microphones and *Variety*'s reviewer said impatiently that 'sooner or later Warners must go outside'. This was a gibe that must have stung. For Warners' sound system still depended on the perfect control of studio acoustics for reproducing dialogue and effects on wax discs. How could one take this set-up to 'the outdoors' and shoot action with the unselective microphones then in use?

It was Fox with its optical track that now significantly advanced the limits of the sound movie, beginning with an unpromisingly titled twenty-two minute short by John Ford. *Napoleon's Barber* (24 November

1928) was based on a stage sketch, a one-joke situation-comedy about Napoleon stopping en route for Waterloo for a shave from a country barber who doesn't recognise his illustrious customer and keeps bragging about what he would do to the Emperor given the chance, all the time plying his razor close to the imperial jugular. The film incorporated flashbacks from Napoleon's thoughts: it was these that allowed Ford to take his Movietone cameras out into the countryside and shoot the action with naturalistic sound effects. He later recalled for Peter Bogdanovich how unwelcome this had been at the time to the sound technicians.

> They said it couldn't be done, and I said, 'Why the hell *can't* it be done?' They said, 'Well, you can't because – ' and they gave me a lot of Master's Degree talk, so I said, 'Well, let's try it.' We had Josephine's coach coming across a bridge and the sound men said, 'That'll never do – it's too loud.' But it was perfect – the sound of the horses and the wheels – perfect.[7]

Sound at that time was just 'a job of work' to Ford. His pragmatic approach was typical of other directors well equipped by their blunt contempt for mystique and finickiness to withstand the autocracy of the sound engineers and insist on things being done their way. To temperaments of this kind, reinforced by the self-confidence of lengthy and successful careers in silent pictures, we owe the increasingly speedy introduction, if not the actual invention, of new methods of shooting with sound.

Ford's contempt for the pliability of the front-office was still hot thirty-seven years later. When sound came in, he said, he and others who supposedly knew nothing about it were all fired and replaced by stage directors from New York. 'We had schedules of three or four weeks in those days – and after eight weeks these fellows had about a half-reel of picture, and the stuff was terrible. They had to hire us all back. . . .' Ford's method with actors was just as forthright. 'What are you supposed to say?' he asked the cast; and when they told him, he barked, 'Well, just say it.' It was perfectly all right, he concluded – 'There was nothing to learn.' Progress needs this kind of rough-shod *chutzpah* to give it a kick in the rear from time to time and tell it to get a move on.

By the end of the year the movies were certainly making progress. Ford's fellow director Raoul Walsh was in a Beverly Hills cinema one night – it must have been about mid-1928 – when on came a Fox Movietone News truck,

> and I saw a fellow interviewing a longshoreman there with all his gorillas and stuff. So I said, 'There's a guy talking outdoors.' I left the theatre fast, I called up Winnie Sheehan (Fox's production chief) at his home and I said, 'I want to make a sound picture.' He said, 'Are you

[7] *John Ford*, by Peter Bogdanovich (Studio Vista, London, 1967), p. 50.

Above, John Ford claimed that *Napoleon's Barber* (1928) was 'the first time anyone ever went outside with a sound system'. This is arguable, but Ford's short talkie about the Emperor hearing a few home truths from an innocent country barber, proved the superiority of the Movietone over the Vitaphone process for location shooting. *Below*, Almost exactly a year after Jolson gave voice in *The Jazz Singer*, another sensational figure gave vent to a whistle. *Steamboat Willie* (1928) was the first cartoon with a fully synchronised sound track. Very soon Mickey Mouse got his voice, too, supplied by Disney himself.

drunk?' I said, 'No. Get me a Movietone News wagon.' He told me, 'Why the hell didn't I think of that? C'mon up to the house.'[8]

Just as speaking pictures had grown out of the Vitaphone musical shorts, outdoor drama came out of the Movietone newsreels. But it needed individualists not in awe of hidebound conventions to seize the chance. Men like Jolson, Ford and Walsh had a habit of dramatising their own feelings, when talking to interviewers, in dialogue that could be set down direct in a shooting script. Dialogue would clearly hold few terrors for such 'natural actors' – their speech was already a script to some extent.

The film that Walsh started out making for Fox, *In Old Arizona*, was premièred on 25 December 1928. Welford Beaton called it 'unquestionably the finest bit of entertainment that the sound device has given us'.[9] For the first time voices and natural sounds were blended naturally and inventively in a full-length feature set frequently out of doors. It was the story of the Cisco Kid, his pursuer and the girl he loves. They were played respectively by Warner Baxter (who replaced Walsh in the star role after an eye injury: at which point Irving Cummings replaced him as director), Edmund Lowe and Dorothy Burgess. Shot in Zion National Park, Cedar City in Utah, the Mojave Desert and the San Fernando Valley, the landscape's authenticity was matched by that of the outdoor sounds which added naturalness and variety to the mood and the characters. The comedy of a jackass's braying synchronised with a man's laugh, or the hero's lip-smacking relish on downing a drink; the suspense added to a gunfight by a ticking clock or the dramatic interruption of mission-station bells; and all the sounds of the open air and isolated life, from the clip-clop of horses' hooves that actually receded when the riders galloped away from the camera to the sizzling of the bacon on the camp-fire skillet. It sounds simple today: in *its* day, it was a revelation. Welford Beaton noted that the dialogue now characterised the personalities as well as conveying the necessities of the plot. Of Warner Baxter's performance he wrote, ' "The warm breath of a few summers, the cold chill of a few winters" is how he sums up life, but a printed title could not put in it the warmth and feeling supplied by the actor's intelligent use of his voice.' With this performance, in broken English, Baxter became the first talking player to win an Oscar at the second annual presentation of the awards in 1930.

It was unusually well-plotted for a Western, being based on an O'Henry type of last-reel twist – the Kid sets up the faithless girl so that the lawman shoots her instead of him. Her scream ends the film, save for a few feet of scenic footage to soften the blow for the audience. About a third of the film was still set indoors and critics complained that it dragged while Baxter made amorous play for Dorothy Burgess; but the outdoor scenes stirred murmurs of appreciation, particularly as a

[8] *The Men Who Made the Movies*, by Richard Schickel (Elm Tree Books, London, 1977), p. 34.   [9] *Film Spectator*, 5 January 1929.

rooster was heard crowing in the distance as Baxter rode away from a corral. 'After I saw *In Old Arizona*,' said Clarence Brown,

> I wanted to go straight back to Hollywood and start work on a Western.' He even knew the story he wanted to make – *The Virginian*. 'When the microphone is gotten out into the open, all sorts of interesting things happen and now that the building of our outdoor equipment is almost completed, I predict a series of Western pictures that will put that type of story back into its favoured position.[10]

Brown was right. *In Old Arizona* restored the movie industry's faith in a film genre that seemed at the time to have reached the end of the trail. The boom years of this staple entertainment of the silent cinema had continued right up to and into 1927, when Western releases were actually double the 1926 figure. A glut then set in; and by 1928 stars like Tom Mix, Hoot Gibson, Buck Jones and Fred Thomson (a former minister and a notable saddle acrobat) were doing only half the work of a year earlier. The budgets and profits of some of these genre movies are revealing: they show how a source of rich and steady income dried up, thereby increasing the companies' desperation to turn to any novelty like sound to make up the short-fall.

Tom Mix pictures cost Fox about 175,000 dollars each and grossed 300,000–375,000 dollars; Buck Jones cost between 50,000–75,000 dollars and grossed around 125,000 dollars. Thomson received about 85,000 dollars per picture from FBO and his movies invariably grossed up to 175,000 dollars. Some Westerns were made for peanuts expressly to keep the goodwill of exhibitors, to whom they were practically given away as programme fillers. But by 1928 the cowboy was no longer the folk hero he had been. Lindbergh's transatlantic flight suddenly made the man in the saddle look old-fashioned and unadventurous compared with the daring pilot flying his small craft into an unknown that was even more boundless than the prairies. 'Tom Mix, Hoot Gibson and Ken Maynard must swap horses for aeroplanes or go to the old actors' home,' wrote James R. Quirk. 'The great open spaces are now landing fields, and the bears in the mountains cannot hurt Little Nell, because Little Nell is thumbing her nose at them as her lover pilots her over the hill tops.'[11] The huge popular success of *In Old Arizona* suddenly added a fresh dimension to the Western and reprieved a market that looked for a time as if it had gone the way of the Old West.

There is evidence that the movies could have overcome their thraldom to a stationary microphone and a boxed-up camera well before the end of 1928 – if they had really wished to do so. Technical advances were leaping ahead: one week's 'insuperable problem' might be solved the next. The sound engineers' dictatorship was crumbling: perhaps the engineers themselves were becoming more like Hollywood natives, anxious to solve difficulties instead of standing pat on their East

[10] *Variety*, 30 January 1929.   [11] *Photoplay*, April 1929.

Coast know-how. Film-makers need not have been shackled by noisy cameras for very long. *American Cinematographer*, as early as August 1928, was advertising: 'The Ideal for Sound Recording Work. The MITCHELL HI-SPEED MOVEMENT, as embodied in our camera, is now being adopted as standard by all the larger producers of the present-day "TALKING PICTURES". The reason is the silent operation. . . .' Bell and Howell also had a nearly noiseless camera on the market, with fibre gears suppressing the whirring of the metal ones; moreover there was a padded covering adhering by suction cups to the camera box, reducing any faint sound still further. Bessie Love noticed this being used in the filming of *Broadway Melody* at the end of 1928 and rather charmingly called it a 'jump suit'; it also got the name of a 'barney', after the strip cartoon character Barney Google whose racehorse wore a protective blanket! By December 1928 Universal were taking credit for designing a revolutionary camera crane with a boom that could carry camera and operators and so noiseless it could go to work on the sound stages. For cameramen who did not have the most up-to-date noiseless equipment there were long-focus lenses available. Why, then, did the talkies not regain their old silent-era fluency much sooner? Kevin Brownlow believes it was partly innate conservatism. The majority of studios still believed that the old sound-proof camera booth was 'satisfactory' for most dialogue pictures. I am sure this is so. Anyone with experience in newspapers and broadcasting knows there is great reluctance in any organisation which has had to lay out huge sums of money on a technological revolution to disburse any additional sums, however small by comparison, on improving the costly new machinery. It is often thought an unnecessary frill, something that fastidious creative people might like to have but not really essential – at least not for the moment. In other words the new sound stages that had been completed in Hollywood in the latter part of 1928 were lumbered with equipment that was becoming obsolete even while it was being installed. The people there had to continue using it until the undeniable cash returns of the talkies enabled yet another outlay to be authorised. There is a parallel here to what happened in the cinemas. Reviews of new films opening in Broadway's sound theatres contain evidence of a multitude of technical break-downs which lasted into 1930. Though these metropolitan cinemas were the industry's 'showcases', they had had the bad luck to be among the first wired for sound. Their systems were probably less 'perfect' than many a smaller cinema elsewhere which had signed on for the new, improved amplifying systems.

It is infinitely harder to fix the moment when the microphone began to follow the players instead of requiring them to grow roots around it, or hush their voices while they crossed the set from one hidden mike to another. So many well-known names claim to have had the idea for the microphone on a boom – or have the claim made for them – that the only polite explanation is spontaneous ignition. The difficulty facing an historian of this period is evident immediately one considers just a few of the better-known claimants. William Wellman told Richard Schickel that

> when we first started (sound) the booms were camouflaged. . . . That burned me up. You can't make a picture that way. You've got to have some flow. So I came in (to the set at Paramount) and I said, 'I've got news for you sound men this morning. I'm moving that god-damned mike.' And I got my grips, got me a big high ladder, and went up and took (the mike) and put it on the end of a broomstick. And I moved it and it worked. And that was the first. Overnight it changed our studio.[12]

But Douglas Shearer tells it differently: he credits the invention of a movable microphone ('It was so simple, but I hadn't thought of it') to Eddie Mannix, then in charge of MGM's new sound department. Arthur Marx in his Goldwyn biography says the travelling microphone boom was invented by Gordon Sawyer, a young UCLA engineer, who installed United Artists' first sound system and became department head. And Marjorie Rosen claims it was Dorothy Arzner who 'improvised the first moving microphone by insisting that sound technicians at Paramount attach a mike to a fishing pole balanced on a ladder and thus follow Clara Bow about the sound stages in *The Wild Party*'.[13] It is quite obvious, from the foregoing, that no one can ever be safely credited with being the first man (or woman) to 'move the mike'.

By March 1929, however, Warners were giving the lie to those who said Vitaphone could never shoot out of doors by doing just that. They used sound trucks from Western Electric, as well as microphones attached to cables and under remote control from the monitor room. Warners had then four sound trucks, and four more on order. At First National, in the Irish village of Colleen Moore's first talkie, *Smiling Irish Eyes*, about 500 yards from the sound stages, cables were laid on to feed the sound back to the studios: it worked well. Harry Cohn was still waiting for Columbia's sound stages to be finished in March 1929 and decreed that his new sound truck, costing 35,000 dollars, must start to pay for its keep at once. Studios were also discovering that sound-proofing need not involve a structure like a medieval arsenal. In fact MGM's two rock-solid stages designed by Professor Knudson came to be used as storehouses rather than places to shoot movies! John Ford, as maverick as ever, believed good luck attended him whenever he shot on the old silent Fox stages on Western Avenue – and that is where he decreed he would shoot *The Black Watch* (22 May 1929), using a Movietone sound truck, instead of going to the brand-new sound-proof complex in Fox Hills. Universal also took to making films on un-proofed stages. *The Wagon Master* was shot in hollow wooden sets

[12] Schickel, op. cit., p. 207.

[13] *Popcorn Venus*, by Marjorie Rosen (Coward, McCann and Geoghegan, New York, 1973), p. 377.

representing a log cabin or saloon bar, the only aid being a few felt screens. One of the sequences was a fight, with yells from the watching throng and the sound of a tinny bar-room piano churning out a continuous waltz as the men slugged each other. No extraneous sound effects would have stood a chance of being heard. The director, Harry J. Brown, tried another innovation. He never permitted any silence to develop in conversations between someone saying something and someone else replying – this was a pretty standard feature of early talkies, for the fallacious reason already indicated. And instead of 'mixing' the voices to an even tone, he chose two men with widely varying voices, hard and soft, to establish a contrast and filmed the scene as naturally as possible. Instead of the precautionary battery of microphones, one only was used for all scenes – the hero's horse being cued silently.

By the last few months of 1928, it is clear how quickly talk had become accepted, how impatient people were for movies to give them more than talk. The voice alone is not wonder enough, especially if its reproduction is off-key. First National at last squeezed three or four random talking sequences into one of its productions, George Fitzmaurice's *The Barker* (5 December 1928), a naïve but pleasing tale of a carnival man's too trusting young son who is seduced by a lady whose name is Lou. Milton Sills, Douglas Fairbanks Jr, Dorothy Mackaill and Betty Compson starred in it – 'the ladies flashing plenty of hosiery and occasionally in various stages of undress', said *Variety*'s 'Sid', adding, in a reference to bluenose censorship boards now flourishing in several states, 'Pennsylvania has yet to be heard from'.[14] Fairbanks drew praise for his resonant speech, so did Sills for his character accent as Nifty the showman, but the dialogue sequences were otherwise so banal that Mordaunt Hall, along with other critics, judged it 'a relief when scenes were silent, accompanied by the now much-despised sub-titles'.[15] In its annual round-up of the past year, *Variety* said, 'No one has yet denied that a bad talker is inferior to a bad silent picture.' A good silent could still hold its own, and more. MGM's synchronised *Our Dancing Daughters* outpaced the studio's first ambitious part-talkie, *Alias Jimmy Valentine* (14 November 1928), in which Lionel Barrymore yet again used his stage training to steady the nerves of a cast of vocal debutants including William Haines as the cracksman whose magic touch finds the combination of a walk-in safe in time to save the child trapped inside. Haines's voice unfortunately recorded with a surprisingly light tone which did not go at all with his he-man looks. If any star has to accept the claim that talkies severely damaged his career, he is probably the first – though there were personal factors in his case which caused the studio to pause before selecting fresh star vehicles for him. He retired in the mid-1930s.

Along with this MGM feature was shown one of the studio's

[14] *Variety*, 12 December 1928.   [15] *The New York Times*, 6 December 1928.

Movietone shorts in which, for probably the first time, John Gilbert's voice was heard on the screen. Along with other MGM stars like Joan Crawford, Norma Shearer and George K. Arthur, he was seen and heard talking to Ernest Torrence who was (or pretended to be: it's uncertain which) at the opening of MGM's new cinema, the Empire, in Leicester Square, London. The film was called *Voices Across the Sea* and Gilbert used words like 'colossal, amazing and wonderful', all characteristic of his hyperactive personality, to describe the occasion. In view of the fate' that was less than a year away from him, it is important to note that no reviewer who noticed the film remarked on the star's voice being anything but satisfactory.[16]

Dialogue certainly was not part of the appeal of a star who made his sound debut a few days later at another New York theatre. But Mickey Mouse's third movie and Walt Disney's first sound cartoon, *Steamboat Willie* (18 November 1928), was an immediate success with audiences and critics – 'It growls, whines, squeaks and makes various other sounds that add to its mirthful quality,' the *Times* said. It was also the most imaginative use of sound to be heard on the screen at that date – and for a long time to come. Disney had certain natural advantages. No problems with camera noise, for his movies were hand-drawn and photographed frame by frame – this one had an optical sound-track. No worries about recording actors' voices, for music and sound effects were the 'dialogue' of his films. Above all his films moved – at a pace that made the flesh-and-blood of other producers' movies look positively paralysed. But Richard Schickel has suggested that sound, as well as being used with freedom, disciplined Disney's animation and marshalled it into more careful rhythms than earlier silent cartoonists had felt the need for, or perhaps had the ability to achieve. And this increased the audience's pleasure in a retrospective way that had nothing directly to do with the novelty of sound. '(It) was able to rediscover some of the joys that had first attracted it to film – a sense of delight that, with the exception of the work of the silent comedians, it had been increasingly denied as movies grew more literary in orientation throughout the twenties.'[17]

As audiences grew used to sound, they became more intolerant of its infelicities. The reactions some of these received, of course, were to be expected. In John Ford's *The Black Watch*, Myrna Loy played an Indian girl with the name 'Yasmani'. It may have looked innocuous in the script, but when it started to come out of Victor McLaglen's lips as 'Yes Minny' it provoked hysterical laughter – and was expunged from most copies of the film before too long.[18] Dolores Costello innocently evoked

[16] See Chapter 10.

[17] *Walt Disney*, by Richard Schickel (Weidenfeld and Nicolson, London, 1968), p. 131.

[18] Ford was said not to have been too displeased. The dialogue scenes in the film, his first feature-length talkie, had been directed by Lumsden Hare and were 'talky' in the extreme.

laughter in another movie by demanding 'the jewels' – a vernacular word for 'genitals'. And there was a surprising outburst against the flip deployment of dialogue, which was resented because it broke the illusion of reality which was now fast replacing the convention of silence. Conrad Nagel was rapped for addressing the audience directly at the end of Howard Bretherton's *Caught in the Fog* (2 December 1928), a jewel-theft drama set aboard a fog-bound Florida houseboat. 'Well, folks, that's all there is,' said Nagel: reviewers were not as tolerant of this as they were when the lines came a little later from Bugs Bunny's lips. Snorted one, who had been embarrassed to be addressed from the screen, 'The dialogue pushover period can't and won't last forever.' Indeed there was plenty of evidence that it was over already. Increasing sophistication made plenty of people impatient of Warners' fourth all-talkie, *On Trial* (14 November 1928), starring the stage actress Pauline Frederick and directed by Archie Mayo, which evoked the caustic comment that talkies were simply a dry-cleaning medium for the older Hollywood material. A particularly imperfect sound system seems to have been used to record (or reproduce) *On Trial*. The star was judged 'so throaty and her talking efforts so obvious that they were no more than muffled sounds, almost indistinct in their entirety and imperfectly synchronised'.[19] Even worse, a revolver shot that should have been chilling sounded like snapping a peanut. Achieving authentic-sounding gun noises was a problem which would plague the talkies for a long time. Mordaunt Hall wrote of *A Dangerous Woman* (19 May 1929): 'Soon after the picture starts, a boom, supposed to be a pistol shot, is heard and the body. . . .' Filmgoers were demanding greater authenticity all round: in the early days of the talkies, animal-noise imitators flourished, including a man who 'did mosquitoes', but now the appropriate roars, growls, grunts and cheeps had to be faithfully recorded from the birds and beasts themselves. The demand for more accurate slang in pictures was forcing studios to consult experts, 'slang directors', they were called, versed in the argot of theatreland, dance halls, campuses, the Army, the Navy, boxing rings, railroads, circuses, high society, Sunday schools – and motion pictures. Paramount claimed to have found the underworld slang in Chicago meant little to the criminal classes of New York.

A Fox film went into production by the end of the year that showed the sophistication rapidly colouring both technique and audience appreciation. This was *The Ghost Talks* (17 February 1929) directed by Lew Seiler who had done 'the mawkish dialogue stuff' in Howard Hawks's *The Air Circus* earlier in the year. As plots went, it was not much: the usual Old Dark House comedy-melodrama. But its sound techniques were now unusually refined. More than one contemporary critic commented on the authenticity of the opening sequences, the sound of a train arriving in the station, a taxi motor idling over, a coach

[19] *Variety*, 21 November 1928.

Above, *On Trial* (1928), a court-room drama, was Warners' fourth all-talkie. It wasn't an auspicious occasion for Pauline Frederick (with Richard Tucker) as the sound recording appears to have been so poor that 'her talking efforts . . . were no more than muffled sounds'. *Below*, 'It conveyed the impression that the microphone was left to look after itself', said a critic about the comedy-thriller *The Ghost Talks* (1928). And everyone praised the 'incidental sounds' of trains arriving, cabs ticking over and coaches driving off in the opening scene at the railroad depot.

drawing off' '. . . the incidental sounds produced without the slightest distortion', wrote Welford Beaton, adding, 'In several shots there are as many as six people, each of whom takes up the conversation, and close-ups are not inserted to show us who is speaking. They are not necessary, for at no time is there any doubt about the identity of the speaker.'[20] This suggests a much more directional type of microphone than had hitherto been generally available. In fact the feature that most interested Beaton was how the microphone was left to look after itself, instead of making the audience uneasily conscious of it lurking somewhere in the vicinity of the characters. Even in long shots, when it was obviously some distance away, there was no loss of volume. Instead of chiefly concerning itself with the accurate reproduction of voices, the sound film was now bent on restoring a sense of movement to the screen. The apparently mobile microphone 'follows the characters along a street and allows us to hear their conversation, and it picks up the yelps of a gang of dogs that provide hilarious comedy by chasing a terrified colored gentleman from a haunted house to a police station'. The 'colored gentleman' was none other than Stepin Fetchit, the white man's favourite black in those early, insensitive days of cinema. If we cringe at the implied comedy of dogs pursuing a black, remember that the talkies had already familiarised a peculiar feature on the sound stages in the shape of an upright, narrow, black-painted 'flat' on which players, uttering their lines without anyone else actually present to be addressed, might fix their gaze. This object was called familiarly 'a nigger'. It may have been because of its non-reflecting ebony colour; but a cynic might suspect it also got that distasteful name because it alone of all the characters in the talkie was not expected to answer back.

[20] *Film Spectator*, 8 December 1928.

9

'The English accent doesn't mean a thing out here.'

One has a sense of the film industry recovering its breath at the start of 1929. The previous year had been decision year: the next twelve months was a period of amazingly rapid advance and consolidation. The ink was dry on the cheques that had underwritten the enormously expensive change-over from silent movies to 'the audible photoplay'. In the eight months up to February 1929, twenty-four million dollars had been spent reshaping the studios: three million dollars more were earmarked for experiment alone during this year. Already huge returns were apparent in some quarters. Studios that had for a time abandoned the talkies to the two front-runners, Warners and Fox, were now panting to catch up – which meant spend, spend, spend. Sound alone was responsible for an estimated three-hundred million dollars now being spent on theatres, amplifying systems, sound recording apparatus. Western Electric's profit for wiring cinemas for sound was an amazing 300–500 per cent per house: the manufacturing cost was only a quarter of the renting price. Many exhibitors who had signed their Faustian compact with the wiring companies in haste or panic were now waking up to the penalties for putting themselves in the power of the communications people. 'America's picture business looks to be owned by Western Electric,' said *Variety* in a by-lined report by 'Sid', under the headline 'THE SMOTHERING TALKER'.[1]

Film company heads don't like to think about it, but this has become the trade's belief and those men who have read the Western Electric contracts with their production studio are convinced that the A.T. & T. subsidiary doesn't want anything more than the film industry's heart for the privilege of the new novelty. If the big wire and

[1] *Variety*, 2 January 1929.

amplification men lose interest, it will be very much as if Western Electric tipped its hat to the pictures saying 'Thanks for the use of the hall,' and walked out with heavy dough.

As well as the wire companies, the studios had passed heavily into the hands of the bankers whose loans had been vital for the talkie refurbishment. By the start of 1929, over forty banking and electrical company presidents sat on the boards of the ten largest film companies. Paramount had eight bankers; and RKO, because of its birth as an alliance of several business interests, had no fewer than nineteen bank representatives. No wonder the people who actually made the films felt unusually pressured by the front office. To have nineteen bankers overseeing your latest talkie wonder, applying their own yardsticks to your budgets, was cruel and unusual punishment even in an industry with a large element of latent sadism. But the bankers had their worries, too. There were now sufficient talkies around to imperil seriously the lucrative foreign market. Louis B. Mayer announced that a fifth of it had already been lost and more would vanish as talkie output increased. He proposed one way out. In future MGM would offer to sell an exact 'blueprint' of a new talkie – location of the cameras, lighting details, dialogue, shooting directions, casting suggestions – all laid out in script form. The foreign producer would only have to translate the dialogue into his own tongue and shoot 'as instructed'. (Needless to say, export sales were not brisk.) Warners began using their New York stages for foreign-language shorts, mostly in French and German, destined for overseas sales and some ethnic districts in America. Paramount were considering going into Spanish, with an eye on South America. Fox announced on 24 March 1929 that they would make no more silent pictures; and as the electric signs in Times Square flashed it on the front of buildings, the crowds paused to see yet another piece of evidence of how swiftly an era was passing away in front of their eyes, or, rather, their ears. Fox still had enough silent films finished or in production to take care of the overseas markets for more than a year; but Winfield Sheehan, Vice-President in charge of production, announced a scheme for partially recouping the export market that did not basically differ from Louis B. Mayer's.

The desire to minimise the blow to the export market had its good side. Until dubbing a film into a foreign language became a practical possibility, it was used as an argument for reducing the overabundance of talk that now swamped the auditoriums. The silent versions of the talkies that were still being turned out were increasingly just the talkie versions with scrappily shot bits of mime supplemented by sub-titles. But it was being appreciated that a combination of dialogue and silent footage would become standard, the dramatic or comedy sequences rating 'talk', while the rest of the film would give the director and photographer a chance to work out the action in terms of silent-movie mobility with synchronised music. Though this dichotomy was crude, and still more generally *felt* to be so than actually articulated as studio policy, it did presage what the 'modern' talkies would become as they picked up pace, perfected their sound recording, and were able to do more skilful editing and mixing. Already there was more flexibility. Some companies which had been using the wax disc recording system began flirting with, or deserting to, optical sound tracks. Even Warners, the disc pioneers, were trying out optical tracks by the end of February 1929. United Artists had made the same decision a few weeks earlier after an exceptionally painful experience with the great D. W. Griffith's first sound film, *Lady of the Pavements*.

This was a period story, in essence the same Diderot *conte* as Bresson later used in *Les Dames aux Bois de Boulogne*. Griffith shot several scenes in cafés and beer-cellars with dialogue and songs. His stars were Lupe Velez, Jetta Goudal and William Boyd, later the cowboy star Hopalong Cassidy, though now clad in Ruritanian uniform, with marcelled white hair, for this tale of a jilted woman bent on revenge. Wax discs were used and the Griffith script referred to sequences that would be 'perfectly synchronised'. It did not work out so perfectly. The laboratories not only printed the sound sequences in the film so poorly that their imperfections were plainly visible, but also imperfectly recorded the songs to the extent that the only sounds which could be heard were the high notes. It took three days to rush substitute discs out to the cinemas.

The start of 1929 also brought home to the studios the effects of their early, panicky extravagances on both coasts of America. Winfield Sheehan, at his news conference in March, announced the names of those legitimate players, directors and writers whom Fox had brought West since 1 September 1928. If anything clinched the wastefulness of this raiding technique it was the large number of names who never amounted to anything once they got to Hollywood. There are too many to quote in detail; but of thirty-two performers listed, the only ones to thrive in the talkies were Will Rogers, George Jessel, Paul Muni, and Louise Dresser; of twenty-five writers, only the composing team of DeSylva, Brown and Henderson was a conspicuous success; and as for the directors promised employment and fame in the movies, the list speaks only for the obscurity of, amongst others, A. H. Van Buren, Edward Royce, Campbell Gullan, Lester Lonergan, Seymour Felix, Ira Hards and Guthrie McClintock.

Things were just as disenchanting in the East. The studios which had been opened there, to be near the source of talent, were either under-employed, or else were abandoning full-length features for a variety of humbler tasks. By January 1929 First National and Universal had decided to make none of their talkies in New York. Though MGM were still synchronising all their Coast-made films in New York until as late as March 1929, their sound stages in Culver City were expanding rapidly and anchoring production more firmly than ever in Hollywood. The spell of Hollywood was proving just too potent – as it always would – for the East Coast to maintain the panic-stricken momentum that had made it look for a few months in 1928 as if the film pioneers were about to trek back there again.

Another reason why the East Coast studios were being abandoned has a bearing on the general direction that film-making was now about to take. It was swinging back to the old screen favourites and away from the notion that a glamorous East Coast stage name was the one that could bring in the people to hear 'the talk'. Jean de Limur's version of *The Letter* (27 February 1929) fared badly at the box-office for a number of reasons. Though de Limur created good Oriental atmosphere, with packed, sweating courtrooms, labyrinthine alleyways, sinister coolies and menacing shadows, signs of nervousness showed in the decision to cut a bit of emblematic evil into the film in the shape of a wild-life short produced by Germany's UFA studios in which a mongoose mastered a cobra. The short had already been shown in America and would have got even wider exhibition had some managers not feared that 'women are often shocked at seeing snakes on the screen'. But the real reason why *The Letter* did poorish business was the fact that its star, Jeanne Eagels, though much more acceptable in Middle America than hooded cobras, was almost as unfamiliar to Main Street audiences in search of stars whom the movies had made. She followed *The Letter* with *Jealousy*, which had closed on Broadway as a two-character play starring Fay Bainter, and was rushed into production fourteen days later as a nine-character vehicle for Jeanne Eagels with de Limur again directing. It did nothing to help establish her as a screen presence – and by the end of 1929 she was dead. Ruth Chatterton's early career also showed how hard it was to graft a stage star on to the filmgoers' affections. An import from Broadway, she had been put into *The Doctor's Secret* (20 February 1929), the first sound film directed by William C. de Mille after he had served his apprenticeship at Paramount to Roy Pomeroy.

De Mille's film was a sixty-one-minute adaptation of J. M. Barrie's *Half-an-Hour*, which had been written as a parody of American melodrama but was here done straight. De Mille photographed it as an intelligently directed stage play: the notices were respectful, but scarcely enthusiastic. Partly to blame was its lack of action. 'Movie audiences expect emotion,' wrote Herbert Cruikshank, 'and in *The Doctor's Secret* they get long photographic discussions between characters and a plot which is rather too mental for a movie-trained fan.'[2] Mordaunt Hall called it 'a most intelligent combination of shadow and voice' – which was a kind of soft put-down. But what many critics agreed on was the poor showing made by Ruth Chatterton, playing the runaway wife whose lover is killed a few minutes before they are due to leave England together. 'She is . . . the first of the invading stage players to appear on the talkie screen,' added Cruikshank, 'and to me she proves that Hollywood does not need to send to Broadway for its talent.' Embarrassment was experienced by some audiences over Ruth

[2] *Motion Picture*, March 1929.

Above, Ethel Wales, Wilfred Noy and H. B. Warner in *The Doctor's Secret* (1929), directed by William C. de Mille, which continued the drawing-room tradition of Paramount's first all-talkie, *Interference*. By now, though, audiences were beginning to find that endless conversation pieces, even when the people conversing came out of the top bracket of society, were smothering the old-time virtues of the movie *as movie*. *Below*, Apprehensive about how his protégé Vilma Banky, who had come from Hungary, might sound in the talkies, Sam Goldwyn took the canny step of 'Americanizing' her. In *This is Heaven* (1929) she played an immigrant, oddly enough from Hungary, who takes quite naturally to tossing buckwheat cakes as a short-order cook. She made herself understood, too.

Chatterton's audible love scene; but Jesse Lasky probably diagnosed the real reason why this stage star got a cool welcome. 'Ruth (Chatterton's) poise was almost poison in the hinterland. Those who had never had the opportunity of hearing a cultivated, well modulated voice thought that she was putting on airs. . . . Our salesmen demanded, "No more accents. The public doesn't like accents." '[3] Her next film, *The Dummy*, a child-kidnapping melodrama, was unworthy material: she had only a bit part, while Fredric March as her husband had even a bit less than a bit part and did not get a single close-up. The blame fell tellingly on the *stage* talents who had shaped the film, particularly Robert Milton. Ruth Chatterton scored a popular hit soon afterwards with *Madame X* and Fredric March was not long in winning a movie following but it was evident by March 1929 that ready-made stars from the stage were not ready-made hits on the screen. In any case, Hollywood was having second thoughts about the need to replace its silent-era idols.

With every talkie produced, fresh discoveries were made among the colony's own members. Legitimate stage players, in contrast, were flunking their screen tests in alarming numbers. MGM had tested over one hundred Broadway-ites by the start of the year and found only one of them, Gwynne Stratford, remotely suitable for a movie contract. She signed one and departed for the Coast – and instant oblivion. Except in the newer crafts associated with musicals, Hollywood had not immediately gained from raids on Broadway: though the position would be modified by the end of the year when hardier stage players would be assuming the mantles of film stardom that they would wear with style in the next decade. By mid-March it was being trumpeted that 'screen personalities are triumphing over stage stars in dialogue films'. Of the fifty or so part- or all-talkie films so far made, featuring over two hundred players, fewer than a dozen had come directly off the legitimate stage, and an equally small number from vaudeville. 'The predictions that a complete change in screen personalities would occur with the production of talkers has failed to develop,' *Variety* reported.

The producers' attitude has changed. Most film people had better recording voices than expected – some of them better even than the stage replacements. Theater managers report that the fans would rather hear a weak-voiced screen favorite than an unknown, not photographing so well, with a cultivated voice. The English accent doesn't mean a thing out here. Personality still sways audiences; and voice is only one of the calculating factors. Most of the existing screen celebrities have found that all they need is a little gargle water. The differences in speech in the early talkies, which made Wise Broadway laugh, brought an entirely different response out of town. . . . It has been found that legit. means little. Ruth Chatterton, Richard

[3] *I Blow My Own Horn*, by Jesse Lasky, with Don Weldon (Gollancz, London, 1957), pp. 217–8.

Bennett, Jeanne Eagels are not known to the great multitude of film fans and the new people can't be built up in one performance. The only proven exception to this has been Al Jolson.'[4]

Actually this was overstating the case in one direction as much as the forecast of the havoc talkies would cause among the stars had overstated it in the other. There was still much nervousness in Hollywood among those with most to lose. A sign of the insecurity was the great influx of star gazers, palmists, crystal ponderers and card-readers into the colony. Advice was sought anxiously and expensively from them by those under the threat of speech. It was noted, by the sceptical, that the reigning period of the birth star was seven years – the term of several star contracts.

For some players it was too late. Emil Jannings had given up wrestling with English and was taking the boat home. Pola Negri had temporarily severed relations with the screen. Sam Goldwyn's Hungarian *protégée*, Vilma Banky, was putting up stiff resistance to a talking picture. She had refused to submit to voice tutoring and now turned down, point blank, the vehicle that Goldwyn had constructed for her debut, *Child's of Fifth Avenue* (retitled *This Is Heaven*: 26 May 1929), because she felt her accent would be submerged in an accentless (i.e. American) cast. Goldwyn, who was then paying her 250,000 dollars a year on a contract that had the most of two years to run, presented her with a choice of evils. Either talk or quit. Banky talked. Actually the film had been quite cleverly devised to exploit her 'foreign-ness'. She played a Hungarian immigrant working as a short-order cook in Child's restaurant, flipping buckwheat cakes on to the waitresses' plates with the best of the local girls and soon flipping small-talk more rewardingly in the direction of a millionaire's son whom she has mistaken for a chauffeur. Yes, it was a *very* American plot! Her line 'Don't be funny' was a guttural put-down that apparently caused a lot of mirth in cinemas: it may have anticipated Greta Garbo's line in the same brand of humourless humour a year or so later. As far as her voice went, Banky was more than passable – though most of her talking was confined to one main sequence. Another passable foreign talent was Baclanova. Though *The Wolf of Wall Street* (27 January 1929) was generally adjudged 'a set-back for the talkies', Mordaunt Hall called her voice 'fascinating'. At least one writer, John Farrow at Paramount, had the special assignment of creating purpose-built dialogue that players who did not speak English too well could handle without difficulty.

Some stars had special problems, however. Lon Chaney was adamant in 1929 that he would never talk on the screen. He had made his reputation as a wizard of make-up and mime, switching form and physiognomy from film to film at sometimes fearful cost to the composure of his limbs and features. Now he could not possibly manage the vocal range to go with the change of characters. 'I have a thousand faces, but only one voice,' he said predictably.

[4] *Variety*, 20 March 1929.

Olga Baclanova in *The Wolf of Wall Street*
(1929). A ballerina who came to
Hollywood from Russia, she had the
good sense to play a Russian *femme fatale*
in her talkie debut and was rewarded by
a *New York Times* notice which found her
accent 'quite fascinating'. The film,
though, was judged 'a set-back to the
talkies'.

In *A Dangerous Woman* (1929) Baclanova
played a faithless wife with a fascination
for men in a relatively dark part of
Africa. It took such exotic roles (and
backgrounds) to render her character
plausible; but the vamp did not last long
into the sound era.

But the fiercest rearguard action against the talkies was fought by the man whose un-American origins would become painfully clear the moment he opened his lips and give to his immortal creation a handicapping local habitation. This was Charlie Chaplin. He gave Gladys Hall, a reporter from *Motion Picture*, an interview on the set of *City Lights* in March 1929, and to her question, 'What shall I tell our readers you think of the talkies?' he snorted, 'You can tell 'em I loathe them.'[5] He then vented his dislike of this usurper in an interview that reads almost like a parody of the criticism that talkies were then getting from highbrow critics and others who realised by now that an art form had been lost for good to a rackety novelty which had come to stay. It is Chaplin speaking in the high-flown vein of an offended Verdoux.

> They are spoiling the oldest art in the world – the art of pantomime. They are ruining the great beauty of silence. They are defeating the meaning of the screen, the appeal that has created the star system, the fan system, the vast popularity of the whole – the appeal of beauty. It's beauty that matters in pictures – nothing else. The screen is pictorial. Pictures! Lovely looking girls, handsome young men in adequate scenes. What if the girls can't act? Of course they can't. They never have. But what of it? Who has cared? Who has known the difference? Certainly I prefer to see, say, Dolores Costello, in a thin tale than some aged actress of the stage doing dialogue with revolting close-ups.

His own pictures, he said, would use synchronised music ('music . . . a universal language . . . will raise up a whole new school of people writing scores and librettos for individual pictures'). But talk – never. 'For me, it would be fatal.' But a few months later, in the same magazine, there came a counterblast from a star with an ego as large as Chaplin's, though with less hot air circulating inside. 'If Charlie Chaplin doesn't make talkies, he won't make anything,'[6] Al Jolson proclaimed to Cedric Belfrage, on the set of *his* new picture, his third talkie, *Little Pal*.

> 'The great beauty of silence!' I was at a party the other night, and from eight-thirty till around five a.m., Charlie never stopped talking and singing. . . . If Charlie wants to keep what he calls 'the great beauty of silence', let him go lock himself in a room – become a nun's brother, or something. . . . Charlie goes on record as loathing talkies. Well, I'm just the opposite. I think he'd better get to like 'em – or he'll find out the public don't like him. . . . What he's really got is a gentleman complex. He's afraid he talks too nice to fit in with the characterisation he has built up on the screen.

There was more than a little truth in this concluding remark, as must have been evident to anyone who heard Chaplin's genteel, rather mincing English accent off-screen. It later transpired that at one time he

[5] *Motion Picture*, May 1929. [6] Ibid., August 1929.

had cogitated hard and long over what accent he would give 'The Tramp', if the worst came to the worst and he *had* to talk: he decided that since 'the little fellow' was a run-down gentleman, an Oxford accent would not be out of the way. It is worth recalling that, years later, Chaplin remarked about Jolson with equal justice in his *Autobiography*: 'Whatever he sang, he brought you up or down to his level.' If 'The Tramp' had had to talk in the 1920s, one wonders what level American audiences would have placed *him* on. Fortunately Chaplin avoided the uncomfortable necessity to open his mouth in movies for nearly seven more years – and then averted criticism by singing a 'nonsense song' as the waiter in *Modern Times*.

One does not know whether those stars still suffering from 'mike nerves' found it consoling or condescending to be assured that voice-doubling was now practicable. It reached its peak at this turn-of-the-year period. *Variety* had even rebuked the studios early in February 1929 for advertising their own cleverness at the deception of 'looping' voices other than the performers' on to their lip movements in the post-production stage or sometimes even dubbing during shooting. It broke the public's sense of illusion, the trade paper said, and it counselled silence on the subject. But January had seen a particularly noteworthy example in Richard Barthelmess's first talkie, *Weary River* (24 January 1929), directed by Frank Lloyd, the tale of a gangster who develops a singing talent while languishing behind bars, achieves nation-wide fame in a radio broadcast and earns the governor's pardon for melody – with which, of course, went reform. Barthelmess was then being paid 9,375 dollars a week by First National on a two-year, three-picture-a-year contract, so he represented a considerable investment. Though such a tale as a felon finding harmony in his soul was deemed a bit beneath a man who had been D. W. Griffith's greatest male performer, with such classics as Henry King's *Tol'able David* in his recent past, his vocal performance in *Weary River* was well received. '(He) emerges as possibly the first of the veteran stars to register a clear-cut wow in the articulate cinema,' was *Variety*'s verdict. 'His voice is always natural, sincere, nicely repressed, carrying by deft suggestion the shades of meaning which speak to the sympathies.'[7] He was discovered to have a melodious, vibrant tenor when he sang the title song: 'Poets say our lives are like the rivers that flow / They surely know, too / Everyone is a different kind of stream, so they say, / And now I know that every weary river / Some day meets the sea.' But at least one reviewer qualified his compliments with the *caveat* '. . . if he sings it'. Though never openly admitted by the studio, it was quite soon accepted that *he* didn't. A voice double had been used for the song, one Johnny Murray. The star of *Show Boat*, Laura La Plante, was also suspected of being 'doubled' a few months later. But the first case of voice 'doubling' actually exposed publicly was,

[7] *Variety*, 30 January 1929.

Above, Hair and toe-caps gleaming, well-pressed suit, concert grand. . . . Thus the gangster whose melodious singing voice – a discovery he made in State pen – got him from behind the bars to behind the footlights in *Weary River* (1929), Richard Barthelmess's first talkie. *Below*, Jean Arthur shapes up to the merciless little blackmailer played by Louise Brooks in *The Canary Murder Case* (1929). Miss Brooks's voice was dubbed by another actress.

suitably enough, in Malcolm St Clair's detective movie *The Canary Murder Case* (9 March 1929), in which William Powell did so well as Philo Vance. Louise Brooks played a ruthless little blackmailer. Mordaunt Hall suspected, however, that the voice did not belong to her; and soon it was admitted that not only was the voice that of Margaret Livingstone, but the 'doubler' had stood in for Miss Brooks in some scenes when the actress was not available! The magazine publisher George Kent Shuler, sensing or possibly whipping up the fans' outrage at this practice, thundered, 'It is bad art and bad entertainment.' After which outburst, voice doubling was either more carefully effected, or more likely, except in such special cases as a non-singing star having to sing, became unnecessary.

The old line of screen stars to whom Barthelmess belonged sat up attentively when they saw the success attending those second-magnitude stars or featured players who had been pushed early and sacrificially into the talkie machine. Reference has been made already to Conrad Nagel's ascent from a 1,500 dollars a week silent star to a much-in-demand talkie actor in the 5,000 dollars a week class. Walter Pidgeon had the same good fortune after playing a song writer who follows his buddy into the Army and composes ditties on the hottest stretch of the Eastern Front. This was in the film *Melody of Love* (the Universal picture whipped together for 40,000 dollars by A. B. Heath with that 'borrowed' Fox sound truck). Pidgeon, who had been getting 700 dollars a week as a useful but not outstanding silent actor, climbed to the 1,500 dollars a week level after *Melody of Love* demonstrated his all-round usefulness with dialogue and songs. Despite his talkie success, Lionel Barrymore soon opted for the director's chair. But others profited (for a time) from the talkie touch – Betty Compson was soon pointed out as one particularly lucky recipient of a talkie bonanza. It had been figured she was through when she quit Paramount in 1926, where she had been earning 3,500 dollars weekly. Her fees subsequently touched as low as 500 dollars weekly. But after her impact in such films as *The Singing Fool* and *Weary River* ('She has a feminine cuteness . . . though she never descends to baby talk') she was up again to 2,500 dollars weekly and much sought after. By early 1929 she had been engaged to make no fewer than thirteen talkies, three for Columbia, four for FBO and six for Warners.

Confirmation of what sound could do for the right kind of Hollywood talent was sensationally provided at the Los Angeles première of MGM's first all-talkie, *Broadway Melody* (1 February 1929). It was also the first Hollywood musical in the modern sense of the term – a movie with songs and music specially written for it. And it helped set the shape of a new genre that has not substantially altered ever since. Edmund Goulding's story was about a sister act from the Mid-West who hit Broadway ('The place we've dreamed and talked about') and swiftly lose their illusions about the power of Eddie (Charles King), the song-

and-dance man already wearing the gold-plated sock-suspenders of success, to get them star parts. They settle for the chorus line ('We ain't never had to get by on our legs before'). But Queenie (Anita Page) opts for the 'security' seductively dangled by a Broadway 'angel' called Jack Worriner (whose name the sound system kept reproducing, to Hollywood insiders' delight, as 'Jack Warner') to the distress ('I guess the bright lights got under her skin') of her tough little trouper sister Hank (Bessie Love). True affections and sisterly self-sacrifice, though the ending with good-time Queenie and big-time Eddie settling for what looks like an awfully short-lived marriage and Hank getting herself a helpfully hard-bitten new dancing partner has more realism to it than the formula plot deserves or perhaps the makers intended. What was to become convention in every backstage musical is present here in pristine simplicity: the imperious impresario, his cohorts of yes-men, the dilettante backers, the star of the show breaking her leg at rehearsal, her replacement wowing the audience by apparently not even singing a note or swinging a limb or doing anything else except simply stand there, and the big-hearted heroine surrendering her own chance of stardom and happiness for the sake of her kid sister. It is already parody-cliché: but we must see it through the novelty-struck eyes of contemporary filmgoers who were paying ticket touts more than twice the admission prices to get in and see it when it opened in New York on 8 February 1929.

Arthur Freed and Nacio Herb Brown wrote the score which, with one notable exception, had to be recorded on the set, as it was being sung, with an orchestra just out of camera range. 'Broadway Melody', 'Love Boat', 'Boy Friend', 'You Were Meant for Me': they had (and have) a freshness and tunefulness closely tied into the small, intense world of backstage emotions. They explain who the characters are, where they come from. Though not serving to advance the plot very much, they exemplify it and define the characters in a way *The Jazz Singer*'s score didn't quite do – the songs in *it* told one about Al Jolson. It was 'the first flash New York has had as to how the studios are going after musical comedy numbers, and there's no question of the potent threat to the stage producer,' said *Variety*'s critic 'Sid'.[8] He viewed it as stunning evidence of how Hollywood, 'if . . . (it) can get the camera close enough to make the ensemble effects seem to be in the same theatre' as the filmgoers, could replicate a Broadway musical for 75 cents (then the average cinema admission price) instead of 4.40 dollars. This we now know was a mistaken, though understandable interpretation: but the novelty value of a *screen* musical gave a lift to the talkies at just the right moment, when a jaded public was demanding more than dialogue and a perplexed Hollywood was wondering what to provide.

Viewed today, *Broadway Melody* does not provide the most visible evidence of one contemporary reviewer's declaration that 'in it the

[8] Ibid., 13 February 1929.

Bessie Love stretches the limbs that danced her into a new phase of her long Hollywood career in 1929, when she co-starred as half of a little sister team who loves and loses in the backstage musical *Broadway Melody*. A *Photoplay* reviewer said she gave 'the most astounding emotional performance in many months'. The film, too, was a revelation.

Variety said that *Broadway Melody* was 'the first flash New York has had as to how the studios are going after musical comedy numbers. . . . The possibilities are what jolt the imagination.' It cost 280,000 dollars and by the end of 1929 had made over one million. The imagination of studio chiefs was jolted all right.

talkies find new freedom and speed'.[9] It is true that Harry Beaumont had the camera cabin put on wheels and sound men in their socks tiptoe-ing along with the stars as they moved, holding out microphones in lieu of the movable boom that was still to come into general use. But 'speed' is not a noticeable result. To us, it is visually still a very static film. What does give it a sense of pace and vitality is its dialogue – hard-bitten, slangy, vernacular stuff written by Norman Huston and James Gleason and spoken at the speed of the backstage milieu where to be last with a comeback was to be out of the game altogether. Some critics found this Broadway argot vulgar – 'Broadway's not too edifying parlance', Mordaunt Hall called it apologetically in the *Times* – but its street rhythms liberate the characters from the poses struck by players in other talkies where the deferential delivery gave away the awe they still felt at speaking written lines untouched by human tongue. And then there is Bessie Love. . . . Amidst the serviceable sentimentality of the plot, she contrives to give a striking feeling of real emotion transfusing her part. Her resoluteness gives her small figure a propulsion that makes her appear hyperactive even when she and the camera are at rest. She has an inner conviction that jets to the surface like a fountain. It is extraordinary still to taste the realism of the justly famous scene when she breaks up emotionally at the news of her sister's desertion to the well-heeled cad. She lashes Eddie into counter-action with indignant scorn, then, when he has gone off to bring the girl back, she collapses into her own private flood of grief as she covers her tears with cold cream. Here she is drawing on a richer source of emotion than any story such as this warrants and conducting it directly and unpretentiously to the audience with words and acting that are perhaps the first, and certainly are among the best, examples of the talkie player's successful fusion of voice and performance. Never again could any audience witnessing Bessie Love in this scene say of a talkie, 'Ain't there anything in this picture but lip-movement?'

Accident played its part in the film's innovations. The plot featured a self-contained stage number, 'The Wedding of the Painted Doll', which Irving Thalberg had viewed and decreed to be unsatisfactory. Re-shooting it more imaginatively, he said, would give the film an extra dimension, particularly as the sequence was planned to be in colour. Rather than throw away the already recorded song and music for the sequences, the disc was played back as the cameras again turned on the players going through their routines, which included some alarmingly shaky acrobatic dancing in a pop ballet. Thus was the technique of pre-scoring and playback found to be practicable; and very soon it was standard practice, doing away with the permanent set orchestra and adding flexibility to the shooting and editing. The film's sound also noticeably improves throughout its running time, indicating how the thirty-day shooting schedule was creatively used by the technicians to

[9] *Photoplay*, April 1929.

bring their craft to a finer pitch. It cost between 280,000 and 350,000 dollars and even before the end of 1929 it was to make MGM a million. On the strength of this sensational success, Charles King and Bessie Love got five-year contracts, his increasing from 1,000 to 2,000 dollars weekly and hers from 500 to 3,000 dollars weekly. Its success was so huge, so sudden, that MGM speeded it into general release in March so as to avoid the rush of similar subjects that were now either in preparation or completion. At the best of times Hollywood is not really a creative place: it is an imitative industry in which only a few creative people are tolerated at any one time. What is imitated is the last big success; and in these jittery times, one man's success the night before could be another man's imitation the morning after.

This was being proved by the cycle of courtroom melodramas that had begun to appear at the start of the year. Everyone, it seemed, wanted to go to court. That was where the action was – or, rather, that was where the non-action was. Such movies had obvious attractions: they were cheap and quick to make, required few sets, even when obligatory 'flashbacks' from the evidence were involved; and, above all, they gave the studios ample opportunity to do what they had spent many millions equipping themselves for – namely, talk. The courtroom dramas now swelled the volume of talk already cascading over the public to torrential proportions. The dam really burst in these early months of 1929.

The Bellamy Trial (23 January 1929), an MGM production directed by Monta Bell and starring Leatrice Joy and Betty Bronson, was one long courtroom scene punctuated by flashbacks. But its whodunit plot did have some novelties on display. It opened without title or cast credits: simply a newsreel-type prologue of documentary impact leading up to the court-house and the start of the trial, a device calculated to gain authority from the public's familiarity with the new sound newsreels. There were also whispering scenes in court: for some reason, the use of whispers impressed reviewers of the early talkies and if there are any at all in a film, they are sure to draw comment. First National's *His Captive Woman* (2 April 1929), directed by George Fitzmaurice, also opened in a courtroom where Dorothy Mackaill was on trial for murdering her rich lover who 'had picked her up and for a time fondled her in luxury'. Then into the witness stand stalks Milton Sills, as the lawman who had been sent to arrest her, and the film went from dialogue into a lengthy, and silent, flashback to the couple's shipwreck on a desert island and Dorothy's redemption by strong sea breezes and the love of an honest man. 'Originally this may have been an interesting story,' said one reviewer, 'but in the operation of grafting dialogue into and on to it, First National have so strained, twisted, pummelled and otherwise mistreated plausibility that the resultant product is pretty silly. And now the thoroughly familiar courtroom scene will not qualify as so hot.'[10] Fox's melodrama *Through Different Eyes* (13 April 1929), directed by John

[10] *Variety*, 10 April 1929.

Above, Constance Bennett, wet through, has stripped to flimsy undergarments in order to dry out: Regis Toomey, like all gentlemen film heroes, averts his eyes. *Rich People* (1929) was one of a bunch of sophisticated comedies turned out by Pathé in the early period of the talkies. *Below*, Stage players in a stage grouping, most of them emoting with what one reviewer called 'too much tonsil' English accents, made *Strange Cargo* (1929) into the kind of 'talkie' that made audiences yearn for the days when movies moved.

Blystone, fared a little better because of its ingenious construction. It featured Mary Duncan, Edmund Lowe and Warner Baxter in a series of events that have precipitated a murder trial, then it repeated the events from the different and conflicting viewpoint of each character. A *Rashomon*-type device. *The Trial of Mary Dugan* (29 March 1929) and *Madame X* (24 April 1929) were other examples of the genre which I shall comment on in the next chapter.

The sheer volume of words mostly issuing from poor stories amidst over-familiar sets could not fail to have the effect it did: it generated a second and now more concerted backlash against the talkies, or, rather, the photographed stageplay replete with dialogue that was used to tell the story in the place of cinematic action. Irritation with 'talky' talkies increases in the correspondence columns of the fan magazines in and around March 1929, and the critics and correspondents, taking their cue from readers, reflect it with more considered exasperation in their columns – even those critics who had hitherto gone along with the new invention now begin to wonder what monster they have helped into the world. Welford Beaton does a *volte face* right after Christmas and the New Year finds him crusading against the 'photographed stageplay' with a ferocity that amounts to mania and in fact deprives *Film Spectator* of a great deal of its value until its editor comes to terms with things about a year later. In March 1929 he was noting with relish that 'the dialogue picture seems to be entirely without friends. . . . Every bunch of clippings I receive from the East shows that the newspapers are rapidly losing their enthusiasm for dialogue pictures.'[11] This was an overstatement: the enthusiasm of the newspapers was kept topped up by the huge increase in advertising for the talkies. But they, too, paid attention to disgruntled readers. There were now many of these, mostly, one suspects, belonging to an older generation which now could not avoid the talkies when they went to the pictures.[12] Beaton jubilantly quoted a selection of critics. The *Evening World*'s George Gerhard: 'We have had so many complaints about talking pictures that we asked seventeen friends at random what they thought about them. Fourteen employed the word 'lousy' and not one had a word of praise for the talkies.' Crighton Peet in the *New York Post*: 'The talkies seem to be a tremendous success – and yet – and yet – the number of movie patrons who are complaining and grumbling is amazing.' The *New York Telegram*'s Katherine Zimmerman: 'The appeal of the talking picture to the general public will never be through profound or scintillating dialogue.'

Now the severe disenchantment of such sentiments springs not from the sheer quality of the voices doing the talking, but from the sheer quantity of the talk itself. It is indicative of what was happening on the Hollywood scene. A shift of obligation was taking place – a shift away

[11] *Film Spectator*, 18 March 1929.
[12] See Chapter 12 for a fuller discussion of the audiences' attitudes.

from the screen performers to prove they had voices which suited the talkies and towards the screen directors to prove that *they* had the skill to mix judicious amounts of talk with the desire for action which the public was now increasingly missing. People throughout 1929 began to hear the real stars talking for the first time. It was a novel experience. But like most novelties connected with the talkies, it hardly lasted overnight. No sooner had the gods and goddesses proved they, or most of them, had voices than the cry went up, 'Don't just stand there talking – *do* something.'

10 'Kiss scenes have them rolling in the aisles.'

A lot of the panic among the stars facing the prospect of 'talking' was self-induced. Actors, and film actors more than most, live in a fairly permanent state of anxiety; and it did not help the Hollywood stars to cope with their crises when they discovered that they were not first on the list of worries at the front-office. One can only imagine the endless process of decision-making that sound required of harassed company executives aware that if they made the wrong choice, or missed the right opportunity, it would not be simply a set-back for their studio – it might be utter extinction. The last name on their lists of the day's appointments in those early months was liable to be that of a star, pampered at the best of times, now hysterically demanding answers to questions that had not even been formulated. Stars in any case were as safe as contracts could make them: which was usually very safe. They could wait. They would still be around when the dust settled and one could count the casualties. And if they themselves were among the casualties, then thank God one had not wasted precious time or money in pacifying and reassuring a wasting asset. Moreover, the argument ran, wasn't it good for stars to be made to feel dependent on the hand that rewarded them, and which some of them consistently tried to bite? Either way, it wouldn't be harmful to leave them aside for the moment while it was determined how many metres of cement were needed for the new sound stage, and whether disc or optical recording was the better bet. It is often alleged that sound was used as a weapon to ruin the stars. This is baseless. To tame and in some instances humiliate them – yes. But no studio with any corporate responsibility set out deliberately to wreck its own valued and fragile assets in whom so many years of grooming and promotion had been invested and to whom the public stayed extraordinarily loyal.

Alibi (1929) was praised for the realism of characters 'who appear to mean what they say'. A crook melodrama, it was largely cast from stage folk imported for the film version and they included Regis Toomey (with Irma Harrison) playing a 'smiling cop' and 'setting a new style in film heroes', according to one reviewer.

Nancy Carroll in *The Dance of Life* (1929) – 'natural and charming,' said *Photoplay*, 'and uses her head for something besides her permanent wave.'

Of course the front office was mesmerised for a few months by the stage candidates for movie stardom coming from Broadway. But it would not have taken long for Mayer, Thalberg, Zukor, Fox, Laemmle, Lasky and the rest of the moguls to see where the fans' affections were directed. A few signal successes from the movie veterans' ranks confirmed that stars whose voices registered well – and as sound improved, so did the numbers of the 'reprieved' increase – could actually add to their popularity, as well as their employers' profitability: which was another reason for holding on to contract artists. Even in present-day Hollywood some things are only done for the negative purpose of denying a rival the chance of doing them. But the businessmen would not have been acting according to their own initiative if they had not kept their stars in a state of uneasy dependence so that stiffer terms could be exacted from them for an assured future in the talkies. Sound was a great disciplining force: it had arrived at the handiest possible moment when many stars were demanding fees that the box-office recession of 1926–27 could not have gone on sustaining. Sound gave the front office a technological purchase on the ever-shifting demands of stars and agents for more and still more money. Sound enabled them to be shaken from their haughty and costly perch – and made grateful for the cheaper seed at the bottom of the cage.

Unfortunately we possess very few candid accounts of what it felt like to be a silent-picture star in the brief transition era. But one who has recorded it is Adolphe Menjou. He was in his last year of his Paramount contract in 1929, being paid 8,500 dollars a week, therefore highly vulnerable to the economics of sound. 'I was a silent film actor,' he later wrote,

> so nobody thought I could act in the talkies. . . . I knew that unless I proved I could talk before my contract expired, I would be a dead pigeon. I went after every Paramount big-shot in Hollywood demanding a voice test. Finally it was arranged. . . . What a painful experience that was! I came out of the projection room a chastened man. Only one thought consoled me: the test proved that I could talk; there was nothing wrong with my voice. . . . So I knew there was still hope for me if Paramount would fit me into a picture. But that was something of a hurdle, for Paramount was busy making pictures with people who had stage experience. The pictures weren't very good, but they talked, and that was all the fans wanted. I sat around drawing my salary for quite a while before somebody decided that I was an expensive bit of overhead and that, good or bad, I ought to draw at the box-office.[1]

But this is not the whole story. Menjou did not actually 'sit around'. He played the moguls at their own game. He was a good tactician. Though

[1] *It Took Nine Tailors*, by Adolphe Menjou (Sampson Low, Marston & Co., London, 1950), pp. 184–5.

Above, 'Ann Harding's superb performance belongs on the stage, not on the screen', wrote a critic of her in *Her Private Affair* (1929), in which she played a woman who stumbles into a killing. 'If I were to spend an evening discussing matters with Miss Harding,' the reviewer continued, 'and she spoke to me in exactly the same manner as she speaks in *Her Private Affair* . . . I would do one of two things: I would rush screaming from the house, or remain a little while longer and choke her to death.' *Below*, 'I knew that unless I proved I could talk before my contract expired, I would be a dead pigeon.' *Fashions in Love* (1929) provided Adolphe Menjou with the chance, playing a temperamental musician who flirted with women. He also appeared in the film playing the piano and singing – obviously covering all his options. The girl is Miriam Seegar.

Pittsburgh-born, his screen image of an elegant philanderer, as well as earlier acting experience in silent French films, had made European audiences think of him as one of them; and he now began hinting to the Press that, failing a new contract, he would be off to France 'where my type of picture is flourishing better than in the United States'. He had this advantage: he spoke fluent French. His chance came when Jannings departed in a huff – Jannings, as has been mentioned, *did not* speak fluent English – and Menjou inherited his role of a temperamental musical genius in *Fashions in Love* (30 June 1929). He played it with such personal command of its eccentricities that it is impossible to imagine the ponderous Jannings as the polished philanderer whose power over women is as much a part of his life as the onion soup prepared for him by a patient wife. Audiences relished the sight of the egocentric composer having his grey hairs touched up by this naïve woman, who also feeds him warm milk for his singing voice and sees that he looks his best when he departs for a secret interlude with a vivacious but maddening flapper who suggests mountain-climbing as an amusement for the maestro. Menjou sang and played the piano in the film. His deft self-satirising touch, aided by a French accent, was best revealed in the mountain-hut scene where the girl is slipping into something looser and Menjou, tinkering with the concert grand in this rustic hideout, is distracted from impending seduction by the discovery of an unbearably wrong note.

But even after the good notices he got – 'His wonderful command of gesture and emotion are more than ever admirable,' wrote an English critic, 'as is his ability to express a wealth of meaning in the smallest movement.'[2] – Paramount remained silent. 'It had decided that if it waited long enough it could get me back at a reduced salary.' To create attention, the wily Menjou now gave out that he was going into partnership with American Sound Records Ltd, to direct and star in pictures, and would receive twenty per cent of the world net. This was good strategy, as the last thing studio executives like is an actor obtaining commmercial advantage: it is liable to give other stars ideas. Menjou, right-wing by inclination although a man who loyally supported fellow actors in Equity's abortive attempt in 1927 to unionise the movie colony, now called on his friend William Randolph Hearst. The connection paid off. The *Los Angeles Examiner*, one of Hearst's two papers in that city, came out with an editorial in praise of Menjou, alleging he might have been the victim of discrimination on account of his support for the actors and deploring any attempts by a conclave of producers to blacklist 'this good American and . . . leading screen actor'. After that thunderous hint from a paper that lavished free column-space on the movie studios, Menjou was swiftly back into the talkies. In view of his stance in the 1947 McCarthy-ite enquiry, when he blithely informed on artists whose Communist sympathies *he* suspected,

[2] *Film Weekly*, 28 August 1929.

his own threatened blacklisting in the 1920s is a piquant and little-known episode.

Douglas Fairbanks Sr talked in his first talkie with such characteristic energy that his voice shattered a valve in the recording room and the microphone had to be moved well away from him till he learned to modulate his ringing tones. The film was *The Iron Mask* (21 February 1929), directed by Allan Dwan. As far as its sound qualities were concerned, this swashbuckler was a more prudent step for Fairbanks than he was accustomed to taking, for he feared that words would get in the way of his acrobatics. The compromise was to make a film that was a 'declamatory' rather than a 'talkie'. It had a spoken prologue and epilogue in which Fairbanks, as D'Artagnan, talked direct to the audience and made great use of a rousing verse which ended, 'Come stir your souls / With our ringing call / Of "All for one / And one for all." ' He spoke, in all, no more than about one and a half minutes: it must be added, though, that some historians now believe he used a voice double. In the re-issue of the film, Doug Jr. 'played' his father's voice.

Fairbanks's wife Mary Pickford took more of a risk in *her* first talkie, *Coquette* (5 April 1929), in which she not only used a Deep South accent (which irritated some of her fans) but also stepped out of the image of the 'little mother', the Victorian child laden with curls and responsibilities, which had assured her the affections of millions in the cinema's more innocent days. Shedding her curls for a shingled style and opening her mouth for speech were both liberating gestures, Mary felt, in tune with 'the modern age' when she might actually experience grown-up love. She was then in her mid-thirties and had been more or less 'playing the child' since she entered movies. The novelty of hearing 'America's Sweetheart' speak on the screen compensated fans for the occasion she had picked: for Mary and tragedy did not mix well. She played a girl who flirts with a young man a social notch below her; her father objects and shoots the youth. To save her parent, the daughter pleads she was being assaulted – whereupon Papa seizes the gun, a courtroom exhibit, and shoots himself. Sam Taylor's style of direction was coeval with the melodrama. 'Mary appears too austere for the unsophisticated character she is supposed to represent,' one English critic complained; but it was conceded that 'she talks fairly well, considering she is asked to assume an affected Southern accent.'[3] Obviously the voice-tests made with the original Broadway cast of *Coquette* had repaid study. Mordaunt Hall wrote:

> Miss Pickford's bobbed hair improves her looks. She is the woman, too grown up for this particular (role), but none the less attractive. Occasionally one perceives in her walk the shy shape of the Mary with curls. She wears gowns instead of frocks and does not permit herself to pout, although she has a pleasing child-like smile.[4]

[3] Ibid., 30 September 1929.   [4] *The New York Times*, 6 April 1929.

For Mary Pickford, sound films meant growing up in other ways, too. Long confined by her fans to 'little girl' roles, America's Sweetheart shingled her hair and sought a role that demanded no 'little girl's' voice, but a young woman's – and a Southern drawl at that. *Coquette* (1929) also featured a bevy of male admirers.

'Gloria Swanson is going to be paralysing picturegoers with her voice', was one trade prediction of her first talkie, *The Trespasser* (1929). And she did, with her singing voice as well as the one she reserved for speech. She played a wife who was left in the lurch with a young child by her weak-willed husband. The limbs here belong to the child actor, Wally Albright.

The performance won her an Oscar at the 1930 awards. But there is evidence of what even a superstar like Mary Pickford had to put up with at this date in the talkie revolution, for a fuse blew two minutes after the première started at the Rivoli Theater, New York. The organist gamely tried to cover up the loss of sound, but a start had to be made again. At the second attempt to project the film, all the audience heard at first were flashes of dialogue, accompanied by faint music. It was a perceptible time before words could be distinguished; and even when intelligible, they were unsatisfactory as regards sound.

Confident of their individual talkie successes, but conscious of the need to keep their audiences, especially as their marriage was under strain and would soon break up, Fairbanks and Pickford ran their respective appeals together in *The Taming of the Shrew* (30 November 1929), the first time they had shared the screen, if one excepts Mary's fleeting appearance in Fairbanks's *The Gaucho* as a visionary Madonna with a penny sparkler throwing a halo around her. The film is surprisingly successful, within its own terms, which were not Shakespeare's. Speaking verse was a disciplining experience for Doug: he makes an excellent shrew-tamer. Pickford proves an unexpectedly resilient slapstick artist, being slapped, taking pratfalls and landing in the mud among the pigs and, as *Variety* said, 'all for 75 cents'. Reports that the two superstars were going to essay Shakespeare caused misgivings to exhibitors – the Bard was traditionally box-office poison. United Artists replied – whether naïvely or not, one can't be sure – that it would be done *as comedy*. 'Then that's okay,' was the reply from 'the sticks'. Just to make sure the film was not contaminated in advance by highbrow expectations, it was publicised with the aid of four railroad cars plastered with bills for the film in the style of a travelling circus. The cost was 75,000 dollars; but United Artists hoped to redeem this by asking exhibitors to pay rentals half as high again for a film with the two stars in it as for one with Mary or Doug as the sole attraction. *The Taming of the Shrew* had its sneak preview at Knoxville, Tennessee, since it was claimed that more Elizabethan pronounciation was used in the Appalachians than anywhere else in America. This promotional wheeze fixed attention on the fact, which might have escaped the hinterland, that it was *a talkie*; but scholars who might have been taken in by it were jolted when they read amongst the credits 'Additional Dialogue by Sam Taylor', scarcely an Elizabethan talent. Though a good deal of snide fun has been had with this example of Hollywood persiflage, the severely shortened version of Shakespeare's play – sixty-five minutes which whizz by due to the performers' brio – has a fairly honourable ancestry. It is the version toured by David Garrick under the title *Katharine and Petruchio*, and even on the boards was only a third of the full text (and probably had some of Garrick's 'additional dialogue', too!) James Agate made a pithy observation on Mary's 'new' image as the shrew. 'No actress who looks like the flower should really hope to be convincing as

Above, Clara Bow, in her first talkie *The Wild Party* (1929), was judged to have 'enough of a voice to reinsure the general belief that (she) can speak as well as look – not so well, but enough'. She played what was described as 'a champ necker and flame of the campus' who got her sights on her professor, Fredric March. *Below*, Bingo, child of the jungle . . . otherwise Joan Crawford in her first talkie, *Untamed* (1929). Her talkie debut, opening with some snappy steps in the fetid swamplands, cannily capitalised on her most popular attribute, which had nothing to do with her voice. She gained culture in succeeding reels.

the serpent under it. . . . Miss Pickford cannot hope to be at once the world's sweetheart and the world's worst-tempered woman.'[5] But he conceded that 'it is enormously to her credit that she tries to forget about the first, and pretends to be the second'.

Clara Bow picked her talkie debut wisely: she played a 'champ necker and flame of the campus' in Dorothy Arzner's *The Wild Party* (1 April 1929). Her voice proved rather flat; but it was 'good enough to reinsure the general belief that she can speak as well as look – not so well, but enough'.[6] Fredric March, as the professor she makes a play for, 'reigns supreme' in the voice department. But it is pretty certain that Clara's fans did not prove fussy about the vocal tones of a film declared by Mordaunt Hall to be 'a production for dwarfed intellects'. What gave Clara Bow most trouble was not her vocal shortcomings, but her restlessness. Even when she stood still in her films, she seemed to be in motion – as if the Jazz Age was galvanising her bones. This constant anticipatory jiggle while men were around (which they generally were) was a handicap when she had to stay close to the still immobile (and immobilising) microphones. She would be all over the set before the monitor cabin signalled her voice was not registering: then she would stand and curse the mike. Perhaps it is this kind of tantrum that persuaded Dorothy Arzner to take the mike to her in *The Wild Party*. In any case, her capricious physicality carries her vocal weakness: 'when Clara flashes a gam,' said *Variety*, 'all senses are deadened'.

Another Paramount star, George Bancroft, a star of three silent films about the underworld all directed by Josef von Sternberg, was successfully ushered into the sound era by the same director in a fourth gangster movie. *Thunderbolt* (20 June 1929) allowed him to personify a sort of primitive manhood charged with potent but corrupt energy, as a gang boss sent to the Big House before he can murder the kid his moll has fallen for: he intrigues to have the boy sent to the opposite cell on Death Row. Herman J. Mankiewicz wrote the dialogue, but von Sternberg's own mischievous cynicism probably infected it. Contemporary reviewers reacted with a certain moral confusion to the inclusion of such characters as a piano-playing, hymn-singing black killer and a comic warder talking cosily about the electric chair as if it were a suite of rooms in a particularly choice hotel. Ordered by the front office to work light relief into the film, von Sternberg responded with characteristic contempt – and had a convict sing 'Rock-a-bye Baby' as Bancroft bludgeons a fellow felon. At the height of his fame in the early talkies, Bancroft was being paid 5,000–6,000 dollars weekly.

Over at MGM, where Douglas Shearer was chief sound engineer, his sister Norma received particularly careful treatment when she made her first all-talkie. (It was also no handicap to have married the studio's

[5] *Around Cinemas, Second Series,* by James Agate (Home & Van Thal, London, 1948), p. 26.

[6] *Variety,* 3 April 1929.

production chief, Irving Thalberg, in 1927.) *The Trial of Mary Dugan*, adapted and directed by Bayard Veillier from his own play, was a 'foolproof' vehicle, a murder-trial plot with a visual twist at the end when the real killer is exposed as he instinctively catches a knife with his *left* hand. To make things doubly sure, the film was rehearsed intensively for two weeks in front of a studio audience, as if it were still a play, before being committed to the cameras. Mordaunt Hall thought it 'highly effective. . . . The vocal reproduction and the acting are capital, in fact there is a marked naturalism in the voices throughout nearly all the scenes', although he tut-tutted over incidental sounds like the courtroom laughter 'which reaches a point where it is dangerously near that of an audience watching a comedy'.[7] It is interesting that several critics comment adversely on Norma Shearer's 'whimpering hysterics' in the prologue, when she is taken out of her cell into court. Some doubted if audiences could stand such unfettered emotion. Dialogue was one thing: but screen passions might embarrass if rendered audible. We shall shortly see how just this unappreciated bit of group psychology proved to be in the case of the talkies' most renowned fatality.

Joan Crawford met the talkies with her usual brand of determination and confidence. *Untamed* (29 November 1929) directed by Jack Conway, wasn't released till the end of the year; and her fans did not care if the English spoken by Bingo, child of the jungle and daughter of a father almost permanently stunned by booze and heat, did rather ape a lady striving for poise rather than a girl reared in a foetid swampland. Crawford's physical animation compensated for vocal deficiencies; and by applying her strenuous mastery to the novel demands made on her, she soon improved.

Gloria Swanson must have turned with relief to her first talkie, *The Trespasser* (1 November 1929) after the ordeal of *Queen Kelly*. Von Stroheim had begun directing the latter as a silent drama in October 1928, at the FBO Studios which were part-owned by Swanson's good friend Joseph P. Kennedy. The intended budget was 228,000 dollars, though this didn't include Swanson's salary which was then around 10,000 dollars weekly. Shooting was two-thirds completed by the New Year, at a cost of 750,000 dollars, when von Stroheim was abruptly dismissed. It seems that Swanson and Kennedy (a prominent Roman Catholic layman) were nervous of the erotic content that the director had succeeded in putting back into scenes which the Hays Office had cleansed before officially blessing for filming. But the arrival of the talkies also made the producer nervous of releasing a movie with just a synchronised music-track. Thus *Queen Kelly* became the sound era's most prominent victim, though at first Edmund Goulding, Hollywood's adroit film 'doctor', was assigned to prepare a talkie version of it. But by February 1929, he had given up any idea of a talking version and settled for grafting dialogue on to about forty-five per cent

[7] *The New York Times*, 29 March 1929.

of the already shot material. By March 1929, when Benjamin Glazer was reported to be writing a new ending, the cost had climbed to over 800,000 dollars. By April 1929 desperate attempts were being made to cut the film to about five reels – von Stroheim is said to have planned thirty reels – which would have brought the budget up to the million mark. Thereafter the film drops out of the news, until Swanson had a tragic ending written for the first part – the prince's abduction of a convent girl and her suicide – and filmed under Irving Thalberg's direction. It was shown in Europe in the early 1930s. But by then Swanson had enjoyed the consolation of making one of the most sensational talkie debuts of the 1920s.

Goulding directed her in *The Trespasser*, in which she played a working-class girl who marries a rich youth. The boy's father objects, separation follows and Swanson holds on to their child, eventually doing battle with her father-in-law. If it seems weary, unpropitious material, that is not how it played. The psychology of its characters was well developed: it stayed on this side of Victorian melodrama. And Swanson received more praise for her devoted mother than many an earlier role had brought her. Her voice particularly was a triumph: at least after she got over her initial 'mike fright' which caused her to forget her lines, by having them written on the shirt front or pinned to the jacket of the man she was addressing. She had also been taking singing lessons: this paid off handsomely with a song called 'Love, Your Magic Spell is Everywhere'. 'She sings like a *prima*. . . . In all of the talkers, all of the controversy about voice and delivery, from stage to screen, there has been no better surprise than this singing voice. With her dialogue after that, of course, there is no question.'[8] It was the first major American talkie to open in Europe first. It also exhibited the flexibility that was becoming part of every inventive director's approach to talkies. Goulding managed to shoot fifteen minutes of film in one day, using twelve cameras and filming nine set-ups on one stage all at once. The scene was a large office; and the players carried the dialogue from place to place as the camera and its microphone travelled together while desks, mounted on castors, were silently pushed out of their way. It anticipated Hitchcock's famous ten-minute take by quite a few decades: it also took nine hours to set up and two to shoot.

As already mentioned, Ruth Chatterton had to wait for *Madame X* to gain popular acclaim. It was a near-perfect formula melodrama – mother defended by a lawyer who, unknown to him, is actually her son. But she had not been slow to learn camera techniques. As *Fortune* magazine commented, 'She has picked up the tricks of posture and facial angle that the stars use to make the camera kind to them, so that . . . she has even appeared to have a beauty she was thought to lack before.'[9] She had wisely adopted a little more of the 'common touch'. The plot permitted her 'aristocratic tones' to become a little roughened as she

[8] *Variety*, 18 September 1929.   [9] *Fortune*, October 1930.

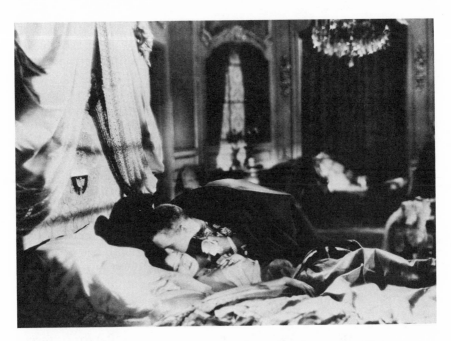

Above, John Barrymore, in his first talkie *General Crack* (1929), was rapped for 'squandering his talent on bedroom twaddle'. *Below*, But the obvious virility of his speaking tones was so satisfactory, compared to poor John Gilbert's, that it aroused less comment than the shapeliness of his lower limbs and his left profile. He played a mercenary who hires his army out to the Emperor of Austria and learns, too late, that his gipsy wife has been part of the deal. Barrymore's love scenes were so intense that his partner (Marion Nixon) had a hard job getting in a word of her own.

came down the social scale and took to drink, becoming a teeny bit *louche* and interjecting a few slang words, with only an occasional sentence or turn of phrase that bespoke her well-bred past. She became in fact more like the fans who went to her films, rather less like the *grande dame* of Broadway she had been.

John Barrymore had delayed quite a few months before letting himself be heard on the screen: then it was in *General Crack* (3 December 1929), an historical potboiler about a mercenary who hires out his armies to the Emperor of Austria but neglects to recognise the essential lightness of his gypsy wife's morals till he learns, too late, that she is part of the deal. The direction was hack-work, skimping on every chance of spectacle for the kind of token action summed up by one critic who wrote that 'a few expert passes and side-swipes and the Hussars control the country'. Barrymore was rapped for squandering his histrionic talents on 'bedroom twaddle'. His shapely limbs were shown off to such advantage by his tight breeches that they evoked more comment than his very satisfactory voice – though James Shelley Hamilton, editor of a perceptive but short-lived monthly called *Cinema*, shrewdly commented,

> It appears – as some have suspected – that the Barrymore voice is more important than the Barrymore profile. Mr Barrymore went blonde in more senses than of donning a wig in some of the costumed contraptions he has been exhibiting himself in, but the sound of his voice puts something gritty and muscular back into him. He is a credible leader of an army, a credible defier of emperors, when he can be heard. His fondness for grimacing, as it seemed when he was silent, becomes an effective method of acting when words from his mouth accompany it.[10]

If anyone exceeded Barrymore in the sort of personal cachet and stage distinction he used to give status to the talkies it was George Arliss. His success story is almost incredible, particularly as he is held in fairly low esteem when his films are viewed today. Talkies not only gave him a second Hollywood career – he had made silent films there – but a pre-eminence he could never otherwise have achieved in the film colony. What studios were hungering for in mid-1929 was the sort of prestige for sound pictures that Adolph Zukor had gained for silent features in the first decade of the century by signing up 'famous players' from the stage. (Of course he soon found it was screen stars who gave him his profit.) Arliss gave the talkies what the industry called 'class'. When the American Academy of Arts and Letters awarded him their gold medal for diction, he said in reply,

> What we actors should do is set a worthy example which the youth of today may be inspired to follow. . . . Not that the masses go to the movies to learn how to speak; but young people are inclined to be

[10] *Cinema*, February 1930.

Above, Ruth Chatterton (here in the arms of Ulrich Haupt) was one of the greatest successes to come from the Broadway stage and take on the 'talkers' on the strength of her skill with dialogue. She had Lionel Barrymore directing her, too, in *Madame X* (1929), described as 'the tale of a thoroughbred woman going down the line to become an absinthe wretch'. *Below*, Sound gave George Arliss a pre-eminence in Hollywood he never attained in the silent era. His precise diction and English accent gave the new invention the stamp of 'class' – and his recognisably 'superior' speaking powers were in turn given contractual status by his billing as 'Mr' George Arliss in the credits of his films. *Disraeli* (1929), in which he played with his compatriot Anthony Bushell, retained the staginess of his Victorian gestures, but made him into the mouthpiece of the new medium.

very imitative, particularly of those actors whom they especially admire.[11]

It is doubtful if Warner Brothers saw themselves as speech therapists for underprivileged youth; but it did not matter greatly since the talkie Arliss made for them, *Disraeli* (2 October 1929), drew universal praise and profits. It conferred on Arliss the prestige that had lately fallen from Jannings, and allowed Hollywood in general to pose as a patron of art.

Variety turned sniffily from consideration of *General Crack* to *Disraeli* with the remark that the latter 'is demonstrating that film audiences can be exhilarated without aphrodisiacs'.[12] The film was a series of sketches featuring Arliss as Disraeli, relishing his various plots and stratagems to obtain control of the Suez Canal. Between statesman-like acts of cunning, were seen a love of gardening and peacocks, and a tenderly blossoming romance of a Government colleague played by that equally gentlemanly English actor, Anthony Bushell. The scenes were dingy, the House of Commons (or the part of it shown) had the cramped dimensions of a jury box in a local court. But Arliss held it all together with his nuanced voice, steely egoism and stage reputation, so that even Frank T. Daugherty, a tough judge of what unlettered exhibitors could profitably show in their cinemas, wrote, 'It will certainly make exhibition history . . . it has shown us the talking picture is no hindrance to intelligence, but, as a medium, is capable of the very highest artistic achievement.'[13]

Something of the same prestige was brought into films by an American actor who also became a status-object. Paul Muni had been signed up by William Fox after viewing a screen test made in New York by this actor from the Yiddish Art Theater. It was an eight-minute sketch – but it found room for seven different impersonations. Fox belatedly boasted of having found 'a Chaney who talks', and offered him a seven-year contract, starting at 500 dollars and rising to three times that in the third year: big money for a beginner. But Muni was rushed into a prosaic adaptation of a one-act play about a heroic prisoner called *The Valiant* (12 May 1929). When Fox viewed the real Muni without his transforming make-up, he wanted to junk the film and release the screen test: its budget was slashed, so was its running time to just sixty-six minutes. To everyone's surprise, Muni was singled out by the critics for his rich, pleasant, strongly resonant voice. 'If he is not pretty,' said one, 'neither is Lon Chaney nor Emil Jannings, and Muni has what these fellows have not: dialogue utility.'[14] Despite this endorsement, the movie was faltering in its initial screenings till advertisements suddenly appeared in the New York papers signed 'S. L. Rothafel' – 'Roxy', as he

[11] *George Arliss, by himself* (John Murray, London, 1940), pp. 127–8.
[12] *Variety*, 31 December 1930.
[13] *Film Spectator*, 30 November 1930.
[14] *Variety*, 15 May 1929.

'What was I? Rugged, maybe. Not handsome. Leading men had to be Adonises. I didn't qualify.' Thus Paul Muni on his debut in *The Valiant* (1929) with Marguerite Churchill. Critics disagreed. 'Paul Muni is splendid', said *The New York Times*.

Who could ever have doubted that Greta Garbo and the talkies would take to each other? Prudently, though, she delayed her debut till sound recording and reproduction had improved, then played the title role of *Anna Christie* (1930), a Swede like herself. Her surprisingly low, husky voice added a mystery to her already vivid screen presence, although the lady herself later said sceptically, 'Did you ever hear any Swede talk like that?'

was known, after his super-cinema. The showman declared his faith in the film and, more significantly, underlined the 'local boy' starring in it – 'Paul Muni, formerly known on the stage as Muni Wiesenfriend'.[15] The support of Jewish audiences, particularly in a showbusiness capital, was crucial for many an impresario's success: *The Jazz Singer*'s earliest appeal had been an ethnic one, even before it became a Jolson one, and the *Disraeli* film had gained custom by being advertised as 'The tale of a wily Oriental (a period euphemism for 'Jew') who had the Western World where he wanted it'. Response to the appeal on behalf of Muni was instantaneous and cumulative – so big that Fox hastily scheduled another movie for him, this time exploiting his chameleon-like capacity for character changes in the amply named *Seven Faces* (15 November 1929) in which he played Don Juan, a cockney, Franz Schubert, Diablero (a Svengali-type hypnotist), Napoleon, a black boxer and a museum caretaker. This production was released in November 1929 – and it is said to have swiftly decided Lon Chaney to change his mind and talk for the first time in his own multiple-character films.

Talk, as has been mentioned, was a crucial problem for a man with a thousand faces, none of which the public believed to be his own. To hear a person's voice was to begin to know him – voices dissipated Chaney's kind of mystery. 'How do I keep the illusion?' he asked Thalberg whose answer, as frequently happened, was the sort of solution that stares everyone in the face. Use several voices – keep them guessing which one is really yours. It meant reverting to the career he had before he appeared in films, as a stock company 'utility man', able to jump into any part, from a 'Dutch' comic to an English dude. 'I was always afraid we'd play *Uncle Tom's Cabin*,' he said once, 'and I'd have to fill in for one of the bloodhounds.' His earlier insistence that he would 'never' do talkies diminished rapidly when he got a new contract in 1929, giving him 5,000 dollars a week.

The film destined to be his first – and only – talkie was a remake of one of his greatest silent successes, *The Unholy Three* (4 July 1930), first directed by Todd Browning in 1925 with Chaney as Professor Echo, a sideshow ventriloquist in public, a ruthless gang leader offstage and a master of multiple disguises including that of a sweet little old lady. It was a clever choice for a talkie. It allowed him five voices in all, including a smooth and mellow one for the stage illusionist (who even throws his voice amongst the audience), a rougher one for ordering the gang about and, finally, highpitched, tremulous tones for the old lady. This last disguise proves his undoing – when his voice drops accidentally to its normal male register while he is under intensive courtroom questioning. 'Doubling', or dubbing, was still so suspect by filmgoers that Pete Smith, then MGM's publicity chief, who was soon to be succeeded by Howard Strickling, actually made Chaney sign an affidavit swearing that all the voices were his own. How he would have developed

[15] One of numerous variations on the spelling of the family name 'Weisenfreund'.

Above, The caption reads: 'Thumbs Up! This is the signal sound experts use to okay a scene. Lon Chaney and Jack Conway, his director, used it as a regular greeting while filming MGM's *The Unholy Three*, Chaney's first talkie.' It was also his last film: he died in August 1930, a few weeks after its release. *Below*, Talk didn't stop Harold Lloyd's visual slapstick. One reviewer of *Welcome Danger* (1929), his first talkie, found 'a consciousness of culture' when the comedian talked; but fortunately this was confined to his 'calmer' scenes.

in the talkie decade is unanswerable: for he died within weeks of *The Unholy Three*'s release. There is a horrible irony in the cause of death: throat cancer.

By coincidence Erich von Stroheim took his talkie test as a ventriloquist in *The Great Gabbo* (12 September 1929); and like Chaney he cleverly hooked the story's interest on to his vocal performance, rather than on to the Ben Hecht–Hugh Herbert story of an arrogant stage illusionist with Pagliacci heartbreak provoked by 'Otto' his stage dummy. Through the dummy's lips is enunciated the philosophy ('You get out of life what you put into it') of the girl, played by Betty Compson, for whom the ventriloquist has an unrequited love: there is more than a hint that the master believes he has endowed the dummy with a soul. Von Stroheim's guttural, bragging tones made a dramatic contrast with the *pianissimo* voice of the stage prop. They held the interest in a film whose director, James Cruze, may have mistrusted his star's appeal, since he kept interrupting the main story with a series of coloured sequences devoted to song-and-dance numbers from the accompanying stage acts. It was a symptom of 'Von's' low esteem in Hollywood at that date that the centre of the stage was being denied to him even when he confined his flamboyant talent to acting, not directing.

Talk did not inhibit Harold Lloyd's visual gags in his first sound film, *Welcome Danger* (20 October 1929): he remade it as a talkie after he had finished shooting it silent. Lloyd's voice wasn't any too strong and there was in it what *Variety* rather damningly called 'a consciousness of culture' – but fortunately this only obtruded in the 'calmer scenes'. The 'cultured undertones' could be overlooked when the slapstick took over. Playing his usual mild-mannered chap mixed up this time with Chinese cut-throats, he cleverly set some of the Chinatown scenes in darkened cellars so that the audience concentrated on the sound effects.

Marion Davies found the talkies no problem to her. If anything, her debut in *Marianne* (18 October 1929), a comedy about a French girl's adventures among the Doughboys in the First World War, proved she was as finely shaded a talking comedienne as she had been a silent mime. Offscreen, among her friends, she had a not unattractive little voice impediment. But there was no sign of a stutter when it came to speaking her lines.

One talent which the talkies suddenly inflated – only to collapse it later to its proper limits – was Jackie Oakie. By 1930 some people were calling him 'the only front-rank comic talent developed by the talkies'. *Fortune* magazine, whose business forecasts, we may hope, were more accurate than its comedy predictions, said, 'Oakie is on the way up, while the great foolers of the silent era like Lloyd and Chaplin are on the way out. He is the precursor of the great arch-clown of the future talkies who will some day convulse the world.'[16]

[16] *Fortune*, October 1930.

Three of the greatest female stars waited till very late in the day before letting themselves be heard in a talkie. One was Greta Garbo. A few forecasts had suggested that her strong Swedish accent would limit her possibilities. Instead, it intensified her exoticism – and MGM carefully chose *Anna Christie* (14 March 1930) for her debut after a sound-test taken in mid-1929 revealed an intriguing new dimension to her personality. Her accent, dour and fateful, was perfect for O'Neill's Swedish immigrant: Garbo, though, as ever apathetic about success, said later, 'Did you ever hear any Swede talk like that?' Certainly no one ever heard any eighteenth-century French aristocrat talk like Norma Talmadge in *Du Barry, Woman of Passion* (2 November 1930), her second talkie after a try-out in *New York Nights*. Her twangy tones aroused laughter when she attempted the title role in David Belasco's nineteen-year-old play, interlarded with hushed pauses and tableaux reminiscent of amateur theatricals. Mordaunt Hall gallantly decided to damn by omission when all he chose to discern in her performance was that she was at her best 'in scenes where her dark hair is covered with a powdered wig, which offers a most pleasing contrast to her bright, brown eyes'.[17] On seeing the film, her sister Constance is said to have cabled her: 'QUIT WHILE YOU'VE STILL GOT YOUR LOOKS AND BE THANKFUL FOR THE TRUST FUND MOTHER SET UP.' The advice was taken.

Lillian Gish waited till late in 1929 before committing herself to a talkie, and then chose none too wisely either, a version of Molnar's play *The Swan* entitled *One Romantic Night* (20 May 1930). Mordaunt Hall believed that her speaking role, as the little goose whom matrimony turns into a royal swan, rendered her acting more interesting than in the silent days. This was a distinctly minority view. James Shelley Hamilton said, 'Her voice is no notable addition to her power.' But what particularly dismayed admirers was her unaccustomed repose in the role. The poised, self-possessed princess was not the most sympathetic part for the bird-like, hoppity skippings escalating into frenzied hysteria which she had played with so many fine, subtle gradations in her silent movies like *The Scarlet Letter* and that masterpiece of pre-talkie days, *The Wind*. 'Her placid Alexandra is a negative person', said the discerning Hamilton, 'with no effect upon the action that centers on her, and people who are not acquainted with the character in the play may well wonder at the complacency with which she lets herself be handed from the tutor (who loves her) to the prince (who marries her).'[18] Molnar plays that took their material from a period now well and truly dead, except in the Middle-European hearts of Hollywood's immigrant moguls, proved antiquated vehicles for carrying stars into a new, more realistic sound era.

If one needed evidence of one silent star who recognised this and expertly adapted to the demands of the talkies, while another even greater star neglected it and was ruined by his fatal oversight, one has

[17] *The New York Times*, 3 November 1930. [18] *Cinema*, May 1930.

163

Above, Lillian Gish, like John Gilbert, chose Molnar for her talkie debut; and *One Romantic Night* (1930), a version of *The Swan*, though not as disastrous as *His Glorious Night*, cost her some of her magic, too. 'Rod La Rocque's uniform', the critic of *Cinema* added, 'is the most princely thing about him.' *Below*, John Gilbert, then at the peak of his celebrity, earning 250,000 dollars a film as the screen's pre-eminent 'Great Lover', leans confidently on the shoulder of Lionel Barrymore, his director, on the set of *His Glorious Night* (1929).

Gilbert's prowess at love-making, which had held the stones breathless on the silent screen, took on an unintentionally comic aspect at the very first ring of the repeated 'I love you' phrases designed to climax his passion for Catherine Dale Owen in *His Glorious Night*.

Ronald Colman felt justly confident about making the transition to sound in *Bulldog Drummond* (1929). Stills from the film betray the awkwardness of the studio photographer rather than Colman's bravado and brio. Ever the gentleman, he kept his jacket buttoned while he deigned to plant straight rights on jaws of assorted Orientals, one of whom must be having a hard time holding his pose.

only to look at the talkie debuts of Ronald Colman and John Gilbert. Both were prime examples of the silent screen's romantic archetype, the Great Lover: but only one of them realised the danger when love at last not only dared, but also *could* speak its name.

Sound had already split up Sam Goldwyn's amorous teaming of Colman and Banky. After four silent romances together, her thick Hungarian accent, while not disqualifying her for screen work, seemed more suited to a future as a Garbo-esque comedienne. Goldwyn's solution was shrewd. He deliberately turned Colman's style away from the ardours that silent films could project and into the insouciant charm that talkies could do so well, provided the actor had the looks and deftness. Sidney Howard, a leading Broadway playwright, adapted *Bulldog Drummond* (2 May 1929) and Richard Jones, a good 'service' director, put it through intensive rehearsals before Colman was committed to the microphone. Seeing the film today, one suspects he was instantly at ease: indeed it is his urbane, self-deprecating yet gallant, cultivated yet throw-away brand of charm that preserves the entertainment value of a film that opens wittily as the camera tracks up to the forbidding doors of a London club where the notice 'SILENCE' provides its own 'in' joke at that time. The members look either asleep or maybe dead until a servant drops a spoon. 'What is the meaning of this infernal din!' cries one of the blimps. This was followed by Colman's deliberately shattering the restored quiet of clubland by whistling – a sign of how fed up he is with stuffy inactivity, how eager he is for adventure. Then the film swiftly and disappointingly declines into stagey repartee largely confined to two sets, the kidnappers' mansion and the hero's nearby outpost in an inn. The acting in some cases is a throwback to the retarded delivery of *The Lights of New York* and a comedy flirtation between Drummond's ally Algy and a villainess is a crude and misjudged interlude. The ending is woeful anticlimax. Yet the film was immensely popular. It must have been almost entirely due to Colman's virile yet understated attitude to events and his total naturalness of speech. The talkies were here creating a new kind of hero, one whom you could tell was a gentleman just by the sound of his voice. Until the more brutal sexist appeal of Clark Gable came along, Colman was the leading male star of the new era. Crowds besieged the Apollo Theater at the New York première and Colman, escorting Mrs Goldwyn, bowed modestly to a huge audience that included Henry King, the director who had given him his chance of stardom opposite Lillian Gish in *The White Sister* (1923). At the end, to thunderous applause, he bowed again just as bashfully, then retired to his hotel leaving a specially imported English bulldog to do the brash work of publicity.

There could not have been a starker contrast with the scene a few months later at another New York première when Hollywood's most popular leading man of the times made his talkie debut – to the annihilating sound of derisive laughter.

John Gilbert's name is the one most frequently quoted as evidence of how sound 'ruined the stars'. That Gilbert's career declined precipitately and pathetically in the sound era cannot be denied: what is arguable, though, is whether his voice was the cause of it. My own contention is that it was not. If his voice was so unsatisfactory as to elicit laughter from those who heard its reputedly piping tones, why was such a fallen idol co-starring five years later with Greta Garbo in *Queen Christina*? That film demonstrates what a perfectly satisfactory voice he had *then*, in 1934. Yet it certainly is true that his first full-length talkie, *His Glorious Night* (5 October 1929), a Ruritanian-like romance drawn from Molnar, provoked such laughter that Gilbert was said to have turned ashen when he read the opening lines of *Variety*'s review. 'A few more talker productions like this and John Gilbert will be able to change places with Harry Langdon. His prowess at love-making which has held the stones breathless takes on a comedy aspect . . . that gets (them) tittering at first and then laughing outright at the very first ring of the couple of dozen "I love you" phrases designed to climax . . . the thrill of the Gilbert lines.'[19] One feels an awesome nemesis at work here. There Gilbert was, one minute the outstanding male on the screen, successor to Valentino, leading man to Greta Garbo in their silent movies, a love-object to millions who succumbed to his dash, chivalry and self-charging energy, being paid 10,000 dollars a week in 1929, 250,000 dollars a picture, with an iron-clad contract guaranteeing him a million dollars inside two years, in short the pride, joy and a good part of the corporate profit of MGM – and then, the next minute, without an interval, without warning, he is struck down, humbled, humiliated, rendered utterly ridiculous by that most withering weapon, the laughter of his once-adoring public.

Such, anyhow, is the myth. Like many myths, and nearly all movie myths, truth lies elsewhere. It was not an inadequate voice that ruined Gilbert: it was something lodged, unsuspected, in the audience's reaction to a certain kind of talkie. To understand that 'something', one must go back a few months. Gilbert's voice was not entirely unknown to movie-goers. He had already made that 'trailer' for MGM's new Empire Cinema, London, in which the hyperbole of the words he used was simply an audible rendering of the heightened vitality that Gilbert could produce in himself, like an erotic friction, when the part called for it in, say, *Flesh and the Devil* (1927) or *The Cossacks* (1928). John Gilbert was a romantic by conviction, whereas Rudolph Valentino had been one by adoption. In love scenes, Valentino always held something of himself in reserve; Gilbert gave all of himself to his fans, generously. On such a temperament, sound would be a constraint. A physical one, too, since such a passionate lover's vocal chords were liable to be tense when panting words as well as burning looks were the end products. But though Gilbert's voice in MGM's early all-star movie, *Hollywood Revue*

[19] *Variety*, 9 October 1929.

Above, Marianne (1929), a comedy about a French girl's adventures among the Doughboys, gave Marion Davies (with Lawrence Gray) the opportunity to prove that she was as finely shaded a talkie comedienne as she had been a silent-film mime. 'She does not need a series of planned "gags" because she *is* funny', wrote a reviewer. No doubt the prop moustache helped, however. *Below*, Ramon Novarro had taken over Valentino's mantle of the male sex symbol, and sound added a dimension to his well-exposed physique in *The Pagan* (1929) (with Dorothy Janis and Donald Crisp) by permitting him to sing 'The Pagan Love Song' so successfully that, as John Howard Lawson said, 'it choked the air waves for the next year or so'.

(dealt with in the next chapter) is certainly light-toned and high-pitched, there is nothing in any of the reports of this production to indicate that it aroused derisive laughter. Maybe filmgoers extended tolerance to the sound in general: the sound was on disc, therefore not as sharp or clear as it would be even a few months later. Another reason was perhaps to do with the sequence in *Hollywood Revue* in which Gilbert and Norma Shearer appeared. They did the balcony scene from *Romeo and Juliet*, first of all 'straight', then 'guying' it in modern paraphrase as a response to head office's orders to 'pep it up'. 'Julie, baby, . . . you're the cream in my Mocha and Java, the berries in my pie.' The joke's crudity is obvious; but what is also noticeable is how Gilbert's voice grows more relaxed as the scene turns into a running gag. In colloquial comedy like this, he feels, he *sounds* at ease. Audiences were cued that they were meant to laugh with him; perhaps they did not laugh *at* him in the more sober recitation because this was, well, Shakespeare. . . .

But when he made *His Glorious Night* he did not have the protection of a sacred text. No one apparently appreciated the risks they were running in putting Gilbert into a film where the one element that had never before counted for anything in his movies, romantic *dialogue*, would be pre-eminent. But then *His Glorious Night* was a rushed production in every sense. It was not the first full-length talkie Gilbert had *made*, though it was the first to be shown. MGM had put him into *Redemption*, an adaptation of Tolstoy's *The Living Corpse*, which was made in 1928–29 by Fred Niblo, then had sequences re-shot and re-edited with the participation of Lionel Barrymore. This story of a man's self-destruction, assisted by gambling fever, guilty hangovers, alcoholic intoxication and dialogue that sounded in every other line like oblique, prophetic comments on Gilbert's own coming ruin, so depressed the star that he pleaded successfully with MGM to shelve it. It appears to have been Press-shown to some magazine critics in 1929, for *Motion Picture* carries an adverse review of it, but not screened publicly till May 1930, when Mordaunt Hall called it 'halting and artificial' and added, 'Mr Gilbert's cheerfulness is not rational and his habit of smiling and laughing strikes one as though he did so to conceal his own nervousness.'[20] But by then, of course, the worst had happened to Gilbert. *His Glorious Night* was hustled through production in four weeks, perhaps to compensate exhibitors for the withdrawn *Redemption*; and the haste showed up in noticeably poor continuity. But what damned it most effectively were the words that had been put into Gilbert's mouth.

Audiences still relatively new to the talkies found it embarrassing to hear, to *overhear*, a man declare his passion for a woman. The very strangeness of hearing love uttered in so many words – blurted out, too, not nuanced – seems to have had an effect on the audience similar to that of first hearing four-letter words spoken on a public stage several

[20] *The New York Times*, 3 May 1930.

decades later. They were embarrassed; and because they were embarrassed, they laughed.

The mood had been building up for months. 'Audible osculation', as some called it, was chided by critics who were in every other respect worldly and sceptical men. Perhaps they toed the line of prudishness they suspected their readers (or their editors) would follow. But even Welford Beaton, in April 1929, censured kissing that was 'plainly audible' in reel after reel of *Sonny Boy*. And reviewing *Weary River* in January 1929, Mordaunt Hall had noted without pleasure that 'you even hear a kiss in this effusion'. Again and again in reading the records of the period, one comes across small but telling comments like this: and not just in America. 'Is Screen Kissing Indecent?' asked the British periodical, *Film Weekly*, in mid-1929 when the last wave of Hollywood's silent movies was breaking in British cinemas. It quoted a reader's letter referring, by coincidence, to Gilbert's last silent film with Garbo, *Woman of Affairs* (1929). 'I know one cannot judge a film by excerpts shown (in trailers), but it is evident that this picture will be full of the rather nasty exhibitions of osculation which are present in most films featuring this pair and for which, apparently, they are famous. . . . Even modern girls have shreds of modesty left and when seeing films like this accompanied by a man friend, well . . . I simply squirm in my seat. Can't something be done about it?'[21] And this, remember, was a response to a film without audible dialogue! To an average film fan in pre-talkie days, the 'love urge', as it was then called out of an objection to rawer terms like the 'sex urge', was largely acceptable because it was wholly silent: people could empathise with the stars expressing it since the lack of audible words removed any fear in filmgoers of eavesdropping on passions that embarrassed them. With silent lovers they were alone, unseen, unheard. But stars who declared their love audibly came swiftly down to earth, put themselves on the same plane as filmgoers, and were judged by standards one might apply if not to oneself, then to one's neighbours. Here are two people, the interior commentary might run, who maybe have the same emotions as ourselves, but magnified and amplified many times larger and louder than us, making public exhibitions of themselves. George Jean Nathan, in *The American Mercury*, accurately forecast the impact that amorous dialogue would make on the public when it replaced glamorous silence.

For a while the public will get a kick from hearing its favorite dummies speak, but it will not be long before it will yearn again for the days when . . . it could work itself up over houris stretched out langorously on sofas, Brooklyn ex-stenographers coyly showing their backsides, and side-burned former counter-jumpers lighting the incense in their louvred bachelor apartments and licking their chops

[21] *Film Weekly*, 20 July 1929.

over the imminent prospect of bolting the door on one of the Talmadges.

Dialogue writers and sensitive directors would learn before too long how to re-instate love on the screen so that it might be spoken of and not get laughed at. But it was *His Glorious Night,* and especially the scene where Gilbert declaimed 'I love you, I love you,' over and over again to a wooden Catherine Dale Owen as the Princess Orsolini, which taught them the necessity of doing so. A correspondent writing in *Variety* (the issue with the famous 'Wall Street Lays An Egg' headline about the stock market crash), noted that Gilbert was not the only star on the screen who was being 'razzed'.

> Charles Farrell in *Sunny Side Up* draws many a giggle for his mush stuff. . . . Seems the only type of love stuff received as intended since the advent of the talkies is the comedy love scene. The screen comics are becoming the heavy lovers and the heavy lovers, comedians. The normal kiss, delivered with the usual smack, sounds like an explosion. For that reason, kiss scenes in the early talkers have them rolling in the aisles.[22]

A Hollywood correspondent in the same issue added,

> Soft-pedal on kissing in romantic love. . . . Hereafter the saccharine stuff will be put over by pantomime. . . . Studios have found that the hooey going over in (sub-) titles won't go in talkers. Someone in the audience titters and it's all off. Hereafter the love passages will be suggested with the romantic note conveyed with properly pitched music. Metro, the first to learn by experience, is heading that way: others will follow for their own protection.

Had Gilbert been given better dialogue, more suitably pitched mood music, perhaps a more responsive *inamorata* than Catherine Dale Owen, and a softer-toned director than Lionel Barrymore, it is quite on the cards that his talkie career would have been devoid of ignominy. It is difficult to find any critic who sets down as a fact that his voice was inadequate. It is easy to find some who testify to the contrary. '(His) responsibility does not lie with his lines and therefore he is to be congratulated on the manner in which he handles his speaking role', wrote Mordaunt Hall, and conceding that his voice was not rich in nuances, he nevertheless found it 'pleasant'.[23] *Motion Picture Classic*'s critic supports this view. 'Obviously John has been spending some time with voice teachers. His accents are a trifle affected and self-conscious. But his voice is pleasing to hear, and is not lacking in a certain warmth which may well be considered essential to his portrayal.'[24] Welford Beaton said, 'Gilbert reads his lines intelligently, with a crispness that

[22] *Variety*, 31 October 1929.   [23] *The New York Times*, 5 October 1929.
[24] *Motion Picture Classic*, January 1930.

underlines his characterisation and with a clear enunciation that makes his most rapid utterances distinct.'[25] William C. de Mille has said, 'It was not that Jack's voice was bad: it was not. It was just not the voice his audience had heard in their minds in *The Big Parade*, or the voice that made love to Garbo in *Flesh and the Devil*.'[26] Jesse Lasky is equally emphatic: 'There was nothing wrong with Gilbert's voice.' It is Frank T. Daugherty, *Film Spectator*'s 'Exhibitor', who seems to balance the pros and cons perfectly in the report he wrote at the time for cinema managers who might be faced with the resentment or disenchantment of cinema audiences at *His Glorious Night*.

Gilbert's entry into the ranks of the talking picture is not an unalloyed success. Gone is the gallant lover and in its place is a young male who looks like John Gilbert, but whose supposedly fiery speeches have all the amorous passion of an assistant director asking another . . . to stake him to a lunch at Henry's. White-hot love speeches brought only snickers from the first-run audience at Loew's here. Snickers, too, which threatened more than once to become a gale of laughter. Quite obviously they were at a loss to know what had happened to their idol and most of them seemed a little ashamed of themselves for laughing – but they laughed, and all the talking pictures in the world, all the fine salary, all the publicity puffs, all the paid reviews, can never undo that laugh.[27]

[25] *Film Spectator*, 19 October 1929.
[26] William C. de Mille, op. cit., p. 288.
[27] *Film Spectator*, 14 November 1929.

11 'Negroes are funny that way about their pictures.'

The bankers who had moved on to the boards of so many movie companies knew where they were with cinemas. Cinemas were tangible assets, their values linked to sites and property: not like the pictures shown in them, frail, intangible collateral dependent on fickle public taste and swollen star egos. So it is not surprising in this immensely turbulent time to find the new men from Wall Street and the electrical companies moving first to guard their investment in bricks and mortar rather than flesh and fantasy. Looking at the early contracts some of the theatre owners had been compelled to sign with the wire companies, Welford Beaton observed that, compared to the latter, Jesse James and Captain Kidd had been 'tame, unimaginative fellows'.

Yet surprisingly few exhibitors had defaulted on rental payments: a mere 35,700 dollars had been checked into the red by mid-1929 for Western Electric sound systems removed from debt-ridden cinemas. The financial strain on independent exhibitors was certainly acute. Film rentals were up: even short features which they could have rented at 250 dollars a week in pre-talkie days now cost them 700 dollars. Projectionists' wage scales were soaring. Talkies brought some unexpected expenses, too. As summer approached, cinemas found they needed to put in new ventilation systems. In the days of silence, they had simply opened the doors to let in draughts of cooling air: with sound on the screen, they now had to shut out the sounds of the street. Many cinemas discovered they must triple attendance to make up the profits eaten away by equipment charges and maintenance premiums. 'The future of the small, singly owned box-office is like that of the Indian', *Variety* commented ominously in June 1929, claiming that thirty per cent of the 'indies' were headed for extinction by the end of the year. At this time there were about 3,200 independent cinemas in America belonging to about 370 mini-circuits; and another 2,000 were in amusement arcades. Of this total, only about 1,500 were in fit condition to be wired. The result was that the Hollywood majors, aware that there were increasingly fewer cinemas they could acquire and add to the circuits they already owned, fell back once again on the logic of their own cannibalistic development. They began eating one another.

Warners had already acquired most of First National in 1928: but this was swallowing a minnow compared to the huge take-over announced in New York, at midday, on Sunday, 3 March 1929, to a roomful of impatient Pressmen. Two of the industry's biggest moguls, Nicholas Schenck, president of Loew's Inc., who owned MGM, and William Fox, president of the company that bore his name, stated that henceforth Fox controlled Loew's – and along with it, 750 of the country's choicest cinemas and the studio with the biggest star roster in Hollywood. Fox claimed he had paid fifty million dollars for the shares held by the family of the late movie magnate Marcus Loew, and had acquired the rest needed for control from various individuals with money borrowed from Electrical Research Products Inc. (ERPI), the marketing subsidiary of Western Electric. News of this colossal coup had been rumoured for months; but Schenck had denied it publicly, and privately, too, backed by his word of honour, to the three MGM executives who now seethed with impotent fury at being left out of the lucrative deal. They were Louis B. Mayer, head of MGM, his production chief Irving Thalberg, and J. Robert Rubin, the studio lawyer. Had they been able to sell the stock they owned before the deal, they would have made millions. Bosley Crowther in his book *The Lion's Share* and William Fox himself through his amanuensis Upton Sinclair in *his* privately printed account of Fox's life, have recounted the embittered confrontation between Schenck and the studio triad. Seldom has the East Coast's desire and ability to act independently of the West Coast studios been better exemplified than in the angry accusations that flew between the parties. Some things were now very clear to Mayer: among them a matter which had seemed peripheral to the deal, but had actually played a vital part in its going through. A headline in *Variety*, on 19 December 1928, had read: 'Louis B. Mayer Leaving MGM in March with John Gilbert Remaining as Its Film Star'. The story reported that Mayer's retirement was imminent, but Gilbert was being retained as the studio's most valued asset. Now of course Mayer did not retire: he had had no intention. But the other part of the story was accurate and, as it turned out, damning. Gilbert was then in the last few months of his MGM contract and had authorised his manager Harry Eddington, a highpowered deal-maker who also looked after Garbo, a privilege only the topmost MGM stars were permitted, to open talks with United Artists with a view to joining them as a producer-director-star of the hyphenate kind Fairbanks and Chaplin had pioneered to their own enrichment. In spite of its illustrious board of stars, the output of UA's films had been paltry in recent years; Joseph M. Schenck, its president, wanted to beef it up and thought Gilbert a most desirable acquisition.

But Nicholas Schenck, Joseph's brother, wanted at all costs to retain Gilbert at MGM; if he lost this prized star, his secret deal with Fox might begin to sour. Nicholas Schenck even negotiated the renewal of Gilbert's contract himself: a sign of its importance and of his desire not to let the studio in on the secret. He gave Gilbert a three-year iron-clad deal at 250,000 dollars a picture. This had to be concluded without delay; and the haste and need for diplomacy may explain why Gilbert was not required to make a test to see if his voice suited the talkies. This omission, in view of his impending ruin, which has already been described, indicates the extent to which his personal fame was inextricably linked with the spectacular deal now ready to be clinched. There will always be speculation whether Mayer's anger at seeing an MGM star ranked above him in importance, both in *Variety*'s published headline and in the subsequent wheeling-and-dealing, played a sinister part in Gilbert's decline and fall once Mayer was back on the MGM throne. For the fact is that the Fox-Loew's deal never went through. Mayer was partly responsible for this: the slighted magnate now proved his muscle as the first film boss who deployed political connections to retrieve corporate power. The Hollywood moguls were probably all Republicans; but they traditionally steered their businesses clear of politics, suspecting accurately that Federal Government was more of a threat than a patron. Mayer was an exception. He had come out publicly in support of Herbert Hoover as early as December 1927, when he told the then Commerce Secretary that all California, and naturally Hollywood, wanted to see him as Presidential candidate – then as President. Mayer was the first picture man to attend a nominating convention as a delegate: he gave his vote to Hoover in Kansas City in May 1928, and was an honoured guest at his inaugural in 1929. The new President showed his support of the film industry in even more practical form: he ordered the White House cinema to be wired for sound, thus indicating his approval of the medium.

It was to this powerful and indebted friend that Mayer now turned. We know he attended talkie auditions in New York City: but the real reason for his visit East was to pay court to Hoover. The White House guest book shows he was there twice inside ten days in July 1929. William Fox believed he had the tacit agreement of the Justice Department to the Loew's deal. Maybe he had: but this was under the last Administration. Fox may now have scented trouble, as he offered Mayer two million dollars to smooth the way with the Justice Department which now found grounds for looking anew at the deal. There is no evidence that Mayer helped Fox; and every reason to suspect the contrary. The result was that the reinvigorated Justice Department began making things difficult for other movie corporations as well at the very moment they were trying to gobble each other up in the search for cinemas.

Warner Brothers, flush with cash, were going after United Artists. Warners' assets were then valued at a staggering fourteen million dollars (which would rise to one hundred and sixty million dollars by the end of 1929). Not only did they want theatres; Jack Warner, ever the pace-setter for others, wanted to impose output quotas on UA's privileged star-producers. Fairbanks would have had to make seven films inside five years; Pickford, Goldwyn and Swanson four each; and that slowcoach Charlie Chaplin would have also had to commit himself for seven. In addition, to sweeten the deal, Al Jolson would go over to UA for 500,000 dollars a picture, plus ten per cent of the net. Sound had indeed generated huge rewards – for some.

In addition to this area of turbulence, Paramount wanted to merge completely with the Publix theatre chain to protect its outlets. It took evasive action. The issue of *Variety*, on 7 August 1929, carried one of the costliest-ever advertising supplements, a huge 184-page paean of praise in copy and advertising that described Paramount in the most extravagant terms. ('No company in any of the other major industries of the country holds a position of such close relations to so many people . . . the world's greatest story-teller . . . any little girl, obscure and unknown, may become a star at Paramount . . . wherever music and songs are played and sung, the tunes of Paramount songs are heard.') It was beyond any doubt part of a campaign to stifle any objections the Justice Department might have to the proposed merger by insisting that what was good for Paramount was good for the USA. Justice did not see it that way. Though the deal did eventually go through, it was on far less aggressive terms. The opposition of the UA celebrities, in particular Chaplin, who feared being hustled to produce a picture beyond his now normal gestation rate of four to five years, killed the attempt by Warners to take over that corporation. The threat or existence of anti-trust suits under the Sherman or the easier-to-prove Clayton Acts effectively dissuaded any other attempts at Hollywood cannibalism. And William Fox was choked by his own gluttony. . . . For the most megalomaniac of all the moguls found he had put his head in a financial noose which his enemies pulled tight. ERPI had lent him fifteen million dollars to finance his share purchase as evidence of their good faith in negotiations over various sound patents which Fox contended he owned. But on 17 July Fox was almost fatally injured in a car crash; while he lay recuperating in his up-state retreat, Fox Hall, his business rivals closed round him. In October came the stock market's collapse. Fox could not round up the extra cash to protect his falling margins. Stripped of his financial power, he was soon denuded of his corporate identity by Western Electric and Government anti-trust suits. In July 1931, a ruined man, he was ordered to divest himself of the Loew's shares he had hoped would crown his career; and by then MGM was master of its own roar again, Louis B. Mayer was back in power and John Gilbert was languishing in the anguished limbo of fallen stars.

While the film companies were fighting among themselves, Equity, the actors' union, was fighting the film companies. An actors' strike was possibly the last thing the studios wanted, now that they were forging ahead with the talkies. But an actors' strike they got in mid-1929; or, at least, they would have got it, had Equity succeeded in declaring a closed shop in the talkies. The union had last tried this in 1927, aided by the ten per cent cut in salaries that the studios were then forcing their personnel to accept. But the leading film actors had reneged on support for Equity's proposed standard contract when the producers withdrew their insistence on a salary cut. Equity closed down its West Coast office, yielding to AMPAS the right to negotiate on film actors' contracts, and retired to New York to lick its wounds. Sound now gave Equity a second chance: the influx of Equity members from the New York stage into Hollywood looked like a desirable 'Fifth Column'. And in June 1929, Frank Gillmore, Equity's executive secretary, called for a closed shop in the talkies, plus such benefits as a forty-eight-hour week, a one-week minimum engagement term, rehearsals to be considered as actual time worked, no Sunday filming save by agreement and no voice substitution (dubbing) except by consent. (It would appear that even then sound recording had taken on a sinister modern flavour, since Equity's Hollywood meetings were expressly held in places where there was no possibility of a Dictaphone to bug the proceedings.) Equity members in Hollywood were immediately ordered not to accept film work – there were about 2,000 of them on the Coast. It looked like a long, grim siege.

In fact Equity's position was very vulnerable. Gillmore was not an aggressive activist, simply a good peacetime negotiator. The union's funds were stretched within a very short time: the campaign cost 4,500 dollars weekly, relief funds to members were running at 1,000 dollars daily by the end of July. Equity had no Hollywood headquarters; and to the film people, already resentful of Broadway interlopers, the union's demands looked like those of a distant alien outfit in New York which had little understanding of the threat already posed by the talkies. Welford Beaton was scathing about the likely outcome: 'Producers will grant Equity the privilege of wearing their button in studio cafés. This will be considered by Equity a great victory, and it will yield on all the other points.'[1] Well, not on all – but on most. By mid-August, after spending three months and 550,000 dollars in a futile attempt to drive its wedge into the studios, using the talkies as its opportunity, Equity had to lift its ban. It was no match for producers driven by apprehension to take the desperate measure of actually aiding each other; for very swiftly they put their heads together and evolved emergency plans for an interchange of non-Equity stars and contract artists. Perhaps Equity's opposition even persuaded the studios that many more of their artists could 'learn' to talk than they had anticipated. Opposition to Equity was fiercest among film stars who had safely passed their voice tests, notably

[1] *Film Spectator*, 10 August 1929.

Conrad Nagel. But the threat of a prolonged ban would have been fatal to those very special talents already holding Equity cards, the chorus girls (and boys), singers and dancers, who had rushed to Hollywood to join in the booming cycle of musicals. These 'little people' eventually weighted the vote in defeating their own union. And the crucial factor was Equity's failure to secure support from the American Federation of Labor, with which it was affiliated, before calling the strike. Everyone realised that to halt the talkie revolution just when it was hitting its stride would repeat the economic disarray that the industry was just then sorting out. Having found its voice, the film industry spoke up for its security: it was an omen.

These mergers and disputes caught the film studios just when they were striving to outdo each other in the most prolific film cycle of the whole transition period – the Hollywood musical. It would be too simple an explanation to attribute this to the proof supplied by the enormously profitable *Broadway Melody*. Most of the studios had musicals in various stages of production while the MGM picture was being shot: its success simply confirmed to them that they had guessed right. The eruption of musicals was in part a response to public dissatisfaction with the surfeit of talk on the screen. Even though the cameras had not attained anything like the quicksilver fluency the next year would bring, musicals had this advantage over the 'talky' talkies – their performers at least *moved*. Melodies gave them an appeal to the ear that was more tuneful than paragraphs of dialogue. Then, again, colour was another way of jumping ahead of your rival – and the spectacular production numbers in a musical were more appropriate for colour then the domestic interiors of the talkies. (The Western was thought to have no future, until *In Old Arizona* proved otherwise, or else colour might have been used first on horse operas, not stage operas.) Colour could also take an audience's mind off the imperfections of synchronisation. So it was largely re-discovered – for of course various colour processes had been in use much earlier than 1929. Twenty-five of the films released in 1928 had used colour – tinted or Technicolor – but none of them was a talkie of any importance; yet in 1929 there were twenty-two all- or part-talkie films released, mostly in two-strip Technicolor or in Multicolor (a process discontinued in 1933) and among these were a dozen major musicals and nearly half-a-dozen films with musical numbers. Ultimately the rush into colour to disguise the deficiencies of sound, or freshen a jaded public appetite, did the process a disservice. Restricted tints (red and green were Technicolor's only hues at that date) and rushed laboratory work (to match the rushed productions, some of them done in three or four weeks) resulted in blurred tints that discomforted the retina as much as poor sound reproduction pained the ear; and the production of Technicolor films had almost stopped by 1932. But in 1929 it was regarded as a vital additive to the all-singing, all-dancing genre. Warners contracted with

Technicolor to do forty movies: they would have to be made fast because they were not cheap – Technicolor was paid eight cents a foot for printing, compared with two cents for black-and-white, and since Technicolor insisted on manning its own cameras, just to shoot a film in colour might mean an extra 100,000 dollars on the budget.

Another cause of the musical efflorescence was the huge profit in the movie companies' ownership of music-publishing or phonograph companies. Between 100,000 and 500,000 sheets of a song could be sold, and an equal number of discs, within a month of a successful musical's release. (Without a film behind it, a song was usually lucky to sell 30,000 copies in three months.) Hollywood's raid on Broadway had really only been successful in the territory of the Broadway musical. The reason was primitively simple. Many musical talents *wanted* to work in Hollywood and found out, once they got there, that they could do the work better than anyone already there. The money was infinitely greater, too. The standard East Coast practice was to pay composers on a royalty basis which fluctuated with sales: in Hollywood they were paid *a regular salary* plus royalties. Hollywood's weekly pay-cheques to song-writers and composers in 1929 varied between 200 and 750 dollars weekly, though in some outstanding cases they were a real bonanza. For writing the book, score and lyrics of Fox's *Sunny Side Up*, DeSylva, Brown and Henderson split a fee of 150,000 dollars and *still* shared in the music publishing royalties. Hollywood's instant and guaranteed money provided a bluer sky over the composers' heads than Broadway – and they rushed West.

Ironically, two of the most successful of them, Arthur Freed and Nacio Herb Brown, were on the Coast all the time, writing and producing stage shows there till *Broadway Melody* gave them their break in films. They consolidated it with the composition 'Singin' in the Rain', selected as the 'plug' or lead number in *Hollywood Revue*, and 'The Pagan Love Song' which 'choked the air waves' for the next year or so when a loincloth-clad Ramon Novarro sang it in *The Pagan*. Soon they were running their own music publishing company. The mad scramble for Broadway performers with good speaking voices was now succeeded by expeditions of rapine intensity for boys and girls from the chorus line and for good-looking hoofers, as the studios had now found that the café tap-dancers and 'suit and collar' boys they had recruited in Los Angeles for scene-dressing simply could not dance well enough for the musical spectaculars.

April, May and June were the 'musical months' of 1929. Every week brought fresh proof of the imitative, and sometimes innovative, industry's commitment to the song-and-dance cycle. As before, Warners stole a march on their competitors. *The Desert Song* (1 May 1929), directed by Roy del Ruth, was described as the screen's first operetta. It starred John Boles, Carlotta King, a 132-member chorus, 109 musicians (the early musicals might have been as justly called

John Gilbert (with Renée Adorée) hits the bottle in *Redemption*, a talkie version of Tolstoy's *The Living Corpse*, about a young Russian who cannot cure himself of gambling fever and takes up with a gypsy girl. Made before *His Glorious Night*, in 1929, this film was not screened publicly till May 1930. By then people realised how horribly prescient its lines were about the self-destruction that Gilbert's own ruined career had brought about.

Carlotta King and John Boles in *The Desert Song* (1929), one of the tremendously successful cycle of operettas transferred 'from the Broadway hit of the same name', as the credits assured patrons. Imagination did not run riot, but generally everything else did.

Jack Cameron and Helen Morgan in Rouben Mamoulian's *Applause* (1929). Disliked by critics at the time for its emphasis on the 'sordid' life of a cabaret singer, the film in retrospect is remarkable for many aural and visual inventions – and in particular for a performance by Miss Morgan that suggests the ravaged desperation of a Judy Garland.

180

'mathematicals') and had an unshakeable addiction to conventions of the proscenium stage so that the characters, as Mordaunt Hall complained, 'seem to seize upon song at inopportune moments' and 'utter lines of dialogue that cannot be listened to with a straight face'.[2] As the film had been shot nearly six months before it opened, its sound showed up poorly at a time when improvements were weekly events. It was much better in Universal's *Show Boat* (17 April 1929), directed by Harry Pollard; but here again the approach was slavishly theatrical, the recipe being to follow the stage production in detail, get in the entire musical score and plug all the songs. At its Miami première in March, the film ran to two hours twenty-seven minutes, with Jerome Kern's music still to be 'interpolated' in some scenes, and even ten minutes shorter at its New York opening, it got a reception that was restrained to say the least. 'The dragginess . . . through paralysed love scenes would have annoyed the inmates of a deaf, dumb and blind asylum,' said *Variety*.[3]

Much more important for the future shape of the new musical was Paramount's *Innocents of Paris* (26 April 1929), the first American film of Maurice Chevalier ('Say it "She-val-yay",' the worried publicists told the public.) Chevalier's talents had already brought him several offers while he was in Paris; but his 'foreign-ness' and the risk he might not 'go over' in America caused them to fall through. One suitor had been Irving Thalberg. He got as far as persuading the Frenchman to make a screen test in Paris, but then could not persuade MGM to pay him more than he got in his own beloved capital. When Jesse Lasky next put in his bid, Chevalier said, 'I will do more than talk it over. I will save you the money and the trouble of making a test. I will show you the test that was made of me two months ago.' Thus did Maurice Chevalier get his Paramount contract on the strength of a screen test for MGM. Lasky acted shrewdly. While the film script was being doctored to suit Chevalier's repertoire of songs, which was to include 'Louise', he put him into the show at the New Amsterdam Hotel's after-theatre resort, the Ziegfeld Roof. This *ad hoc* act neatly familiarised Broadway with the Frenchman, as well as defraying his *per diem* expenses. (Lasky even got a bonus; for he offered a contract to a girl who appeared before Chevalier to sing a blues number: she was Lillian Roth.) An undemanding artist while he was on his own soil – 'Will I get to meet Mary and Doug?' he asked, like any fan, when Lasky proposed Hollywood to him – Chevalier turned unexpectedly resistant to the limp script of *Innocents of Paris*, a tale of a singing junkman whom it is proposed to pass off as a singing prince. Only the guarantee of having his famous songs inserted in the tale mollified him. He need not have worried. *The New York Times* hailed him as 'the whole show'. Charming, unaffected, happy-go-lucky: such qualities were the reverse of Jolson's aggressive, go-getting, ego-boosting persona. But the two men did have one thing in common – the quality of being a

[2] *New York Times*, 2 May 1929.　　　　[3] *Variety*, 24 April 1929.

Above, 'Girls, you'll have me blushing', says Maurice Chevalier in *Innocents of Paris* (1929). The sexiness of his accent survived even an inferior musical like this. *Below*, 'In *Close Harmony* (1929) we have two excited youngsters agreeing to get married and what they say during the love scene is absolutely of no importance whatsoever. And that is the theory upon which all screen dialogue should be written.' An overdose of talkative talkies provoked this rather extreme view in a contemporary critic, but everyone agreed on the charm of Buddy Rogers, as a youthful orchestra leader, and Nancy Carroll as his best girl.

success. It was one that the camera loved. Chevalier's preferred approach to film roles was set in these early Hollywood days and never varied. 'I am not the lady-killer type,' he said in one unusually intelligent interview, '"I think women like me because I make them smile, but they do not say –" here he dropped his chin into his palm and rolled his eyes heavenward – "'Oh, that Chevalier!' . . . When the big dramatic scene comes, I do not feel it in my shoes. I try to play it naturally – as I feel it – as it would happen in life – with a little humour, if possible – because, though all my life has not been so funny, I find there is a funny side in many serious things. But still I do not like these romantic roles."' He is referring to the Prince in *The Love Parade*, which at first he rejected because of the starched uniform and elegant manners he thought it entailed. '"I like best to play the part of a plain fellow that women understand and that men understand, too."'[4] Despite a certain streak of chauvinism in some reviews – he was reminded that while his French accent 'ought to make it good for New Orleans . . . there are two sides to the Mississippi' – the public had no difficulty understanding his appeal. And in the hands of Lubitsch and Mamoulian, Chevalier's European bonhomie, seemingly weightless and uncreasable, was exactly the kind that could dance on the breeze of the liberated musicals just months ahead.

Charles (Buddy) Rogers was an All-American boy with a sweeter centre; but he had the same sympathetic effect on Paramount's *Close Harmony* (28 April 1929). Directed by John Cromwell and Edward Sutherland, its story of a shy young orchestra leader getting helped to Broadway fame by a sophisticated chorus girl played by Nancy Carroll was conventional backstage stuff. But it not only captures the re-retouched spontaneity of the affections between the young lovers in a way that Paul Fejos's *Lonesome* managed to do in its silent passages before the sweethearts opened their mouths and broke the spell: but also it shows how swing music and 'natural' talk, colloquial, illuminating and never verbose, can loosen up the whole feel of a musical. Its good fortune was also to come out at the same time as Warners' first all-colour musical, *On With the Show* (28 May 1929), directed by Alan Crosland, a backstage story stuffed with painfully reiterative wisecracking dialogue about a leading lady who demands too much money and the understudy who goes up to the footlights, sings in her place and comes back a star. 'One almost imagines the lovely hues writhing in agony at being called upon to decorate such a story', Mordaunt Hall said sadly.

It was becoming clear by mid-1929 that Warners were swiftly losing the lead they had built up in artistic and technical innovation. And this was confirmed when Universal at last brought *Broadway* (27 May 1929) to the screen. The tale of an innocent hoofer embroiled in bootlegging and murder, it was the original inspiration of most of the underworld and night club dramas and might have looked distinctly weary had it not

[4] *Photoplay*, interviewed by Ida Zeitlin, September 1930.

been for Paul Fejos's direction. This is an exemplary piece of film-making. It builds comedy out of dialogue, drama out of situations, and expands the screenplay well beyond the stage proscenium by a spellbindingly unfettered camera that keeps swooping from all heights and angles above and across the straight-lined art-deco sets which include the interior of the Paradise Night Club, some seventy feet high and a city block wide. Fejos, that odd blend of artist and scientist (on the première programme he is still described as a 'Hungarian bacteriologist'), had had the camera crane built at a cost of 75,000 dollars to travel six hundred feet a minute. The film anticipated the inflationary tendencies of the Busby Berkeley style in its replication effect of geometrical patterns and look-alike chorines. It was as if the spirit of Henry Ford's Detroit assembly line had somehow been built into the Hollywood musical. On stage, it had been scaled down to the size of the sets; on screen it threw in everything the producers then believed was crowd-pulling. To be populous was to be popular: so the night-club sequence, which was in colour, had a chorus of 30 as well as 100 extras on call. 'Illustrate, enlarge, multiply', was the script direction. Such was the element of excess that one reviewer complained, 'it even gives us both sides of a telephone conversation'.

The compulsion to throw in everything (and everyone) on the lot was carried out most strikingly in the all-star revues that were a feature of most major studios in these months. They were the sound showcase of the contract talent, proof positive that everyone could now talk, sing and dance at least passably well. They were the Vitaphone music and vaudeville shorts grown up as far as dimensions went, even if they were unengagingly immature in other respects. *Hollywood Revue* (14 April 1929) is the most famous of them; but apart from showing who was at MGM at the time, its virtues are few. It is filmed almost constantly head-on, in a proscenium setting, and features some twenty numbers, twenty-five personalities and two 'interlocutors', Jack Benny and (the well-nigh inevitable) Conrad Nagel. Act follows act with monotonous gaucheness relieved only – and then almost reluctantly – by a couple of panning shots and once by an overhead shot of the sort that Berkeley's choreography would soon make into a dazzling speciality. Benny plays the violin when given a chance (not often), Nagel does some ham-handed comic introductions, of the put-down kind, Laurel and Hardy at least juggle with endearing ineptness, Keaton dresses as an Egyptian gal in King Canute's court, a poorly photographed Joan Crawford sings 'Low Down Rhythm', and Marion Davies, diminished by trick photography, swaggers through the giant legs of guardsmen singing 'Tommy Atkins on Parade'.

Quite the best bits of *Hollywood Revue* are the novelty numbers: Bessie Love, for instance, likewise scaled down in size to come out of Benny's waistcoat pocket, steps off his hand singing 'I Never Knew I Could Do a Thing Like That' and is flip-flopped along a line of hair-raisingly

Above, Edward G. Robinson was one of the most capable stage stars to make a successful transition to the talkies. Contrary to what he usually did later on the sound screen he is here on the receiving end of some rough stuff in Paramount's kidnapped-child thriller, *Hole in the Wall* (1929). *Below*, Filming outdoor location scenes like this in King Vidor's *Hallelujah* (1929) was a landmark achievement in the history of the sound movies. He decided, in the main, to 'shoot silent' and put the sound in later. This entailed agonies of experiment in the cutting rooms; but enabled the film to retain the fluidity of the great silent era.

unsychronised male choristers. Sandwiched into this low-brow affair was the Gilbert-Shearer excerpt from Shakespeare filmed in muted hues of salmon and greenish blue. The finale was also in colour: ballet girls in green tutus against an orange grove, while the stars parade around in transparent rainwear reprising 'Singin' in the Rain' as if the Ark bearing all MGM's two-footed talents had just that minute come to rest on the Ararat of sound musicals.

If *Hollywood Revue* is indeed a landmark, it is of historical importance only. One trade-paper reviewer acknowledged its ineradicable staginess when he advised the MGM Press department to make diplomatic requests to newspapers for the dramatic critics to be assigned to review it 'in all spots'. Clumsy and static though it is, it was one of the first sound movies to be promoted into what we would now call 'an event'. Cinema façades in Los Angeles and on Broadway were turned into 'Human Billboards' with long-legged girls in satin shorts standing on the title's capital letters, anchored by safety harness around their waists so as to leave their legs free to give two alfresco shows nightly of somewhat restricted vivacity, backed up by eighteen unfettered chorines at pavement level, all of them paid five dollars a performance and the upper tiers protected by group liability insurance. It had cost MGM about 7,000 dollars to erect the 'sign', and the non-human source of energy would have run up supplementary bills of 4,000 dollars monthly if the police had not intervened to stop the show. A judge, who was applied to for relief by the studio, delivered the Solomon-like decision that the 'Human Billboard' might remain intact, so long as the girls did not move their legs. They were replaced by cardboard cut-outs.

Warners answer to the *Revue* was its own *Show of Shows* (20 November 1929) with no fewer than seventy-seven names; Fox made *Movietone Follies*, where two lavishly staged musical numbers, 'Break Away' and 'Big City Blues' were the main attraction; and Paramount came out with *Paramount on Parade*, released in April 1930, and clearly showing what beneficial differences the intervening months had made: it was more good-humoured, relaxed, rhythmical, sophisticated, confident of itself and far more *risqué* as well than *Hollywood Revue*. One item had Chevalier having a lovers' bust-up, arguing 'on pitch' with Evelyn Brent as they undress in their bedroom, and then appearing as a genially lubricious *flic* chasing a dozing greybeard off a park bench to make way for Bright (and smooching) Young Things. In another, Clara Bow danced and sang on a ship's quarterdeck backed by a matelots' chorus; Nancy Carroll emulated Bessie Love by apparently coming out of a slipper and singing to an orchestra that fits into a shoe box; and though George Bancroft, not the most flexible talent for musicals, looks awkward in a heavy-handed comic turn about a man who loses his cocktail party inhibitions and tells everyone the truth, there is an agreeably self-kidding number featuring Gary Cooper, Richard Arlen and a bunch of other boys in hunting pink singing a drinking song to Mary Brian and Fay Wray.

But if these studio 'menus' were generally one-off affairs, the grip of the Broadway production style on Hollywood musicals was not. It was evident in the film acclaimed as 'in every aspect . . . the finest of the screen musicals'. It was RKO's presentation of *Rio Rita* (6 October 1929), directed by Luther Reed with stage direction by Russell Mack. The movie retained all the old Flo Ziegfeld stage pageantry, the Mexican fiesta, the pirate barge, as well as the stage comedy act of Wheeler and Woolsey. John Boles acted and sang the role of 'Jim the Ranger Captain'; and Bebe Daniels gave a tremendous boost to her manifestly flagging career by revealing a melodious singing voice in the role of Rio Rita. She had been one of the silent screen's best-known, highest-paid tom-boy comediennes; but when 'mike panic' was at its height, Paramount agreed to dispose of her services over the remaining ten months of her contract provided she could find some other company to employ her in the talkies – i.e. compensate them for the loss of services they either did not want or could not use. She did. *Photoplay* said of her Rio Rita: 'Despite very strong competition, Bebe Daniels is the most glowing personality. . . . Her voice, untrained as it is, has a rich quality which an experienced *prima donna* might well envy.'[5] Bebe Daniels herself, nearly forty years later, gave a hint about why the film showed such superior recording quality despite the fact that 'we shot it in 24 days . . . some of it on location, which created its share of problems. . . . The musical numbers were shot ordinarily, like the rest of the film. My second cousin was Lee De Forest, the father of sound, and he used to come on to the set and was always doing things to the microphone, moving mikes around to better positions and that sort of thing.'[6] According to John Kobal, who interviewed Walter Plunkett, later one of Hollywood's most noted costume designers, and at that time working behind the scenes on *Rio Rita*, the film's colour sequences – which occupied the second half, after the intermission, the first half being black-and-white – had to be shot at night because the studio's Technicolor camera (of which there were only twenty-five in Hollywood in 1929) was in use during the day on another colour production.

Despite its alfresco location scenes and horse-riding, *Rio Rita* is still a musical firmly committed to proscenium staging. But it shows this slight advance. Its numbers were sung in 'natural surroundings', rather than integrated into a cabaret show as in *Innocents of Paris*, or as the footlights part of a backstage story. The type of number was also dramatically relevant to the mood, ranging from intimate love ballads to comedy and solo numbers and rousing choruses. Progress was painfully slow, but it was being made, towards the freely inventive screen musical such as Lubitsch devised, or David Butler's East Side Cinderella story, *Sunny Side Up* (3 October 1929), with Charles Farrell and Janet Gaynor, which combined sound and image with great technical assurance and, as

[5] *Photoplay*, November 1929.
[6] *Gotta Sing, Gotta Dance*, by John Kobal (Hamlyn, London, 1970), p. 31.

Cinema said, 'experimenting so successfully that the experimental nature of what they did was not perceptible'. The Eskimo musical sequence, where the passions make the snow and ice melt, had already the tongue-in-cheek hyperbole of the very best *Gold Diggers* films.

It may seem slightly stretching the definition of a 'musical' to include King Vidor's *Hallelujah* (20 August 1929). It would in any case be assured of mention, since it is among the finest films produced in this last year of the talkie revolution. Technically, it is among the most fluent sound films of that year, for the paradoxical reason that it was shot silent. But this view of the black race had music, heard and unheard, running through it, determining its form as well as its material. One of Broadway's biggest hits in 1927 had been Rouben Mamoulian's Guild Theater production of *Porgy*; and King Vidor, as Lewis Jacobs shrewdly noted, 'undertook to do its counterpart in *Hallelujah*, spying a grand opportunity for song and dance in the new sound form'.[7] Vidor began writing the scenario in August 1928: it was then untitled. *Variety* stated, 'It will have an all-Negro cast,' but added circumspectly, '(it) is not going to be a propaganda film'. Neither was it going to be a musical travesty of the Deep South blacks, like Fox's *Hearts in Dixie* (27 February 1929), directed by Paul Sloane, which had plenty of tuneful numbers but Stepin Fetchit in his definitive eye-rolling performance. Vidor's would be nearer to opera, but opera based on the black 'as he is'. He jotted down characters and sequences of black life in the South which he felt could be bonded together by music and shot on location: he was himself a Texan, so he knew his territory. But to make an all-black film then which had some pretensions to authenticity was almost heresy: it was practically certain not to get distributed in the South. Vidor won over Nicholas Schenck by a blunt appeal of the kind that seldom failed with movie corporation presidents. He offered to put up his own high fee for directing as investment money if MGM would match it dollar for dollar. He has recorded that Schenck replied, 'If that's the way you feel about it, I'll let you make a picture about whores.'

The sound trucks that Vidor had been expecting when he and the unit moved to Memphis, Tennessee, didn't show up: so he was obliged to start shooting the movie silent. He continued that way. Out of an accident came another leap ahead for sound films. *Hallelujah* thus retained the camera freedom of the silent film at its best: Vidor snapped the mechanical fetters of the microphone as joyfully as the slaves had once broken their chains. The hard labour of matching sound to the silent visuals was suffered in the editing stages afterwards, although Vidor did try to edit the film as he shot it. He was a great admirer of Disney; and his description of using a metronome to provide an evenness of rhythm or to cue a player into dialogue or song has striking

[7] *The Rise of the American Film*, by Lewis Jacobs (Harcourt, Brace & Co., New York, 1939), p. 458.

resemblances to Disney's description of how *he* synchronised sound to his cartoon *Steamboat Willie*. By necessity, Vidor was forced to use sound the way Disney did – non-realistically. Try as he and his editors might, they were unable in the absence of anything like a Movieola to do a precise enough job with the projection room screen and a system of buzzers and grease pencils that they hoped would mark the particular frame on which the actors' lips opened. Vidor's editor suffered a nervous breakdown. For the long tracking shots where the black hero is chased through the Arkansas swamplands, Vidor deliberately overlaid the visuals with heightened and impressionistic sound effects – the cracking of sticks sounding like broken bones, the sucking of the swamp like a greedy quicksand, birds crying savagely and louder than nature intended. Dialogue was reduced to a minimum – as much from necessity as for effect. Only in sequences which were relatively easy to synchronise, like the singing of Irving Berlin's 'The End of the Road' or 'Going Home', is the film affected by the static quality of a proscenium musical. But the music's own dark rhythms transfused it, as the camera moved down the lines of cotton pickers singing 'Swanee', or into the blues numbers, the dance-hall exoticism and the spiritual hosannas at the revivalist meetings. Even its dialogue veers into near-song. One contemporary critic referred to the scene where the hero returns home with his brother's body, to be greeted by a babble of incoherent woe. 'Incoherent, yet Mammy's shrill soprano wailing, the children's whimpering treble, Missy Rose's passionate contralto, and Massa's grief-stricken bass all combine to make a magnificent speaking chord of purest music.'[8]

It is a film that undeniably is better in intention than achievement. The real milestone it represents is one in the history of the sound film, rather than the black race. In trying to show the latter as it was, Vidor got badly entangled in the imperatives of a melodrama – a simple black enticed by a vamp into a fixed craps game, accidentally shooting his brother, atoning for it by turning evangelist, falling for the flesh again, murdering and then expiating the crime before returning to the cotton-pickin' plantation and his own true love. But all this is no more high-keyed than the opera towards which it is always striving. What counts is the scenes that Vidor stages in and around the narrative: the cotton bales arriving at market, the baptismal 'orgies', the chase through the swamps. The fidelity to place and atmosphere has a documentary directness, a topographical truth. The film's tendency to exclude all whites, and to show the Southern black in a historical vacuum, or present him glibly as 'the pathetic symbol of his race', is today a major flaw. But this view has to be countered by reference to the time in which *Hallelujah* was made, when it was customary for even liberal reviews of the film to refer to the blacks as 'darkies', or 'the dusky sons of Ham'. In a naïve and still brutal time for blacks, it impressed audiences and even

[8] *Cinema*, January 1930.

in 1946, when it was revived in London, a sophisticated weekly's reviewer admitted, 'I was black while it lasted . . . it leaves one feeling spent'.

Variety recognised the importance of the fact that Vidor was 'doing something for the race that none of the other directors or producers has ever done' by covering the film's two concurrent New York premières, one at the Embassy Theater in downtown Manhattan, the other at the Layfayette, Harlem. (The use of the Layfayette was shrewd: several of the film's cast, like Nina Mae McKinney as the vamp, Victoria Spivey as the patient true love and Bill Fountaine as Hot Shot the craps shooter, had made their stage debut there; and Harry Gray as the white-whiskered patriarch had been a porter at the New York *Amsterdam News*. To them, and their local audiences, it must have been an intensely moving kind of homecoming.) The reaction of the up-town whites was, perhaps predictably, self-consciously appreciative. The black reaction was more complex and it deserves quoting in full, since it gives the contemporary lie to many later accusations by guilty liberals that the film was exploitatively condescending to a Negro unreality. The proviso one has to make is that the Harlem blacks who saw *Hallelujah* on 20 August were Northern Negroes – and pretty street-wise, too, about their rural Southern contemporaries.

To *Variety*'s correspondent (colour not stated, but surely white), the initial reaction was puzzling. 'Sizing up the all-colored reception of the film from its start to finish, the Negroes just won't take their big dramatic stuff seriously. They laugh. It's a collective laugh and not scattered here and there. Even in the big religious scenes, especially the baptismal, gales of laughter swept the Lafayette up and down.' Conscious that whatever film was screened at this theatre there was always audible comment, the reviewer then itemised the scenes that drew reactions of – of what? Recognition? Appreciation? Possibly both.

> The familiar dice shift by Hot Shot, a gag that every craps shooter in Harlem knows; the row of cat houses in the Southern town with their little outside benches where the guests are entertained in the open; the levee scene as true as Gospel itself; the jug-blowing musicians, the noisy, hotsy-totsy cabaret band with the stick-juggling drummer; the old circus car repainted that hauls Ezekiel the Prophet and his family; the old-fashioned Brunswick stew that Southern Negroes dote on almost as much as possum pie or fried chicken or chidlins; the black Billy Sunday outfit, its evangelist style and method of operating from town to town; the old cannonball express or steamboat gag that the colored preachers used to pep up their meetings; the church scene where Vidor is said to have let the Negroes stage it as if it was real; the saw mill that Vidor used which is just across the river from Memphis; the St Louis Blues crooning that Nina Mae McKinney did which Harlem sheiks know their wives or sweeties

now start singing when they plan to give their hubbies or lovers the air; the stone or rock pile all colored convicts get when they are real bad Down South. All in all, a mass of detail that went to make the picture as close to nature as possible.

To an offay[9] sitting amid the packed Lafayette Theater with blacks, the thought occurred that perhaps the tidal wave of laughter that greeted so many of the big serious scenes – and scenes that had a true aspect and those where tragedy and death stalked hand in hand – was just a sincere form of appreciation, similar to that which affected the race for years either in sorrow or joy, whether receiving religion and making such a show that they go into the holy-roller stuff and keep shouting for a long time, or giving vent to their real rhythmic feeling whether listening to a hot raggedy band or to the handclap that starts the Negro boy or adult moving his feet in time. Up Lafayette way when the show is bad or the picture has been accepted as NG (no good), the colored patrons on their exit not only tell everybody within earshot how punk it is, but stop at the box-office to inform whoever is within how the show smells. None of that Tuesday night. . . . It's tradition at the Layfayette that when the audiences hiss (and they are some hissers in the Black Belt) the show is rotten. No hisses during *Hallelujah*. That perhaps spells its success despite the deluge of laughs . . . when silence should have registered. But the Negroes are funny that way about their pictures.[10]

[9] Vernacular expression, meaning *au fait*, 'in the know'.
[10] *Variety*, 28 August 1929.

12 'Our little old Hollywood was gone.'

One is usually unable to say precisely when a usurping technology has succeeded in supplanting the one it infiltrated and rendered obsolete. No exact date could (or should) be attempted for the beginning of what we now call 'the talkie era'. But there are useful milestones, large and small. Academic acceptance, for instance. Sound gained the movies campus respectability. The University of Southern California's spring semester, 1929, saw a new course 'Appreciation of the Photoplay': it was sandwiched between 'Philosophy' and 'Physical Education'. And in the summer, Stanford followed USC in recognising 'the talkies' as a formal subject of study. In the wider world, one cannot doubt that by the last few months of 1929 the important transition has been made. Hollywood has accepted it: so has America. Facts and figures do not reveal everything: but they register the changed awareness.

By October 1929, relative scarcity had turned into glut: there were between thirty and thirty-five talkies ready for their premières and not enough Broadway cinemas to showcase them in – the producers being reluctant to go into the side-street houses. *Variety* instituted a special section at the start of 1929 for the silent films it reviewed – it was less than two years since it had introduced a similar section for the sound shorts and the rare part-talkie – and this section shrank in size like the remnants counter at a winter sale till it was discontinued in 1930. By the end of 1929 there were over 8,700 cinemas wired for sound in America – most of them could use the disc or optical system. RCA had equipped 1,200 of them, General Electric over 2,000; but the great bulk of them, 4,000, had been wired by Western Electric's ERPI division whose revenues over the three years of installation added up to a staggering thirty-seven million dollars. There were other growth symptoms. ERPI had only 180 people on its payroll in 1928: at the end of 1929 it was paying the wages of 2,400 employees and had set up schools for cinema projectionists in 17 cities as well as laboratories in Hollywood for processing the talkies without the need for a lengthy freight-journey East.

Nothing signals so clearly the irreversible establishment of talkies than the restoration of Hollywood's supremacy as *the* centre of American movie-making. All the efforts, hopes and cash invested during the panic of 1928 in turning New York into the mecca of speaking pictures proved wasted. 'Despite the irrefutable and beautifully reasoned points brought out and forwarded by the Eastern advocates, the bulk of production stubbornly adheres to Hollywood', *Variety* reported at the end of the year.[1] About twenty studios had been built or refurbished for sound in New York. With the exception of Paramount's Long Island lot, hardly any of them made a notable contibution to the talkies. Their activity was sluggish, limited to talking shorts, two-reel comedies and fly-by-night productions by penny-pinching independent outfits with lengthy shut-downs between films. MGM closed down its Cosmopolitan Studios: they were just too expensive to operate. Other studios proved fire hazards, they had been put up in such a hurry: some were shut by the authorities after a spectacular conflagration at Pathé's at the end of 1929. Other drawbacks were the doorstep presence of Equity and the tough Broadway unions, high rentals, stage-trained actors who could not learn movie techniques, the shortage of suitable outdoor locations. All these could have been visualised with a little thought – but foresight would indeed have been unusual in Hollywood. Above all, the stock market crash put the Broadway impresarios out of the notion of managing the East Coast film studios. In short, 'producing East' proved an illusion: its implementation, a fiasco: its history, a set of 'write-off' figures in the balance sheets.

Hollywood, in contrast, was bursting with confidence. It began to be felt that movies were invulnerable to the economic blight of the gathering Depression; and this eupeptic mood lasted for a year or so at least, till box-office figures started telling a different story. One on-the-spot observer, Harold B. Franklin, described the new vigour and optimism in the final pages of his book on cinema management published at the end of 1929. 'Technicians and players are available in sufficiency. They have a full realisation of possibilities and are equipped to use their knowledge to advantage. Moreover, practically every important producer is now engaged in the new venture. We have learned that the entertainment and artistic value of the silent technique need not be sacrificed in the adaptation to sound. What is more, each new sound motion picture will show improvement.'[2] More to the point, so far as movie companies were concerned, was the improvement their revenues were showing – stupendous in some cases. So intense was the public's infatuation with the talkies that almost every producing company in

---

[1] *Variety*, 25 December 1929.   [2] Harold B. Franklin, op. cit., pp. 359–60.

193

1929 made big money, and, far more amazing, nearly every single talkie released made money, too. The net profits for the leading concerns were: Warners: 17,271,805 dollars in 1929 as against 2,044,842 dollars in 1928; Fox: 9,469,050 dollars (5,957,217 dollars); Paramount: 15,544,544 dollars (8,713,063 dollars); MGM: 11,756,956 dollars (8,568,162 dollars). Profits of this order served art as well as enriched Mammon: they helped sweeten the banking and electrical interests that now virtually owned Hollywood, softened their aggressive determination to protect their investment at whatever cost to the artistic pretensions of the film folk. Experience in any case would have cooled Wall Street's ardour to interfere. Bankers soon saw it was the intangible quality of 'entertainment' that provided the profits: the investors could only do so much, and little of that on the studio stages. The boardroom take-over did not transform Hollywood as much as the backroom improvements – the refinement or invention of ever more sophisticated movie-making equipment.

The accelerating trend was towards the recording of sound on film. By mid-summer, 1929, Western Electric was considering discontinuing all sound recording on wax discs, then judged to be sixty per cent imperfect. Warners discontinued using discs in 1930, the year that a great leap ahead occurred with RCA's Noiseless Recording system which eliminated the 'hiss' that had plagued the talkies from their first syllable. When the first film presented in this process, *The Right to Love*, was screened in 1931, the *Times* said that 'the excluding of bothersome noises is highly successful, for, because of the background of silence, the player's voice is more life-like than ever. The quiet may seem at times too noticeable, but this is only because one has become accustomed to hearing the intrusive mechanical undertones.'[3] Even directors still using older talkie techniques shared in the confidence. It is surprising to find William Wyler's first talkie, *Hell's Heroes* (28 December 1929), a raw Western set on the edge of Death Valley, was made with a camera still incarcerated (with its operator) in a padded booth. But then, as has been mentioned, obsolescent equipment stayed in use until the studios could dip into the incoming profits to replace it. It did not kill Wyler's inspiration. The story was an updated religious allegory about three outlaws doing penitence for their crimes by delivering a fatherless infant across unbearably hot desert wastes to the town of New Jerusalem, which they reach on Christmas Day. 'Since the story had the men fleeing or trying to reach civilisation, I couldn't very well have them stop all the time to declaim,' Wyler said. 'So we had to devise *moving* shots with dialogue. That meant putting the padded box on rails. Just imagine a dozen guys pushing this padded shack on rails in Death Valley . . . in absolute silence. Microphones were concealed in cactus and sagebrush every ten feet or so.'[4] *Hell's Heroes* was Universal's first outdoor talkie; its

[3] *The New York Times*, 2 January 1931.
[4] *William Wyler*, by Axel Madsen (W. H. Allen, London, 1974), p. 68.

Stepin Fetchit in *Hearts in Dixie* (1929), one of his definitive performances as the 'lazybones' black.

William Wyler's first all-talkie, *Hell's Heroes* (1929) was also the first outdoor movie made by Universal. Its story of three hold-up men getting an orphaned baby over the baking desert to the town of New Jerusalem was shot in the Mojave Desert and Death Valley and involved putting the camera booth on rails – the cameraman fainted more than once in the heat. Charles Bickford, with baby, had a raw time, too.

Sophistication, up-to-dateness and the looks and rhythm of the big city were elements in the success of the early sound musicals, all present even in Merna Kennedy's head-dress in *Broadway* (1929).

effective use of sound in natural locations got it dubbed 'Wyler's *Hallelujah*'.

It illustrates how slowly technical improvements actually got into the hands of *the directors*: blimped cameras and microphone booms were certainly available when the film was shooting in August 1929. The suspicion must be that techniques were refined more quickly among the backroom boys in the labs and editing rooms than among the front-line craftsmen. Once sophisticated new lab materials and post-production tools like the Movieola had been perfected, their use rapidly affected every other phase of production. But while waiting, the directors and photographers made amazingly swift progress in coming to terms with sound.

The great outdoors had quite lost its recording terrors. Now that it was feared the musical cycle was growing stale, there was a rush outdoors with cameras and microphones. By the end of 1929 virtually every studio was scheduling Westerns for production. Seventeen were in various stages of shooting: the number was thought likely to double in 1930. One cause was the availability of colour, another was the box-office success of films like Wyler's – and Victor Fleming's *The Virginian* (20 December 1929). This Paramount production, filmed with blimped cameras on location around Sonora, freshened up all the old clichés, stock characters and ritual situations of the Western with an injection of new psychology. Dialogue now threw light on the motives of the classic gun duel in the emptying Main Street, on the social setting that produced lynch law. It made telling use of sound like the horses swishing their tails suddenly the moment before the reluctant Virginian, played by Gary Cooper, gives the signal that sends them plunging forward leaving the rustlers, who include his best pal, dangling from the nooses. Fleming handled dialogue with conversational ease. Even Cooper's tongue-tied awkwardness was the vocal expression of a backwoods chivalry every bit as natural and believable as Ronald Colman's more cultivated accents. Above all, as one critic noted approvingly, 'the film *moved*'.

So did Frank Capra's first all-talkie, *Flight* (13 September 1929). 'He gives us the impression that all the air is his', said Welford Beaton, who had been fighting a manic editorial battle against 'The Lack of Motion in Talkies'. He also liked the way Capra handled dialogue. 'There is no suggestion of stage elocution. In one scene he comes nearer realising the possibility of dialogue than any other director has done so far. . . . Lila Lee is a nurse in a hospital and she is trying to quiet Ralph Graves who has been injured in a crash. She speaks to him in a soothing tone and we catch only a few of her words.'[5] This may seem a naïve comment: but it indicates how dialogue was now being used to delineate character and supplement mood. It was definitely supplanting the early use of dialogue simply for the purpose of furthering the story or reciting the characters' feelings to the audience. The fact that such advances into movie

[5] *Film Spectator*, 14 December 1929.

colloquialism occurred so often in films directed by men like John Ford, Raoul Walsh, King Vidor, William Wyler, Frank Capra and Victor Fleming (who had young Henry Hathaway as his assistant on *The Virginian*) is surely not wholly accidental. These men were confident iconoclasts. They were natural story-tellers. They were action-conscious. They were self-dramatising. Their own temperaments bent the new technology to their wills and skills; and when the box-office results showed how well-placed their self-confidence was, studio executives blessed their innovations with new budgets and their peers were emboldened to hitch their talents to these trailblazers or go off on innovative routes of their own. As Richard Schickel has underlined, these men were 'aliterary as well as apolitical . . . when they considered subject matter and how to handle it, they sought not what was most individual about their sensibilities, but what they shared with their audience'. They created 'a direct, brisk way of making a movie'.[6] Sound, talk, dialogue was accepted by them as a totally natural part of that way.

Other directors, more conscious artists, pointed the talkies in the direction of increasing sophistication. Rouben Mamoulian made *Applause* (7 October 1929) on location in New York and at Paramount's Astoria Studios on Long Island, where he had spent days watching Jean de Limur directing Jeanne Eagels in *Jealousy*. His own star, Helen Morgan, a former torch singer in cabaret, took to cinema as if it were her native element. She played an ageing burlesque queen, literally on her last legs, whose self-sacrifice for her daughter was rendered by Mamoulian with an unsparing awareness of what a sordid milieu did to those who toiled in it. But many contemporary critics could not discern the humanity for the harshness and their reviews are pungent with words like 'loathsome', 'vulgar' and 'disgusting'. Possibly for the same reasons, the public were put off by *Applause*. Yet it is a key film for the artist's self-assertion over the film technicians. Mamoulian, his own senses sharpened by apprenticeship to the pictorial and aural rhythms of opera, liberated the camera and curbed the microphone's tyranny so that both should serve emotion, mood and dramatic point, not annihilate them. Right at the start, in a burlesque theatre, the camera moves off a chorus line to pick up a conversation – and lets us hear the talk above the now modulated volume of the chorus number. Even more revolutionary was the scene where the daughter's bedtime prayer and her mother's lullaby 'Give Your Baby Lots of Love' were recorded simultaneously on separate microphones and then combined on the sound track. Everyone assured Mamoulian that 'mixing' of this sort was an impossible feat. 'So I was mad', he later recalled. 'I threw down my megaphone . . . and ran up to Mr Zukor's office. . . . "Look," I said, "nobody does what I ask. . . ." So Zukor came down and told them to do it my way. . . . Next day I went to the studio very nervous. But as I went in, the big Irish doorman, who'd always ignored me before, raised his

[6] Richard Schickel, op. cit., p. 10.

hat and bowed. It seems they'd had a secret 7.30 viewing of the rushes in the studio, and were so pleased with the result that they'd sent it straight off to a Paramount sales conference.'[7] Once a technical innovation like this entered the commercial system, it travelled fast. By the end of 1929 the initiative had passed back to the directors and the speed at which they mastered sound was impressive.

Of course, in a more general sense, the exact opposite proved true. Sound mastered the old Hollywood cinema. It changed it from a marvellously graduated battery of emotions conveyed by mime supplemented by photography, lighting and music to a cinema that mainly relied on dialogue to 'tell a story'. The Mamoulians were very few: not many directors could (or were encouraged to) relate sound and dialogue to a visual design: the microphone could do the work of story-telling for them more swiftly, clearly and cheaply. Sound clarified and defined situations and characters in ways that were frequently seductively entertaining but were bereft of the silent cinema's more felicitous resonances. It is instructive to see what silent movies were actually being shown on Broadway during that fateful week in August 1926, when Vitaphone was presented at the Warner Theater. Next door, or just down the street, were Rex Ingram's *Mare Nostrum* with Alice Terry and Antonio Moreno; Rudolph Valentino's last film *The Son of the Sheik*; King Vidor's *The Big Parade* with John Gilbert; Sjostrom's *The Scarlet Letter* with Lillian Gish; MGM's *Ben-Hur* with Novarro and Bushman; E. A. Dupont's *Variety* from Germany; *The Waltz Dream*, another UFA film; and a whole repertory season of Emil Jannings's pictures. Sophisticated in their narrative-telling, international in understanding, without speech yet intelligible in all languages and to most classes, orchestrating emotions with some of the screen's most nuanced players, each one bearing the individual signature of a director, star or studio: such movies as these represented some of the silent cinema's finest flowering – they would be the pick of the cinematheques today. In their day, however, they were the stuff of popular entertainment, patronised by all social classes linked by common enjoyment and understanding of the silent art's manifold conventions. Yet this was the world that a short selection of Vitaphone concert items and, the next year, a Mammy singer in blackface helped sweep out of common currency though not, fortunately, into total oblivion.

No wonder the intelligentsia felt resentful. The astonishing thing is how many professional critics were still so tolerant of the commercial innovation once they realised how ruthlessly it was dislodging the art form, impoverishing its vocabulary, coarsening its appeal and limiting its international reach. Only the amazingly short time it required for the talkies to take over, their huge novelty value, and the redeeming speed of technical improvements could have made the revolution tolerable. We

[7] Rouben Mamoulian interviewed by David Robinson, *Sight and Sound*, Summer, 1961.

have seen how the initial enthusiasm waned swiftly with the torrent of undifferentiating talk; and this was anticipated and analysed with some pessimism by three film-makers who had in fact welcomed sound. In a statement written in the late spring of 1928 and published in English the same year, Eisenstein, Alexandrov and Pudovkin wrote: 'A first period of sensations does not injure the development of a new art, but it is the second period that is fearful in this case, a second period that will take the place of the fading purity of a first perception of new technical possibilities, and will assert an epoch of its automatic utilisation for "highly cultured dramas" and other photographed performances of a theatrical sort.'[8] Critics and intellectuals came round to a reluctant acceptance of sound just at the time, in 1929, when the talkies were recovering their sophistication – and the possibilities of a *third period* were apparent.

What was this third period? Of what did it consist? The answer must be – a far closer illusion of reality. Particularly an *American* reality. Once voices could be heard, they suggested the society that the speakers inhabited; once the society was shown, its way of life had to be audible as well as visible. The accent of fascination was inevitably put on the American character of people, speech, scenes and events. With the exceptions of *The Big Parade* (though it was set in Europe in the First World War) and *The Scarlet Letter* (though it was directed by one Swede and co-starred another), none of those films in release at the time of the Vitaphone première was essentially American in story or texture: their 'European' bias is manifest. But look at the respective lists of 1929's dozen or more 'outstanding productions' drawn up in January 1930 by Welford Beaton and Frank T. Daugherty who between them represent a reasonable cross-section of art and commerce. There are only two films with a European setting or tone: Garbo's *The Kiss*, set in Lyons and directed by the Belgian Jacques Feyder; and *The Case of Lena Smith*, set mainly in nineteenth-century Vienna and directed by the Viennese immigrant Josef von Sternberg. Both are *non-dialogue* films.

The talking cinema's more realistic impression of American society posed problems that few studios wanted. Problems of content and censorship. The Hays Office had already issued a set of guide lines in 1927, restrictions of the 'Don't' or 'Be Careful' kind, but the silent screen often enabled these to be avoided with ease. Words changed all that. Words made social situations plain and individual intentions positively brazen; and the risk of running into costly trouble from censorship bodies, lay and religious, was measurably increased. It's been noted how early on in the talkies came the demand for cuts – the scene in *Tenderloin*. Events rebuffed Harold B. Franklin's pious optimism that 'when it is fully realised that censorship of speech from the screen is an assault on the most sacred rights guaranteed by the Constitution, the practice will ultimately be abandoned'. That hope was expressed in 1929: it was not

[8] *Close-Up*, London, October 1928.

199

till 1952 (the case of Burstyn *v.* Wilson involving the film *The Miracle*) that the movies gained the Supreme Court's protection in the declaration that they were not just 'a business', but were entitled to the guaranties of free speech and free Press under the First and Fourteenth Amendments.

The sound era's early years offered plenty of provocation to anyone out to abridge the movies' freedom of speech. Sound films were not specifically mentioned in the various Acts creating State boards of censorship or review. But Fox was prosecuted in 1929 for refusing to submit 'the sound portion' of one of its films to the Pennsylvania State Board. The State legislature ruled against the company, saying that 'the recording of the language is only incidental' – in other words, a talkie was 'not fundamentally a new creation'. The result was a sudden increase in the Hays Office's vigilance and arbitration on dialogue matters. The movie-makers had hardly begun to speak on the screen before the emotive force of the words was amending their freedom to utter them. A list of prohibitions grew up at a speed which itself indicates a sense of alarm over the imminence of a civic backlash. By the late summer of 1929 the movies must not say 'Damn, Hell or go to the Devil', or utter 'God, Christ, Jesus or Lord' in a profane sense. In British territories they were forbidden to say 'My God, damnable, or God-forsaken', as well as 'crap and bloody'. Pennsylvania objected to 'harpy and hell-cat' being pronounced inside its State lines; for some reason Virginia took against the word 'fool'. And anywhere in the United States it was most inadvisable for characters in a movie to come out with 'broad, tart, moll, trollop, slut, nance, fairy, louse or lousy, nigger or chink'. Even sounds drew frowns whether or not they were turned into speech: it was forbidden to 'leer' audibly, except 'in light-comedy style'.

By bringing a more realistic view of the world within earshot of audiences, sound set the moralists' alarm bells jangling and helped precipitate the codified restrictions for production that were adopted by the industry on 31 March 1930. A few years later the threat of economic boycott by a newly formed Legion of Decency turned the production Code from a declaration of piety into a dictatorship of virtue. Thus if sound brought more realism into the movies, it indirectly imported more hypocrisy. Its great potential to reflect life accurately in all its aspects was distorted for reasons of commercial prudence into the glamorising of some sections of life and the total exclusion of others.

We have already observed some of the effects the talkies had on audiences. They broke what Richard Griffith has called 'the charmed, hypnotic trance', the dream-like quality of witnessing a silent movie. Many complaints were made in the early months that talkies destroyed 'the sense of relaxation' to be got at a silent movie because they compelled people to concentrate on the new-fangled dialogue. What this signifies is the period of adjustment that filmgoers were experiencing. By 'relaxation' they probably meant subconscious participation. During the silent film's 'dialogue', when the characters' lips were seen moving soundlessly, filmgoers projected their own emotions on to the screen in order to give a sense of closure to the relationship between image and audience – until the sub-title appeared and clinched it. Talkies reversed this process. People were made the recipients of a huge, often redundant amount of information about characters or plot. Talkies substituted passive participation instead of the deeper state of active communion that silence encouraged. What the talkies did was *fix* audiences' attitudes – thus putting a tremendously potent tool (or weapon) into film-makers' hands. The feeling of being 'manipulated' by dialogue, even for one's pleasure, was no doubt partly responsible for those early complaints of 'disturbance'.

Jean Keim, the French critic, described this phenomenon very well when he wrote: 'Sound has generally deeper resonances where a person is concerned than sight; the impressions received by the eye touch the senses rather than the depths of the mind; it is through the ear that deeper and more lasting impressions are received, which trigger off the mental apparatus with more force. Formerly the impressions received did not last long; now they are invariably prolonged.'[9] Anyone can verify this by trying to recall details of a silent film even a few hours after seeing it. They have usually faded from memory in a dismayingly short space of time, leaving only a vague feeling of what was seen, though this, just because it is so unfocused, can frequently act like a spell on the emotions. In a talkie, on the other hand, dialogue becomes a form of mental notation to be relied on for recall – it also tends to confirm one's attitude to the scene and the actors in it.

Photography and lighting in the best of the silent films supplied an emotional ambience that did duty for the lack of audible dialogue. They stimulated filmgoers' imaginations: they conveyed an impression rather than a description. But talkie dialogue quickly usurped the function of photography which dramatically lost, for a time anyhow, its atmospheric power of involvement. Talkies required brighter lights for the sharper, faster film stock in use: 'soft' stock was one of the earliest casualties of the new technique. Moreover the sheer expense of altering cumbersome camera and microphone set-ups abruptly reduced the emotional diffusion of the silent era's movies to the crisp, bright transcription of audible performances in the talkie era.

Perhaps as dismaying, but as inevitable, was the speed at which people forgot what it was like to watch the silents. Silent movie-going suddenly seemed to belong to another age. In any case, choice in the matter rapidly disappeared. In 1929 there were 335 films made in Hollywood with complete dialogue; half of these went out in so-called silent versions to 'service' the 10,000-odd small cinemas still not wired for sound. But by the end of 1930 not one of the Hollywood majors was producing a silent feature of any variety.

[9] *Le Cinéma Sonore*, by Jean A. Keim (Editions Albin Michel, Paris, 1947), p. 45. My translation.

The popularity of the talkies conquered audiences in a series of spasmodic advances, relapses and recoveries. It is evident from preceding chapters that their novelty value was always fortuitously renewed just as it seemed to have worn off. Vitaphone and the novelty of the variety shorts; Jolson's colloquial ad-libbing in *The Jazz Singer*; the 'first all-talking' *Lights of New York*; the well-bred conversation-piece of *Interference*; Fox's speaking newsreels; Jolson at full throttle in *The Singing Fool*; location realism in *In Old Arizona*; *Broadway Melody*; the consecutive excitements of hearing the stars talk; the wave of Hollywood musicals. . . . These are roughly the novelties that sequentially seized people's imagination, freshened their appetites at shorter and shorter intervals, sometimes sharpened their critical discrimination, and in turn spurred Hollywood on to surpass its last effort with its next sensation until, by sheer ubiquitousness, the talkies were established as the *expected* form of mass entertainment.

Hollywood, too, soon forgot what it had been like to *make* silent films. 'After working in synchronous sound films for a number of years, with their usual dependence on dialogue, the techniques of directing actors in silent films began to fade in my memory.'[10] King Vidor made it sound as if he was the slowly recuperating victim of amnesia. 'I wondered what exactly I had told them to do and just how they had accomplished what they did. . . . I remembered that the directors often guided them with brief instructions while the shooting of the scene was actually taking place. Some directors talked during the scene more than others. Commands had to be sharp and clear so that they would penetrate an actor's consciousness without causing confusion. But to what extent was the director responsible for the performance of the actors as compared with today's talk-oriented performances?' This is an extraordinary confession coming from one of the great silent film-makers: no wonder we lack so many first-hand accounts of the pre-talkie era. Sound seems in many cases to have been like a trauma, expunging it from recollection.

Just looking at the best examples of silent screen acting shows how much of value was irrecoverably lost. Sound made acting more naturalistic, but also lazier. Words did the work. They diminished the mobile, finely nuanced quality of the screen mime and began the process in which the sense of people playing parts in a dexterously visible way is lost sight of in a stylised naturalism that requires a dominant personality to make it bearable from film to film. One gets less and less chance in the talkie era to write about acting *performances* as distinct from personality *traits*. Ultimately the latter come to tell us more about the nature of the society that finds them so fascinating than about the actor or actress exhibiting them. The silent stars were mythical figures, not quite human because they didn't speak, yet giving emotions a human shape. The stars of the talkie era are utilitarian icons: they have the properties of go-

[10] *On Film Making*, by King Vidor (W. H. Allen, London, 1973), pp. 63–4.

betweens, connecting a social experience with a narrative one. Once they had dialogue on their lips, the silent idols suffered a grievous loss of divinity. They became more like the audiences watching them. This helps explain why the talkies altered star values so radically. What they did not do – and this needs stressing – was *ruin* the silent stars. It is persistently but erroneously held that many silent stars could not cope with talking roles and sounded, to put it vulgarly, like dumb broads or piping eunuchs. The truth, well illustrated in earlier chapters, is that hardly any major silent stars suffered ruin, or even a relapse from public favour, because of a vocal deficiency. Norma Talmadge was certainly a victim; William Haines as well, perhaps; and the stars from Europe with foreign accents either adapted to conditions or emigrated. But there is no evidence at all of mass carnage. Some careers were made (or remade) because their owners talked so well. Hardly any succumbed to the fancy-vowelled invaders from Broadway. 'Of the 30 or 40 leading faces,' said *Fortune* in October 1930, as it surveyed the first full year of the talkies, 'all but half a dozen are names which had achieved a momentum of public favor over a number of years.' Voice trouble was not really the root cause of careers that soon began to fade. John Gilbert, as we have seen, was not the victim of 'white voice', as high-pitched tones were euphemistically called, but of poor studio thinking that did not foresee how a Great Lover's romantic ardour would sound embarrassingly foolish to latter-day ears. Sound made it essential to show audiences a more authentic view of contemporary life-styles; and quite a few of the silent-era archetypes simply withered away in the glare of realism and the harsher social climate of the Depression.

Clara Bow would have likely been a victim had her voice been adequate or not. The image of the flapper girl swiftly dated as sex took on the economic realism of the gold-digger type. Clara made the transition effectively enough as far as her voice was concerned, but was unable to meet the competition from a new breed of maturer screen ladies like Joan Crawford, Norma Shearer, Bette Davis, Ruth Chatterton and Jean Harlow whose voices contributed so much to defining their roles as worldly women of the 1930s. Some of these names overlapped the two eras; but it was sound that consolidated their prominence. Jean Harlow, for example, owed her good fortune to replacing the Norwegian vamp Greta Nissen when the tireless Howard Hughes re-shot *Hell's Angels* as a talkie after he had lavished over a year and two million dollars on a silent version. Harlow's hoydenish allure, part gold-digger, part good-sport, a playgirl who radiated sex as luminously as her beacon of platinum hair, suggested the Depression era's need for maturer consolation than Clara Bow's Jazz Baby could possibly offer. Other silent stars suffered a variety of misfortunes, few of which had anything to do with speech. Pickford's fans preferred her in her 'Sweetheart' image; Fairbanks was past his physical prime: various female stars like Colleen Moore, Lillian Gish, Gloria Swanson and

Marion Davies were showing their age to the unscrupulous camera and some of them preferred to desert to the softening distance of Broadway's footlights; Barthelmess was up against screen heroes like Cooper, March and very soon Gable and Tracy who personified more modern tastes in leading men than his own conscience-laden manliness. Some stars simply fell victim to over-exposure. Conrad Nagel made thirty-one films inside two years and later commented ruefully, 'That would kill anybody. . . . My wife would say, "Well, let's go out and see a movie tonight." We'd get in the car and discover that I'm playing at the Paramount Theater. And I'm playing at the Universal Theater. And the MGM Theater. We couldn't find a theater where I wasn't playing. So we'd go back home. I was an epidemic.'[11]

Sound humanised and democratised the stars. One swift result of this was an enormous upsurge of fan mail in the 1929–30 period addressed to the stars of the new talkies. It was as if the act of talking established such close rapport with an audience that the stars now became identifiable parts of the audience's consciousness, not dream figures existing in some collective unconscious. But the reverse of this was a loss of divinity. Silent stars who made the transition successfully nevertheless seemed diminished – more vulnerable, life-size and somehow much more ordinary. It was a shock to realise how much the addition of a voice could change the quality of an individual. The actors who *became* stars in the talkies were luckier in this respect. Stage players like Edward G. Robinson, Paul Muni and Claudette Colbert, vaudeville comedians like the Marx Brothers (whose Broadway success *The Coconuts* adapted perfectly to the talkies in 1929), radio stars like Rudy Vallee and stars from the Big Bands like Bing Crosby all brought their voices with them to the screen, inseparable and distinctive parts of their personalities, so that they never had to suffer that temporary but dislocating need for their fans to familiarise themselves afresh with faces of whom they had grown fond. For some of the new stars, of course, sound proved a double-edged blessing. Known as well by their voices as their looks, they discovered that sound simply reinforced type-casting. Cagney, Robinson, Harlow, Davis, Joan Blondell and Lee and Spencer Tracy had voices that seemed to slot them very precisely into the social milieu of the 1930s; and they soon found it as hard as the silent stars had done to manoeuvre their careers into other kinds of roles.

Sound certainly helped save Hollywood from the worst or at least the immediate effects of the economic catastrophe that crippled other industries. It was not till 1932 that cinema box-offices were adversely affected, necessitating fresh economies and rationalisation. If the film industry had waited another twelvemonth to re-equip itself for sound, it is probable that Wall Street's panic would have made it impossible to get the colossal loans needed. Studio bankruptcies would have been savage. And it must be anyone's guess when the talkies would have actually

[11] Rosenberg and Silverstein, op. cit., pp. 189–90.

'arrived'. It is arguable that television might have come into common use as an entertainment medium two decades before it began giving the movie industry a run for its money and its audiences. It was quite practicable by the late 1920s to transmit television programmes: RCA even had a home television set for rent at 7.50 dollars a week in 1929. It is lucky for Hollywood that the banks, wire companies and electrical equipment manufacturers had written out their cheques to the movie industry a year before the Crash – otherwise it might have looked a better bet to them to bring consolation and entertainment into the very homes of the people via talking pictures on a tube. The huge sums already invested in talking pictures for the cinemas gave Hollywood the energy, and bankers the incentive, to weather the worst economic storm in memory and come out enriched and smiling. At least some did.

As the American Depression showed it meant to stay around for years, the new economic system that sound brought into being asserted itself more and more intimately in the lives and careers of everyone in the movie industry. The first change sound had made in Hollywood was to kill the festive atmosphere of movie-making. The ensuing upheaval sponsored a traumatic sense of insecurity among the inhabitants. Such moods are the stuff that tyranny feeds on. With all its insistence on controlling individual fates to a degree never before attempted or possible in the freelancing system of the 1920s, its self-serving collusion with a hypocritical system of censorship, its ruthless gearing-up of the studio system to be an awesomely efficient manufacturer of dreams in the American idiom, the talkie era imposed a form of servitude on the industry for which glamour was only the camouflage and fame the sometimes adequate consolation. The last word should be given to one of the old residents who knew from personal experience the regrets as well as the rewards that the talkies brought in their wake. 'Within two years', wrote William C. de Mille, 'our little old Hollywood was gone and in its place stood a fair, new city, talking a new language, having different manners and customs, a more terrifying city full of strange faces, less friendly, more businesslike, twice as populous – and much more cruel.'[12]

[12] William C. de Mille, op. cit., p. 296.

Bibliography

A complete bibliography of all the works consulted for this study would be too extensive to print here. But the author wishes to express his gratitude to the writers and publishers of the following works quoted in the text:

Agate, James. *Around Cinemas*, First and Second Series (Home & Van Thal, London, 1946, 1948)

Allvine, Glendon. *The Greatest Fox of Them All* (Lyle Stuart Inc., New York, 1969)

Alpert, Hollis. *The Barrymores* (W. H. Allen, London, 1965)

Bogdanovich, Peter. *John Ford* (Studio Vista, London, 1970)

Carneal, Georgette. *A Conqueror of Space* (Liveright, New York, 1947)

Geduld, Harry M. *The Birth of the Talkies* (Indiana University Press, 1975)

Gordon, Jan and Cora. *Star-Dust in Hollywood* (George G. Harrap & Co., London, 1930)

Green, Abel and Laurie, Joe Jr. *Show Biz from Vaude to Video* (Henry Holt, New York, 1951)

Jacobs, Lewis. *The Rise of the American Film* (Harcourt, Brace & Co., New York, 1939)

Keim, Jean A. *Le Cinéma Sonore* (Editions Albin Michel, Paris, 1947)

Kobal, John. *Gotta Sing, Gotta Dance* (Hamlyn, London, 1970)

Lawson, John Howard. *Film: The Creative Process* (Hill & Wang, New York, 1964)

Madsen, Axel. *William Wyler* (W. H. Allen, London, 1974)

Menjou, Adolphe. *It Took Nine Tailors* (Sampson Low, Marston & Co., London, 1950)

de Mille, William C. *Hollywood Saga* (E. P. Dutton & Co., Inc., New York, 1939)

Pudovkin, V. I., ed. and translated by Ivor Montagu. *Film Technique and Film Acting* (Memorial Edition, Vision Mayflower, London, 1958)

Rosen, Marjorie. *Popcorn Venus* (Coward, McCann & Geoghegan, New York, 1973)

Rosenberg, Bernard and Silverstein, Harry, eds. *The Real Tinsel* (The Macmillan Co., New York, 1970)

Schickel, Richard. *The Men Who Made the Movies* (Elm Tree Books, London, 1977)

Schickel, Richard. *Walt Disney* (Weidenfeld & Nicolson, London, 1930)

Thrasher, Frederick. *Okay for Sound* (Duell, Sloan & Pearce, New York, 1946)

Vidor, King. *On Film Making* (W. H. Allen, London, 1973)

Warner, Jack L. and Jennings, Dean. *My First Hundred Years in Hollywood* (Random House, New York, 1965)

White, Llewellyn. *The American Radio* (University of Chicago Press, 1947)

Wilson, Edmund. *The American Earthquake* (W. H. Allen, London, 1958)

A Talkie Chronology

1925

Warner Brothers open radio station KFWB, Los Angeles (3 March). Sam Warner hears sound demonstration at Bell Labs, New York (April). Warners and Western Electric agree to research into sound film possibilities. Tests begun at Warners Vitagraph Studio, New York (June).

1926

Warners set up Vitaphone Corporation to produce sound films (April). Agreement signed with Western Electric for formal use of Vitaphone sound system and its licensing to other movie producers (20 April). Production of synchronised feature *Don Juan* in Hollywood, Vitaphone operatic and concert items in New York. William Fox buys patent rights to Case–Sponable sound system, renamed Movietone (23 July). Sensational New York première of Vitaphone shorts and *Don Juan* (6 August). Radio promoting more 'popular' entertainers. RCA incorporates NBC as radio subsidiary (September). Second Vitaphone bill along with synchronised feature *The Better 'Ole* (5 October). Other film companies envious of Warners, but not committing themselves to sound as yet, though Fox and Zukor making secret overtures. Vitaphone begins big sales drive to equip theatres for sound (December). Hollywood majors meet in defence session, agree not to have dealings with Warners–Vitaphone, or go into sound production till alternative system available (December).

1927

William Fox signs mutually useful licensing agreement with Vitaphone (January), presents first movietone programme of shorts along with silent feature *What Price Glory* (21 January). Vitaphone's third programme, now angled at popular appeal (3 February). Novelty of Vitaphone shorts wearing off by spring. Fox presents second Movietone bill along with *Yankee Clipper* silent feature, creates sensation with West Point cadets and Lindbergh take-off in sound (2 May, repeated in enlarged bill 27 May). Public gripped by verisimilitude of hearing outdoor events. Warners transfer to ERPI right to license other movie producers, announce a 'full-length talking picture'. Negotiations with Jessel to star in *The Jazz Singer* broken off, Jolson signed instead (May–June). General Electric, RCA subsidiary, demonstrates Photophone sound system (September). Première of *The Jazz Singer* evokes wild enthusiasm (6 October). Warners announce lensing of twelve talking pictures in addition to silent-movie roster (November). Rival studios, save Fox, still in state of indecision, conducting experiments, enviously eyeing *Jazz Singer* box-office. Power scramble beginning as year ends.

1928

RCA acquires Keith Orpheum cinema chains, forms RKO to go into Photophone sound production (January). *The Fortune Hunter* in silent and synchronised versions (18 January). Fox releases first of fifteen sound movies this year, *Four Sons* (13 February). Part-talkie *Tenderloin* attracts first example of sound censorship (14 March). United Artists stars make Big Broadcast (29 March). Sound welcomed by Welford Beaton: 'Nothing is sacrificed when we add sound, but something will be missing when we omit it' (March). *Glorious Betsy* première astounds Hollywood with sound possibilities (26 April). Paramount, United Artists, Metro-Goldwyn-Mayer follow First National and sign with Western Electric for use of sound devices (15 May). Studios feverishly impatient to 'go sound' as public demand swells. Three hundred cinemas now wired for sound (mid-summer). Warners announces the 'Vitaphon-ing' of Broadway hit plays, musicals: all future films will have talking sequences. *The Lion and the Mouse* regarded as the shape (and sound) of things to come (18 June). Demand begins for stage talents. George Bernard Shaw makes sensational Movietone short, quite eclipses feature film *The Family Picnic* with outdoors Movietone sound (25 June). Perplexity and anxiety spread through Hollywood craft unions. Projectionists demanding new, higher wage scales point to costs escalation and hasten dismissal of house or studio orchestras. First all-talkie *The Lights of New York* (8 July). Edmund Goulding forecasts future talkie scene, reveals confusion existing between stage and screen (13 July). Fan magazines begin taunting silent stars, elocution teachers in demand, stage experience sought by feature players, gloom in the star colony. 'Sound at any price' response by studios who add effects to silent releases including *Warming Up* (18 July), *The Perfect Crime* (6 August), *Scarlet Lady* (14 August), *Submarine* (30 August), or schedule sound sequences in current production *White Shadows of the South Seas* (31 July). Warner's second all-talkie *The Terror* (16 August) condemned for 'recitation' dialogue, spurs raids on Broadway stage talents, refurbishment of New York film studios for sound productions including *The Letter*. Desperate and vain Hollywood economy measures as sound costs soar in all departments, actors demand better conditions and more pay. Critics becoming less tolerant of poor synchronisation, public more *blasé* about sound effects in films like *The Air Circus* (2 September), *State Street Sadie* (2 September). Great revival of box-office enthusiasm with second Jolson feature *The Singing Fool* (19 September). *Lonesome* (2 October). Warners' third all-talkie *The Home Towners* (23 October). MGM's first part-talkie *Alias Jimmy Valentine* (14 November). Paramount's first all-talkie *Interference* (16 November) praised for skilful sound, but thought likely to suffer from public demand for something more than simply talk. First Mickey Mouse sound cartoon *Steamboat Willie* (18 November) screened with *Gang War* which it eclipses. *Napoleon's Barber* reveals outdoor possibilities of Movietone sound recording (24 November). *Caught in the Fog* (2 December). *The Barker* (5 December). Dip in studio production towards the year's end as studios await start of all-talking production roster. *My Man* (21 December) signals public ignorance of Broadway personalities in movies and confirms studios' disenchantment with many talents imported to Hollywood: exception are song writers, composers, some scriptwriters, a few favoured stage players. Many others packing bags, heading East again. Growing evidence of Hollywood realising talkies must shape their own techniques, cannot simply be Broadway-on-the-screen. *In Old Arizona* proves outdoors sound movies a success, revives interest in Westerns (25 December).

1929

More sophisticated techniques (sound, camera mobility, etc.) coming into play, as in *The Ghost Talks* (17 February). In six months ending February, twenty-four million dollars spent in studio refurbishment, another three million earmarked; over three hundred million dollars already spent wiring cinemas. Bankers, electrical company executives moving on to movie company boards. Concern for foreign versions of talkies. *Lady of the Pavements* (28 January). *The Doctor's Secret* (20 February). Growing disenchantment with wax disc recording, preference beginning for optical sound tracks. William Fox announces control of Loew's Inc. (3 March) and an end to silent features. Louis B. Mayer, head of MGM, begins to mobilise Government opposition to Fox take-over. Rash of take-over attempts as theatre ownership seen as key to talkie prosperity. Warners (who acquired First National, September 1928) make vain bid for United Artists: Paramount closes relationship with Publix Theaters. *Variety* warns studios against peril of losing public trust by dubbing as with Barthelmess in *Weary River* (24 January), Louise Brooks in *The Canary Murder Case* (9 March). Studios now addicted to 'cycles' in sound pictures: *The Bellamy Trial* (23 January), *The Trial of Mary Dugan* (28 March), *His Captive Woman* (2 April), *Through Different Eyes* (13 April), *Madame X* (24 April), all courtroom-accented movies which contribute to public weariness with over-talkative productions. Distractions, novelties sought and found in growth of colour photography, musicals: *The Broadway Melody* (1 February), *Hearts of Dixie* (27 February), *Hollywood Revue* (14 April), *Show Boat* (17 April), *Innocents of Paris* (26 April), *Desert Song* (1 May), *Broadway* (27 May), *On with the Show* (28 May), *Close Harmony* (28 April), *Hallelujah* (20 August), *Rio Rita* (6 October), *Sunny Side Up* (3 October), *Show of Shows* (20 November), but all eventually contribute to glut feeling. Equity attempts closed shop in Hollywood (June). Strike collapses for want of big union support (mid-August). William Fox severely injured in car crash (July). Convalescence and Stock Market crash contribute along with Justice Department enquiry to collapse of attempt to buy control of Loew's and eventual bankruptcy. Public appetite continuously whetted by stars now making talkie debuts: Baclanova: *The Wolf of Wall Street* (27 January), Fairbanks: *The Iron Mask* (21 February), Bow: *The Wild Party* (1 April), Pickford: *Coquette* (5 April), Colman: *Bulldog Drummond* (2 May), Muni: *The Valiant* (12 May), Banky: *This is Heaven* (26 May), Bancroft: *Thunderbolt* (20 June), Menjou: *Fashions in Love* (30 June), von Stroheim: *The Great Gabbo* (12 September), Arliss: *Disraeli* (2 October), Gilbert: *His Glorious Night* (5 October), Davies: *Marianne* (18 October), Lloyd: *Welcome Danger* (20 October), Swanson: *The Trespasser* (1 November), Crawford: *Untamed* (29 November), Pickford–Fairbanks: *The Taming of the Shrew* (30 November), Barrymore: *General Crack* (1 December). All prove vocally adequate or more than adequate, but Gilbert's career slumps due to disastrous casting in amorous role and audience embarrassment over audible passions. (Garbo, Chaney, Gish, Norma Talmadge postpone talkie debuts till 1930: only Talmadge utterly ruined by hers. Chaplin's voice first heard in 1936.) By October relative scarcity of talkies almost turned into over-production: not enough Broadway cinemas to screen them in. More than 8,700 cinemas wired for sound throughout America. Hopes (and cash) invested in turning New York into Hollywood East fade as power returns to the Coast, economics hamstring East-side production. New vigour and optimism in Hollywood bolstered by (temporary) belief that movies will ride out Depression, huge corporate profits being made by almost all studios. Accelerating refinement in sound techniques evidenced in *Applause* (7 October), *The Virginian* (20 December), *Hell's Heroes* (28 December). Artistic control now reverting to the directors, the tyranny of the microphone ending as 'booms', sound-proof cameras, editing benches, etc., become commonplace techniques. Movies more Americanised, more realistic; stars more 'democratic' and less 'divine' as a result of sound. Censorship given boost by the spoken word. Audiences, reacting less to the silent-movie mime, become more passive as talk tells them the plot, cues their responses. New kinds of sound stars come into being whose voices are as characteristic as their looks. Studios, back in good economic shape, profit from sound's dislocation to reinforce their rule, streamline their production, 'Within two years,' writes William C. de Mille, 'our little old Hollywood was gone.'

Index